ENFLAMED BY THE SACRAMENTAL WORD

Enflamed

BY THE SACRAMENTAL WORD

Preaching and the Imagination of the Poor

VINCENT J. PASTRO

Foreword by Gregory Heille, OP

PICKWICK *Publications* · Eugene, Oregon

ENFLAMED BY THE SACRAMENTAL WORD
Preaching and the Imagination of the Poor

Pickwick Publications
An Imprint of Wipf and Stock Publishers
199 W. 8th Ave., Suite 3
Eugene, OR 97401

www.wipfandstock.com

ISBN 13: 978-1-60608-525-7

Cataloguing in Publication data:

Pastro, Vincent J.

Enflamed by the sacramental word : preaching and the imagination of the poor / Vincent J. Pastro.

xii + 206 p. ; 23 cm. Includes bibliographical references and index.

ISBN 13: 978-1-60608-525-7

1. Preaching. 2. Liberation theology. I. Heille, Gregory. II. Title.

BV4211.2 P38 2010

Manufactured in the U.S.A.

And this is eternal life, that they may know you, the only true God,
and Jesus Christ whom you have sent.
(John 17:3)

For
María Teresa Montes Lara, OP
and the Base Ecclesial Communities of
Holy Spirit Parish

In Memory of Dominican Mentors and Mothers
Marygrace and Frank
Emily Agnes

Contents

Foreword

I have read this book, and now I invite you, deserving reader, to meditate on it. Vince Pastro began this intellectual and spiritual journey as a Maryknoll volunteer in Peru. A diocesan priest of the Archdiocese of Seattle, he then returned home to Puget Sound to serve as pastor to a Mexican immigrant parish. He visited his parishioners' home village of Tzintzuntzan in Mexico. He also began to travel back and forth to Saint Louis to pursue doctoral study in preaching, as well as to spend precious vacation time in Mexico and Germany to meet and converse with some of the theologians he loves to read and with pastoral agents such as himself, who love to "do theology."

Father Pastro calls himself a "theologian pastor," and as you will see in this book, he envisions a theological endeavor no longer characterized by the dualistic, fragmenting, silo mentality of a theology broken into disparate university disciplines, but rather a more integral and contextual habit of the pastoral heart. To the reader accustomed to the more abstruse cadencies of much classroom theology, the material found here may seem eclectic and therefore to some disagreeable. Pastro, however, characterizes his work as "nepantlic"—employing Javier Garibay Gómez, SJ's usage of the *Náhuatl* word *nepantla* meaning "situated in the middle" and having to do with discerning the integral unity of important and complimentary opposites. Thusly, Pastro invites us to become equally and dynamically at home in the world of North American and European theology and also the world of Central and South American theology. He also invites us to grasp with both hands the perspectives of men and women, East and West, sin and grace, baptism and ordination, old and new. In doing so, his ministerial and scholarly intent is to introduce us to a theological methodology of the poor, in service to the ministry of preaching in any pastoral context.

As a North American Anglo preacher turned academic, I must say I have learned a lot by reading this book. Notably, I call your attention to the footnotes—in which you will see that Pastro is widely read in American homiletics and theology, in Latin American theology in its original Spanish, and in European theology in English translation. The notes also give repeated insight into how a bright, accomplished pastor-theologian sees and interprets his world.

By organizing the three parts of the book according to three questions—Where have we been? Where are we now? Where are we going?—the book "does" historical theology, ecclesiology, and eschatology in pursuit of an operative theology of preaching from the interpretive viewpoint of the poor. While naturally sympathetic to Pastro's message, at times I questioned what I heard him to be saying. As one of Pastro's teachers, however, it pleases me that my student has gone where I from my social location could not have gone—my student has become my teacher.

As a grateful reader, I have compiled the following list of some elements of Pastro's book that I have found particularly insightful, helpful, and at times refreshingly surprising:

- The story of the first Dominican community in the "new world" of La Española, of the brave preaching of Friar Antonio de Montesinos to the Spanish conquistadors there, of the ensuing and far-flung ministry of Friar Bartolomé de Las Casas, and of the first scholarly articulation of the idea of human rights is one of the great American stories and one of the truly inspiring stories of Christianity. This story deserves to be told and taught well, and Pastro does so elegantly.

- Both in the text and in his notes, Pastro introduces his readers to a broad panoply of theologians and homileticians: European theologians Karl Barth, Karl Rahner, SJ, Edward Schillebeeckx, OP, Dietrich Bonhoeffer (the theologian Pastro believes will lead us into the third millennium), Jürgen Moltmann, Hans Küng, and Otto Semmelroth, SJ; North American homiletic theologians such as Mary Catherine Hilkert, OP, and Paul Janowiak, SJ; Latin American theologians Leonardo Boff, Jon Sobrino, SJ, Ivone Gebara, Elsa Tamez, José Marins, Víctor Codina, SJ (to whom Pastro would award the Noble Prize in Theology), José Comblin, Gustavo Gutiérrez, OP, and Javier

Garibay Gómez, SJ; and North American Protestant homileticians David Buttrick, Barbara Brown Taylor, Henry Mitchell, and Anna Carter Florence—amongst many others.

- Pastro also understands the importance of such "blueprint theologians" as the Cappadocians, Augustine of Hippo, Thomas Aquinas, and Martin Luther—while not being afraid to take a position against a too facile allegiance to the traditional Platonic and Aristotelian categories so often used in scholastic theology.

- I particularly am impressed by Pastro's nepantlic pulling together of the dialectical imagination as represented by Karl Barth and the sacramental or analogical imagination as represented by Karl Rahner, SJ. Neither should easily be dismissed, and both are very important— and Latin American theology seems to appreciate this. Pastro defines the terms beautifully and explains their theological importance to life and ministry. And he goes further, asking what it might mean to preach from the imagination of the indigenous poor.

- Considering a number of themes currently important in homiletic literature, Pastro's consideration of seven homiletic concerns of Pedro de Córdoba and his early Dominican community in La Española is particularly timely: learn the language of the people, emphasize story, preach frequently, live in solidarity with the poor, prepare communally, do not impose on the poor, and employ illustration and drama.

- Pastro explains why in his view the call to preach is by virtue of baptism: preaching is not primarily an office, but a way of life.

- Coining the term *transverbation*, Pastro rewards his reader with an extended and rich Christological meditation: Jesus is God's own sermon, revealed in the *pueblo*.

- Pastro accomplishes a beautiful explanation of the see, judge, act method of theological praxis. Using the words *ver, juzgar, actuar, evaluar,* and *celebrar,* he spells out a theological methodology of the poor. He also discusses the Yes and No theological methodology of Karl Barth, both in its original German social context and in that of contemporary theologizing by and with the poor.

With this book, Vince Pastro makes a valuable contribution by tilling new ground in the theology of preaching. God bless all those "resident theologians" among you who, enflamed by the Sacramental Word, aspire to pursue the preaching way of life with the imagination of the poor. I pray that Vince Pastro's theological exposition and his example of life will inspire and help you on the Way.

Gregory Heille, OP
Professor of Homiletics and Academic Dean
Aquinas Institute of Theology
Saint Louis, Missouri

Introduction

The *Ojo de Agua*

In the beginning was the Word, and the Word was with God, and the Word was God.

—John 1:1

Theology is a critical reflection on praxis in the light of the word of God.

—Gustavo Gutiérrez, OP

Theology is *ministerium verbi divini*. It is nothing more nor less.

—Karl Barth

The hallowing of the holiday (Sunday) takes place through the proclamation of the Word of God and through the willing and reverent hearing of this word. The desecration of the holiday begins with the deterioration of the Christian proclamation . . . Thus the renewal of the holiday hallowing starts with renewal of the preaching.

—Dietrich Bonhoeffer

Theology and preaching revolve wholly around the Word. Their only purpose is the service of the Word. In the academy, this is, perhaps, easier to overlook. But the "resident theologian"[1] in the community of God's people—the preacher—must never forget. Theology and preaching are at the service of the Word.

---

1. The phrase is Anna Carter Florence's. See *Preaching as Testimony*.

Karl Barth's greatest contribution to theology, and the proclamation to which it is intimately related, was his development of the three "words": the Word of God who is Jesus Christ, the word of God in the Holy Scriptures, and the word of God as proclaimed and lived by the Church community. Theology serves these three words whose source is Jesus Christ, the Sacramental Word of the God of the poor. Theology—and we resident theologians who are preachers—must attend primarily to this Word, this Sacrament, which is the source and summit of all words and the life of the poor.

Some years ago, Dominican Mary Catherine Hilkert published a ground-breaking study called *Naming Grace: Preaching and the Sacramental Imagination*. In this book, she proposes that preaching has its source in one of two theological imaginations. These imaginations, developed over the history of Western theology with notable examples in contemporary North Atlantic theology, are called "dialectical" and "sacramental." She maintains that Karl Barth represents the dialectical imagination, while Karl Rahner, SJ, acts as "spokesperson" for the sacramental imagination. In oversimplified summary, dialectical imagination underlies the theology of the word. In the dialectical imagination, the word of God is a two-edged sword (Heb 4:12) cutting through human pretentions. Sacramental imagination is behind sacramental, or "analogical," theology. In the sacramental imagination, divine action in grace is "named" through that which is concrete, contextual, and historical. Preaching happens primarily out of one of these two imaginations, and a major task of the preacher is to discern which imagination is prevalent in his or her preaching.

Hilkert is right. The effective preacher must work, in prayerful reflection, to identify the imagination from which she or he is preaching. However, while Hilkert treats two theological imaginations, there are, in fact, infinite varieties. These imaginations are formed within specific contexts and cultures. I have attempted to identify one such imagination after many years of ministry, study, and reflection in poor Latin American ecclesial communities both overseas and in the United States. Theologically, I describe it as "mystical-indigenous" because of its intimate connection to the language of the mystics and its indigenous roots. But practically, it is the imagination of the poor, whose indigenous mysticism is the shared wisdom of centuries of cultural heritage.

I have, with some hesitation, selected the descriptive phrase "imagination of the poor" for the purposes of this book. But global poverty, and

the image of the poor, has changed. Two Latin American theologians—
among many—have described this transformation: Pablo Richard and
Víctor Codina, SJ. Both recognize that the theological paradigm for Latin
America has dramatically—even radically—changed since the 1970s
and 80s. We can no longer speak exclusively, they say, in terms of the
classic liberation theology developed during those years. Rather, Latin
American theology is looking, in the twenty-first century, for a new biblical paradigm, now no longer the liberation of the exodus but, perhaps,
the experience of the exile, as Víctor Codina suggests.[2] Exile and exclusion are the norm for the poor of the twenty-first century.

Further, poverty can no longer be seen solely in socio-economic
terms. It is, rather, a "new" poverty only witnessed in the last decade of the
twentieth century and more prevalent as we conclude the first decade of
the twenty-first century. The new poverty is a poverty of exile. It is a poverty of the excluded, says Richard,[3] more global and not limited to Latin
America. Richard calls for a dialog of the excluded, Codina for a dialog
of the "different" and the exiled; both begin from the Latin American experience of socio-economic poverty, but now call for an ecumenical and
global conversation among large new sectors of the marginalized. When
I use the terms "poor" and "Latin American liberation theology," then, I
am no longer talking exclusively in terms of the poor of the 1970s and
80s, or the classic liberation theology of the same epoch. I am referring
to twenty-first century theology of the exiled and the twenty-first century
poverty of exclusion, now greatly enlarged from the socio-economic context of a different epoch. It includes the economic poor, but also embraces
women, undocumented immigrant communities, entire racial groups,
indigenous peoples, those whose sexual orientation makes them "different," and many others.

North Atlantic academic theology, as it has been done for centuries in the West, also finds itself seriously deficient as we move into the
third millennium. It, too, like the meaning of poverty and classic Latin
American liberation theology, has experienced the monumental changes
that confront our global community. North Atlantic theology, in short, is
elitist—too devoted to the academy; it is *macho*—too ignoring of the role
of women; and it is culturalist and racist—too patronizing of indigenous
cultures that make up much of Latin American and world reality. What

2. Codina, *No Extingáis el Espíritu*, 190.
3. Richard, *Fuerza Ética*.

is necessary is a critique of Western theology itself. Few in the Church or the academy want to go *there*. If this book is no more than just another theology of preaching, just another book on the "mechanics" of preaching, it will have failed miserably. Perhaps the biggest need, in the twenty-first century, is for the pastor, once again, to become a theologian and the theologian a pastor. When theology is transformed into the "contemplation of the Holy Trinity" of the Fathers and Mothers of the first centuries; when it becomes living ecclesiology; when it moves from academic rigorism that throws it onto a North Atlantic butcher block and chops it with a meat cleaver, like a side of beef, into all kinds of "sub-disciplines"; only then will it address the human needs that the *kerygma* was intended for by the Spirit of the God of Jesus. This book is an invitation to contemplate the Holy Trinity in the inscrutable light of the eternal Sacramental Word (John 8:12, John 9:5), gazing, as St. Gregory of Nazianzus says, while hiding in the "cleft of the rock" (Exod 33:22) who is the incarnate Word. But this contemplation—now not solely done "rationalistically" as in the West, or even "symbolically" as in the East, but "nepantlically" (unity *within* diversity) as in the South—is itself an invitation to turn the contemplative gaze from the ecclesial West (Rome), the ecclesial East (Constantinople), and the ecclesial North (Wittenberg, Geneva, Canterbury), towards the ecclesial South—Mexico City, São Paulo, Lima, La Paz, Michoacán, Oaxaca, Chiapas, and the undocumented Mexican immigrant communities in the United States.

I write from a Latin American mystical-indigenous perspective. But the imagination of the poor seeks a global commonality of the oppressed. So this book, I hope, will be of use to any preacher, in any context, who desires solidarity with the poor, the exiled, the different, and the excluded. Although many have inspired this book, I am especially grateful to the mystically indigenous exiled communities with whom I have ministered over the years. I am also deeply grateful to three mentor preachers and theologians: Gregory Heille, OP, John Heagle, and José Marins; and to my editor Dr. K. C. Hanson of Wipf and Stock Publishers.

The way I have done pastoral ecclesiology the last number of years has not undergone a "paradigm" change. But it has, nevertheless, experienced a shift that has been nothing less than earthshaking. The first shift has been an immersion in Dominican charism of the Word—through my friend and colleague of many years, María Teresa Montes Lara, OP; through my sisters of the Tacoma Dominican community (Congregation of St. Thomas Aquinas) with whom I am associated; and through my friends at Aquinas Institute of Theology in St. Louis, Missouri. The second was provided by the writings of Víctor Codina, SJ, to which Fr. José Marins introduced me some years back. Anything I say in this book about theology as "contemplation of the Holy Trinity," a renewed appreciation of pneumatology and Eastern Orthodox theology, symbolic theology as distinguished from North Atlantic rational theology—all combined with the option for the poor—is wholly due to this great ecclesiologist. It is a real loss to the academy and the Church in English-speaking countries that his theology has been so little translated. If there were a Nobel Prize for theology, Víctor Codina would be my candidate! The third shift is based in newer Latin American theologies, particularly Ivone Gebara's ecofeminist perspective and Mexican indigenous theologies. I am grateful to Ivone Gebara and her love for women, men, creation, and the poor, and to my friends Manuel Arias Montes and Javier Garibay, SJ, without whom I would have never been introduced to indigenous theology (Arias Montes) and *nepantla* (Garibay). All have influenced the direction of my ministry and, of course, this book.

In recent years, I have re-discovered the theology of Dietrich Bonhoeffer thanks to the International Bonhoeffer Society. I am especially grateful to Luís Eduardo Cumaru, President of the Brazilian section of the Society, and to my Brazilian colleagues in the Society; and to my friend Gottfried Brezger, the pastor of *Johanneskirche* in Berlin and the chairperson of the board of directors of the *Bonhoeffer-Haus*. The attentive reader will note the strong influence of Bonhoeffer throughout, who, like the poor in any context, died "before his time" (Gustavo Gutiérrez). I have been particularly touched by what his friend Eberhard Bethge called his "Christological ecclesiology." Bonhoeffer's image of Church and preaching has deeply affected my own: the Church is "Christ existing as Church community,"[4] the Church is "the communion of saints created by the resurrection,"[5] and the primary goal of preaching is that "the congregation of Christ might become the church"[6]—preaching as *epiclesis*, if you will. If I were to choose the twentieth century theologian who has had the greatest influence on my theology of preaching, it would be Dietrich Bonhoeffer.

A preacher accompanying an exiled community must quickly adapt to their imagination if she or he is to proclaim effectively the good news

4. See especially *Sanctorum Communio*.

5. Godsey, *Preface to Bonhoeffer*, 41.

6. Fant, *Bonhoeffer*, 138.

of Jesus in the context of poverty. This book can be especially of service to the preacher ministering in such a community. But I write, as Hilkert, for all preachers. If the preacher who proclaims the good news, like the Master, realizes that the Word always proceeds from the "margins," then this book will have served its purpose. What Latin Americans theologians have referred to as the "option for the poor" is not an option for *some* preachers. *All* preachers reading this book in *any* context will discover, in solidarity with the poor, that it is Jesus Christ Sacramental Word of the God of the poor who, in the creative breath of the Spirit, stands at the center of life, exile, and the preacher's journey.

In the state of Michoacán in Mexico, there is a small town called Tzintzuntzan—or, in the original *Purépecha* language, the "Place of the Hummingbird." Tzintzuntzan is about an hour and a half southwest of Morelia, the capital of Michoacán. The bus trip goes quickly because of the magnificent scenery. Michoacán is much like Washington State where I live, work, and minister. The landscape is filled with evergreens, so that sight never grows tired. Perhaps that is why there are so many people from Michoacán in Washington State.

Tzintzuntzan sits on the shores of Lake Pátzcuaro, a large fresh-water lake in Michoacán. A number of towns surround this lake known for its famous *pescado blanco*, the white fish that is so delicious and a staple of the people who live around this small inland sea. The people are proud of their *Purépecha* culture. The language is still spoken. When visiting Tzintzuntzan, one can still see the archeological ruins of what was—and is—a great indigenous culture.

Ojo de Agua, less than a mile from Tzintzuntzan and the source of the lake, forms practically one town with Tzintzuntzan. Its literal meaning in Spanish is "eye of water," but linguistically it refers to the source of any body of water, whether river or lake. Thus Ojo de Agua is the source of Lake Pátzcuaro. That great lake, from which these two towns take their livelihood, is fed, nourished, and sustained by the *ojo de agua*, the source. Visitors are proudly brought to the source, which is surrounded by a large well. A chapel to Our Lady of Guadalupe was built there long ago. It is said that if one listens intently at the foot of the *Guadalupana*, one can hear, deep below, the rushing of the underground spring which is the source.

Ojo de Agua is a sacred place. Were it not for the source, the people would die. The source is God's gift of life and grace. It is what feeds the lake and is ultimately responsible for its being; the lake, in turn, feeds the people. This imagination, mystical and indigenous, runs through the people's veins and permeates their identity. For the two great town feasts of *Corpus Christi* and *El Señor del Rescate*, Sacred Heart Church in Tacoma, Washington, a parish miles from Tzintzuntzan that I pastored for many years, is decorated with intricate fishing nets which hang from the ceiling. The nets are adorned by artificial *pescados blancos*, boats, fishing floats, and other symbols which bespeak their life as fishing villages. The *ojo de agua* is the source of life for the *pueblo*[7] of Tzintzuntzan.

There is a life-giving *ojo de agua* for the preacher as well: Jesus Christ, the Sacramental Word of the God of the poor. All other preaching fonts—Scripture, the sacraments, the word that is the community, the words of the preacher—have their foundation in this one Source. The Sacramental Word, if the preacher is open to the Spirit hovering over the *ojo de agua* (Gen 1:2), is made known through the inadequate words of the preacher. Jesus the Sacramental Word, source of life and liberation for the poor and the exiled, is the source of the words, because Jesus Christ is the eternal Word of God spoken from before all ages. In this one Word, all words are spoken. God, in *this* Sacramental Word, as St. Thomas Aquinas said centuries ago, speaks God's very being and all creation.

But there is another requisite for the preacher. Through the power of the Sacramental Word, she or he is called to develop a deep communion with the exiled *pueblo* and their imagination. The pages that follow invite the preacher on a journey through the "mystical-indigenous" imagination: the imagination of the poor immersed in the *ojo de agua* who is Jesus Christ Sacramental Word of the God of the poor.

Vincent J. Pastro
Twenty-Eighth Anniversary of the Holy
Martyrs Ita, Maura, Jean, and Dorothy
Vigil of St. Francis Xavier
Kent, Washington, USA

---

7. This is a Spanish word, very popular among grassroots ecclesial communities, which will be used frequently in this book. Its literal meaning is "people," but the English does not capture the nuances expressed by the Spanish. *Pueblo* is generally more descriptive of the communal reality signified by the word. It is especially experienced in poor communities. Phillip Berryman says, "*Pueblo* is really untranslatable: literally, it means 'the people,' but it also means the mass of people—poor people in contrast to the elites." See *Liberation Theology*, 159.

Part One

Where Have We Been?

"History is the greatest teacher," as the saying goes. History tells us where we have been. Where would we be without the lessons of history? What did the ancient Greek philosophers contribute to the history of thought? Did the Roman Empire teach us more than good road building technique? What year did Columbus "discover" America? Questions such as these are typically asked in history books from the perspective of dominant culture and the historical winner. They *must* be the right questions, we say. Seldom is history seen from the point of view of the "historical loser," from the underside of history. The poor and the exiled rarely appear in the pages of history texts used in the schools of the dominant culture.

Edward Schillebeeckx, OP, says that history is, nevertheless, that privileged place where the God of life is sacramentally revealed. We *must* look to history. But he invites us to see history from a different perspective: the perspective of "negative contrast." History, for Schillebeeckx, must be seen from the underside, from that unrecognized place where the victim suffers what is not recorded in the history books. History must tell the story of the exiled and the victim. Only then can it mysteriously reveal to us the presence of the Holy One.

The Sacramental Word speaks through the imagination of the poor, but the poor are always on the margin of history—most often the history of the "winner," the *conquistador*. José María Camorlinga Alcaraz says that the history of Christianity tells the story of the Christianity that "wins," "conquering Christianity." Most history books—even *Church* history books—never tell us about the Christian faith that "loses," the "conquered Christianity." Dare we admit that most ecclesiastical history is recorded by the Eusebiuses of Caesarea who write from the courts of Constantine the Great?

But history from the underside, the "negative contrast experience" of the victim, cries from the margins. The Triune God, through the Sacramental Word and by the power of the Spirit, hears the cry of the exiled (Exod 22:23; Job 34:28; Isa 19:20) and invites the Church community to do the same. The cross has been long used as sword throughout Western history (*in hoc signo vinces*), and the true cross of Jesus that is folly for Paul (1 Cor 1:18ff.) falls victim to the conquering sword. The pages that follow will attempt to return the "cross of folly" to its proper place. The Church is invited to listen to the Sacramental Word as it cries in the Spirit from the wood of the cross of *conquered Christianity*—from the imagination of the poor.

1

The Cry in the Desert

On 8 November 1510, Pedro de Córdoba, prior to the newly arrived group of Dominican friars on La Española (present-day Haiti and the Dominican Republic), preached his first homily to the indigenous *Taíno* in the colonial town of Concepción. The people were poor and literally slaves of the Spanish *encomenderos*. The *encomieda* was an outdated and unjust system of feudal entrustment dating back to Moorish times and imposed by Columbus in 1503 on the indigenous people. Many *Taíno* were sick and dying from the back-breaking labor imposed on men, women, and children alike, and the diseases brought to the island by the Spaniards. Earlier that year, Pedro and two other Dominican friars had arrived. They were horrified by the conditions in which they found the indigenous to be living. Now Pedro was ready to give the first homily, which he had carefully prepared, to the indigenous *Taíno*. Diego Colón, the governor, was present as well as a number of other Spaniards. A young cleric named Bartolomé de Las Casas was also part of the congregation.

The expectation was that Pedro de Córdoba, in the great Dominican tradition of preaching, would deliver a rousing homily from the pulpit. Instead, he sat down on a bench among the people with nothing but a crucifix. Starting with creation and culminating with the cross, he gently spoke to the people of God's love for them.[1]

This was the first of many Dominican homilies given during the next years, mostly to the indigenous *Taíno* but also to the Spanish *encomenderos*. Barely a year later Antonio de Montesinos, on behalf of the

1. This story is adapted from Miguel A. Medina's fine introduction to the catechism by Pedro de Córdoba. See *Doctrina Cristiana*, 23.

11

entire Dominican community of La Española, would deliver his famous cry for justice for the *Taíno*. Pedro de Córdoba and the Dominicans, this unique community dedicated to accompanying the indigenous poor of the island, would develop a style of preaching that attempted to address both the theological imagination of the *Taíno* and the context in which they lived. These were perhaps the first homilies preached from within the mystical-indigenous imagination—a theological imagination unique to the indigenous poor and preached by followers of Jesus in every age who proclaim, in the footsteps of the Master, God's option for the poor and the oppressed.

It must be said, from the outset, that what North Atlantic imagination calls the discovery of America[2] was nothing less than the devastating decimation of an indigenous people. The three great civilizations of America—the *Mexica*, the *Maya*, and the *Inca*—along with many others, were not "discovered" by the Europeans. They were invaded in what was classic unjust war. What is called the discovery of America by the history books of the dominant culture was, in fact, a war of violent aggression. Bartolomé de Las Casas, some five centuries ago, describes the horrific context:

> They [the Spaniards] forced their way into native settlements, slaughtering everyone they found there, including small children, old men, pregnant women, and even women who had just given birth. They hacked them to pieces, slicing open their bellies with their swords as though they were so many sheep herded into a pen. They even laid wagers on whether they could manage to slice a man in two at a stroke, or cut an individual's head from his body, or disembowel him with a single blow of their axes. They grabbed suckling infants by the feet and, ripping them from their mothers' breasts, dashed them headlong against the rocks. Others, laughing and joking all the while, threw them over their shoulders into a river, shouting: 'Wiggle, you little perisher.' They slaughtered anyone and everyone in their path, on occasion running through a mother and her baby with a single thrust of their swords. They spared no one, erecting especially wide gibbets on which they could string their vic-

---

2. I will use "America" consistently to refer to North *and* South America. Other consistencies will be the words "invasion," "incursion," or "conquest" instead of discovery, and *Mexica* instead of "Aztec."

tims up with their feet just off the ground and then burn them alive thirteen at a time, in honour of our Saviour and the twelve Apostles, or tie dry straw to their bodies and set fire to it. Some they chose to keep alive and simply cut their wrists, letting their hands dangling, saying to them: 'Take this letter'—meaning that their sorry condition would act as a warning to those hiding in the hills. The way they normally dealt with the native leaders and nobles was to tie them to a kind of griddle consisting of sticks resting on pitchforks driven into the ground and then grill them over a slow fire, with the result that they howled in agony and despair as they died a lingering death.[3]

The figures for the victims of this invasion are mind-boggling; a modern-day equivalent is the Jewish extermination by the Nazis during World War II or the atomic bombing of the Japanese cities of Hiroshima and Nagasaki.[4] Many indigenous authors are beginning to refer to what happened as nothing less than genocide.

It is within this context that historical theology regarding the evangelization of America by Christian Europe must be viewed. The European invasion and Christian evangelization went hand in hand. The friars accompanied almost every expedition of conquest, and the Europeans—the Spaniards and the Portuguese in the case of Latin America—depended on the work of the friars to "Christianize" the "pagans." It was not the preaching of the good news of liberation in Jesus but a rational for the enslavement and destruction of an entire indigenous culture. José María Camorlinga Alcaraz, a Mexican philosopher and theologian, says that "conquering Christianity" represents the worldview of the Spanish *conquistadores* and the friars who accompanied them in the initial evangelization, and "conquered Christianity" the work of Bartolomé de Las Casas and a very few who took the perspective of the poor.[5] One has its roots

3. Bartolomé de Las Casas, quoted from Hanke and Rausch , eds., *People and Issues*, 103.

4. We have no way of knowing the exact mortality figures from the European invasion. This chapter will refer mostly to the *Taíno* culture. It was all but destroyed by the Spaniards. Gustavo Gutiérrez gives perhaps the most reliable figures in an appendix to his book on Bartolomé de Las Casas. In La Española alone, the figures point to what Gutiérrez refers to as a "total demographic collapse." Gutiérrez says Las Casas estimated the *Taíno* population to be some three million people. The University of California in Berkeley says the figure was closer to eight million. In 1540, there were only three hundred indigenous left on La Española. See *En Busca de los Pobres*, 639.

5. Camorlinga Alcaraz, *Dos Religiones*, 81.

in Constantine and the "theology of glory" (*theologia gloriae*) that has dominated the history of institutional Christianity. Its names are legion—the Crusades, the Inquisition, the Salem witch trials, Hitler's "German Christians"—too many aberrations to list. The other looks solely toward the cross in a *theologia crucis* lived by Pedro de Córdoba, Bartolomé de Las Casas, Dietrich Bonhoeffer, Oscar Romero, and many others.

Within this context, there were few Christian preachers who did not serve both cross and crown. Most, in fact, served not cross at all but rather crown and the interests of the colonizers. While there were defenders of the rights of the indigenous peoples among the friars, most, ultimately, served the needs of the colonizers by their belief that the indigenous practiced "idolatry." Even sympathetic friars felt that local religious practices were idolatrous and should be eradicated. The best solution, in the mind of most missionaries, was to "Christianize" the people as soon as possible through forced baptism.

The first Dominicans to arrive in America believed differently. They practiced an evangelization that was rooted in the word of God and *converted* rather than forced, making theirs the great commission of Jesus: "Go therefore and make disciples of all nations, baptizing them in the name of the Father and of the Son and of the Holy Spirit, and teaching them to obey everything that I have commanded you" (Matt 28:19–20). These friars of the "Sacred Preaching"—as the order was called by Dominic—were filled with passion for the word and a desire to follow the Jesus of the poor. Within a short time, they developed a deep respect for the indigenous *Taíno* and their culture. This was, unfortunately, unique among the missionary friars. Even the Dominicans, once they moved into Mexico and beyond after this initial cry for justice, ignored the evangelical foundation so painstakingly developed by Pedro de Córdoba and the first friars of the Sacred Preaching.[6] Thus, the Dominican community of *Santa Cruz* on the island of La Española was a shining star in the midst of the dark night of forced baptisms and religious justifications of violence and enslavement.

6. In 1558, the Dominicans of a priory in Guatemala founded by Bartolomé de Las Casas supported the use of violence against the indigenous of the area. See O'Gorman, "Prólogo," *Los Indios de México*, xxvii–xxviii.

Who were these men who arrived in La Española almost five centuries ago? They were, in their entirety, Spanish Dominicans who had been attracted by the reform movement of the order. Some years earlier, a number of friars had discovered the need to return to the Dominican rule as envisioned by their founder, Domingo de Guzmán. They were to go back to their roots as the *Sacra Praedicatio*, originally formed by Dominic, and would be dedicated to a life of "Sacred Preaching" in prayer, study, and, of course, Dominican preaching. The first Dominicans in America came out of this reformed vision. They would be concerned for the pastoral care of the Spanish colonists on the island and the *Taíno* indigenous men and women who worked as virtual slaves on the *encomiendas*.

The Dominican reform movement had been afoot since the latter part of the fifteenth century. The center of this *ultrareforma* in Spain was the Dominican priory of San Esteban in Salamanca.[7] The reform was an attempt to return to the "primitive observance" of the first Dominican constitutions, particularly in regards to the charism. Contemplation, study, and, most especially, preaching were to be given priority in the lives of the friars. While considered rigorist by some, it received much inspiration from the movement for reform in Italy (San Marco in Florence) through Girolamo Savonarola. The friars sent as missioners to La Española—almost without exception—had their theological education and Dominican formation at the reformed San Esteban where Antonio de Montesinos had been sub-prior. Salamanca was considered one of the best schools of theology in Europe during the late fifteenth and early sixteenth centuries and was listed with Oxford, Bologna, and Paris. Francisco de Vitoria, Melchor Cano, and Domingo Bañez would teach there (it is unfortunate that Vitoria later disagreed with Las Casas regarding the indigenous in the Americas).

The Dominican chapter of 1508 in Rome supported the *ultrareforma*. The new master general, Tomás de Vío Cayetano, agreed that the mission to the New World should be charged to the Spanish reformed Dominicans.[8] The following year, on November 20, a number of friars from San Esteban were assigned to the newly opened priory of Santo Tomás in Avila. Juan Hurtado, a key figure in the reform at San Esteban and spiritual director to Pedro de Córdoba, was appointed prior of Santo Tomás. Included with Juan were Pedro de Córdoba, Antonio de Mon-

7. Pita Moreda, *Los Predicadores Novohispanos*, 69.

8. Medina, *Doctrina Cristiana*, 18.

tesinos, Bernardo de Santo Domingo, and Domingo de Villamayor—all connected with the primitive observance reform who would, just one year later in September of 1510, be assigned as missionaries to the New World priory of La Española. Of these four, three were known as excellent preachers and were the first to arrive in La Española.[9] Pedro himself had been appointed official preacher for Santo Tomás by Juan Hurtado, and Bernardo de Santo Domingo and Antonio de Montesinos were specially selected because of their homiletic abilities (it has been said that Pedro himself approached Antonio and invited him to consider the mission). In the coming years, three others (among many) would join the newly formed province of *Santa Cruz* in La Española: Domingo de Betanzos, founding provincial of Mexico,[10] the well-known Tomás de Berlanga, and the great Bartolomé de Las Casas.

Spain itself, in the late fifteenth and early sixteenth centuries, was ripe for Church reform. This Spanish reform movement had its great lights and shadows. When the first friars of what would become the Dominican province of *Santa Cruz* arrived with Pedro de Córdoba in 1510, not twenty years had passed since the incursion into America by Christopher Columbus. In Spain the royal couple, Ferdinand of Aragon and Isabella of Castile, were ruling an increasingly united and powerful territory. The queen was particularly interested in Church life (her title in many Hispanic-Latino countries is *Isabel la Católica*—Isabella the Catholic; the two were known as "the Catholic monarchs"). Ferdinand was not interested in reforming the Church except as a means for political expediency, but Isabella seemed genuinely interested in Church reform. The two would have much to do with the growth of modern-day Spain—and, for better or worse, with the history of America from the time of Columbus.

Isabella convinced her spiritual director, the Franciscan Francisco Cisneros de Jiménez, to accept appointment as bishop of Toledo, one of the most powerful ecclesial posts in the country. After conceding to her

9. Ibid., 17.

10. Domingo de Betanzos' record with the indigenous is mixed. He had a good relationship with the *Taíno*, perhaps due to the influence of Pedro de Córdoba. Later assigned to Nueva España (Mexico), he became the founding prior of that province presently known for its commitment to the poor. Unfortunately, Domingo strayed from his original commitment with the *Santa Cruz* community and is associated with an unfavorable attitude towards the indigenous of Mexico. This friar, whom Gutiérrez calls a "great missionary," repented of what he had said about the indigenous and their capacity for evangelization on his deathbed. See Gutiérrez, *En Busca de los Pobres*, 417 n17.

wishes, he proceeded in his project of Church reform in Spain and was responsible for the translation of Scripture into the vernacular. Ferdinand and Isabella, with the help of Cardinal Cisneros, were unrelenting in their efforts towards the unification of Spain under a reformed—and intolerant—Catholic Church. It was during this time that the Inquisition began to take on an important role within Spanish reality. It was also the century of Teresa of Ávila, John of the Cross, and Ignatius of Loyola. Columbus sailed under the auspices of the Spanish royal couple. During these years, Spanish activity in America would be critical to the future of both Spain and the New World. The Spanish Dominican reform, now firmly entrenched, was deeply affected by this religious and civil context.

When the first Dominicans arrived in the New World, they were horrified at the conditions in which they found the indigenous *Taíno*. Children, women, and men were already being subjected to the horrors of which Las Casas later so eloquently wrote. The work in the Spanish mines and on the large *haciendas* killed or incapacitated the great majority of the indigenous. These Dominicans, on fire with the return to their Dominican roots in the word, knew they could not remain silent. Years before our contemporary sensitivity to human rights abuses, Dominican historian Francis MacNutt would write: "Their observation of what was happening around them and of the injustice and cruelty daily practiced on the natives . . . forced upon them the duty of protesting against such violation of all laws, human and divine."[11] For over a year, the newly founded community of the Sacred Preaching prepared an appropriate response to the injustice of the Spanish *encomienda*, which was precisely the system which caused so much scandal to the newly arrived friars. It was built upon an outdated system of "entrustment," adapted from feudal Spain, in which individual Spaniards were given large tracts of Moorish land and serfs as the Iberian peninsula was "retaken" (*La Reconquista*) from Islamic hands. The *encomiendas* in La Española were mostly gold mines covering vast amounts of land. They were "entrusted" to the colonists along with the indigenous *Taíno* and their *caciques* (leaders). The *Taíno* people became the slaves of the foreign colonists and lost their dignity, their culture, their way of life, and their freedom. They died, literally, by the thousands because of war, sickness, and the back-breaking labor of the *encomiendas*.[12]

11. MacNutt, *Bartholomew de Las Casas*, 53.
12. Traboulay, *Columbus and Las Casas*, 27; and Bethel, *The Cambridge History*, 165.

The "appropriate response" that the friars decided upon was preaching. Over the following year, they prepared one of the most important homilies ever given regarding human injustice. The entire community would sign the written text, delivered by Antonio de Montesinos on the Fourth Sunday of Advent.[13] By then, it is thought that the priory had grown to some fifteen friars—all committed to justice for the indigenous *Taíno*. This first and most important chapter in the history of the province of *Santa Cruz* would be an expression of the Sacred Preaching and the reform at its best, for it was not only Montesinos who preached on that Sunday in December of 1511, but every member of the Sacred Preaching. When the authorities came later that day for Antonio, Pedro answered that all the friars were equally "guilty."

Thus it was that on 21 December 1511, over a year after the arrival of the first friars, the unassuming Antonio de Montesinos stood up in the pulpit after the proclamation of the gospel and preached. Lewis Hanke does not exaggerate when he says, "The sermon by Montesinos in 1511 in the straw thatched church in Hispaniola may be considered not only the beginning of the struggle for justice in Spanish America but also a turning point in the history of Christianity."[14] In one of the few references we have to Montesinos, Bartolomé de Las Casas calls him the Dominican's "most important preacher." He goes on to say, "His talent lay in a certain sternness when reproaching faults and a certain way of reading sermons both choleric and efficient, which was thought to reap great benefits."[15] As Montesinos began, no one was expecting anything extraordinary. Perhaps the *encomenderos* were waiting for a regular homily that would leave them with good feelings, for Antonio was known for his preaching abilities. The text for that Sunday was John 1:23: "I am the voice of one crying out in the wilderness, 'Make straight the way of the Lord.'"

What then fell on their ears was nothing less than revolutionary. Unfortunately, we no longer have the text of this preaching, though it is perhaps the most famous of classic social justice homilies. The only

13. See Gutiérrez, *En Busca de los Pobres*, 47. There has been some debate over the date, but contemporary Lascasian scholars identify it as 21 December 1511. See also Pérez Fernández, *El Itinerario Espiritual*, 8.

14. Hanke, *All Mankind Is One*, 8.

15. De Las Casas, *The History of the Indies*, 182.

description is two short paragraphs, written over twenty years later, by his great friend and collaborator Bartolomé de Las Casas:

> In order to make your sins against the [indigenous] known to you I have come up on this pulpit, I who am a voice of Christ crying in the wilderness of this island, and therefore it behooves you to listen, not with careless attention, but with all your heart and senses, so that you may hear it; for this is going to be the strangest voice that ever you hear, the harshest and hardest and most awful and most dangerous that ever you expected to hear … This voice says that you are in mortal sin, that you live and die in it, for the cruelty and tyranny you use in dealing with these innocent people. Tell me, by what right or justice do you keep these [Taíno] in such a cruel and horrible servitude? On what authority have you waged a detestable war against these people, who dwelt quietly and peacefully on their own land?
>
> … Why do you keep them so oppressed and weary, not giving them enough to eat nor taking care of them in their illness? For with the excessive work you demand of them they fall ill and die, or rather you kill them with your desire to extract and acquire gold every day. And what care do you take that they should be instructed in religion? … Are these not humans? Have they not rational souls? Are you not bound to love them as you love yourselves? … Be certain that, in such a state as this, you can no more be saved than the Moors or Turks.[16]

Montesinos became the voice in the desert, which he calls not now the voice of the Baptist but the voice of Christ. Montesinos preached that the Spaniard *encomenderos* must listen. This voice cried in the "sterile desert of the consciences" of the powerful of La Española,[17] demanding justice for the *Taíno*. Bartolomé de Las Casas says that Antonio left the pulpit with "head held straight" and went home to his straw shack "to eat his cabbage soup."[18]

Gustavo Gutiérrez characterizes this preaching as both "juridical and evangelical."[19] It is juridical because of its reliance on scholastic theology. Thus we see the references to the rational soul and the *Taíno* as human. It is mortally sinful, according to this juridical theology, for the

16. Ibid., 183–84.
17. Ibid., 183.
18. Ibid., 184.
19. Gutiérrez, *En Busca de los Pobres*, 49–50.

encomenderos to treat their *Taíno* sisters and brothers in this odious way. But the preaching, according to Gutiérrez, is profoundly evangelical. It relies on the gospel value of love of neighbor: "Are these not humans? . . . Are you not bound to love them as you love yourselves?" Here is not simply a juridical theology about "rational souls" and "mortal sin," but, at an infinitely deeper level, an evangelical theology that forever unites the juridical to the great commandment of sisterly and brotherly love.

The *encomenderos* were furious. A delegation led by the governor, Diego de Colón (the son of Columbus), marched directly to the simple straw priory[20] demanding to speak with Antonio de Montesinos. Pedro de Córdoba answered the door. The homily, he said, had been prepared as a Sacred Preaching—by the entire community of friars. They were all equally responsible and in agreement with what Montesinos had said. If anyone should be accountable, Pedro said, it was him as superior. When the Spaniards threatened to send the friars back on the next boat to Spain, Pedro quipped that that would be fine, as they were all working hard and could use a rest![21] "Of a truth, gentleman," he said, "that will give us little trouble."[22] The tension was high, but Pedro stood his ground. After talking to the colonists for some time, Pedro agreed that another homily would be given the following Sunday—by the same Antonio de Montesinos— clarifying what had been said. To the furor of the Spaniards, the next homily did indeed clarify. Antonio told the *encomenderos* that they were in such a sorry state because of the "mortal sin of injustice" that the friars all agreed to give no one absolution until the indigenous were released from slavery.[23]

This time the Spaniards complained to the king, who wrote to the Dominican provincial in Spain asking that the *Santa Cruz* Dominicans be censured. Pedro de Córdoba later received a letter from the provincial ordering the friars to preach no further on the topic and to retract what had been said. But the die had been cast, and the Dominicans continued to preach strongly against the abuse of the Spaniards. The *Leyes de Burgos* (Laws of Burgos), the first Spanish legislation attempting to protect the

---

20. When Pedro de Córdoba and the first friars arrived in La Española in September of 1510, the Spanish colonists wanted to build them a priory. Pedro insisted the Dominicans temporarily live in a simple straw house until they themselves built a permanent priory.

21. Medina, *Doctrina Cristiana*, 38.

22. MacNutt, *Bartholomew de Las Casas*, 55.

23. Medina, *Doctrina Cristiana*, 38–39.

rights of the indigenous, were passed on 27 December 1512, largely as a result of the preaching of these courageous Dominicans.[24] Unfortunately, these laws changed very little: "That was the sum of the first protest against the *encomienda*: Montesinos had preached, a junta had deliberated, the Laws of Burgos had been proclaimed, and the lot of the natives was no better than before."[25]

The young priest and *encomendero* who was present at Pedro's first preaching in Concepción and Antonio's later cry for justice for the *Taíno* was converted to the Jesus of the poor in 1514 while preparing his Pentecost preaching and reflecting on the following text:[26]

> If one sacrifices ill-gotten goods, the offering is blemished;
>
> The gifts of the lawless are not acceptable.
>
> The Most High is not pleased with the offerings of the ungodly, nor for a multitude of sacrifices does he forgive sins.
>
> Like one who kills a son before his father's eyes is the person who offers a sacrifice from the property of the poor.
>
> The bread of the needy is the life of the poor; whoever deprives them of it is a murderer.
>
> To take away a neighbor's living is to commit murder;
>
> To deprive an employee of wages is to shed blood (Sir 34:21–27).

On the feast of the Assumption that same year in Cuba, he preached to his Spanish parishioners that he had decided to give up his *encomienda* and had set free his enslaved indigenous workers.[27] He encouraged his parishioners to do the same. Thus began Bartolomé de Las Casas' long journey of accompanying the indigenous poor of Latin America. Eight years later, he experienced what he called his "second conversion" and became a Dominican friar. He was to make his religious profession—and receive his Dominican formation—with the community of the *Santa Cruz* on La Española.

24. MacNutt, *Bartholomew de Las Casas*, 58.
25. Wagner, *The Life and Writings*, 11.
26. MacNutt, *Bartholomew de Las Casas*, 59.
27. Gutiérrez, *En Busca de los Pobres*, 72–80.

2

Ill-Gotten Goods

Perhaps there is no more important figure in the history of the Christian theology of the accompaniment of the indigenous poor than Bartolomé de Las Casas. As Gustavo Gutiérrez says of this great Dominican defender of the rights of the poor, "[A] passion animated Las Casas: His love for the living Jesus Christ, scourged, struck, crucified, and died in the poor captives of the Indies, 'not just once, but thousands of times.'"[1] From the time of his conversion to the Jesus of the poor on Pentecost of 1514 through his death—over fifty years of commitment—he tirelessly made the cause of the poor his own.

Not much is known of the early life of Las Casas. He was born in Sevilla, Spain. It was believed for a long time that the year was 1474, but contemporary scholarship points to ten years later, in 1484. Whether or not he studied Church law in Salamanca is still debated. Even his ordination date is disputed. Some place it in Rome around the year 1507. Others think he was ordained in Santo Domingo in the year 1510 by Pedro de Córdoba, who was given special faculties as there was as yet no bishop in the New World. It is, perhaps, Pedro himself, Bartolomé's fast friend and mentor, who helps us conjecture about the dates. If Pedro was his mentor, his "spiritual father," as Bartolomé called him, it is unlikely he would have been ten years younger—arguing against 1474 as the year of birth. In fact, Córdoba was probably older (though not much) than Las Casas. Since Pedro was not only friend but mentor, this gives credence, in my opinion, to his ordination by Córdoba in 1510.

1. Gutiérrez, *En Busca de los Pobres*, 95.

Around 1502, Las Casas came to the New World with his father and his brothers. He received—and accepted—an *encomienda*. But he could have only been deeply affected by what he witnessed during those years as the *Taíno* suffered increasingly at the hands of the colonists. He was present at Pedro de Córdoba's first homily to the indigenous in Concepción and, barely a year later, at the preaching of Antonio de Montesinos.

From their arrival in the New World, Bartolomé was intimately connected with the Dominican Sacred Preaching—for better or for worse. After the Dominicans made the decision to withhold sacramental absolution from colonists who would not give up their *encomiendas* with the *Taíno* slaves, Bartolomé himself—already a priest—was denied absolution, perhaps by Pedro de Córdoba. The commitment of the community of the Sacred Preaching must have touched him deeply, for in four short years he was converted to the Jesus of the poor and left his *encomienda*.

After Bartolomé's conversion in 1514, he collaborated closely with the *Santa Cruz* Dominicans in their support of indigenous rights.[2] During the eight years that passed between his conversion and his entrance into the community of the *Santa Cruz* Dominicans, he journeyed to Spain a number of times—the first with Antonio de Montesinos—to secure official royal protections and legislation on behalf of the indigenous poor.[3] Bonds of friendship and respect were formed between Las Casas and the Dominican community of *Santa Cruz*. Bartolomé often wrote favorably about Pedro de Córdoba, Antonio de Montesinos, Tomás de Berlanga, Domingo de Betanzos, and other Dominicans. While ministering to both Spaniard and *Taíno*, he collaborated with the Dominicans as they sought justice.

These eight years formed an important part of the maturation of his thinking regarding indigenous rights in America, for he participated in two experimental "failures" before full-heartedly joining the Dominican effort.[4] His friend, Pedro de Córdoba, gently tried to discourage the projects, telling Las Casas that "as long as the king lived" the pacifistic colonization proposed by Las Casas would be impossible.[5] Perhaps Pedro

2. Pérez Fernández, *El Itinerario Espiritual*, 8.

3. Ibid., 9; O'Gorman, "Prólogo," *Los Indios de México*, xxv.

4. See Pérez Fernández, *El Itinerario Espiritual*, 9–15, Camorlinga Alcaraz, *Dos Religiones*, 84–87, and Gutiérrez, *En Busca de los Pobres*, 83–85, 112–19, for a summary of these two early Lascasian projects.

5. Pérez Fernández, *El Itinerario Espiritual*, 9.

was able to see the latent patronizing in any project—even pacifistic—dominated by Europeans.

First, Bartolomé obtained approbation from the regent Cardinal Cisneros (Ferdinand had died in 1516) of a project of "pacifistic evangelization" of the indigenous.[6] In this plan, formulated around the time of the king's death, the *Taíno* were to be given tracts of land and led by an indigenous *cacique*. They would be under the ultimate authority of the Spanish crown and would pay tribute to Spain. All would be supervised by a commission of friars. This failed quickly, because the Jeromian friars who were appointed to supervise soon came under the affect of the *encomenderos*, and the Spanish colonists, in their greed for wealth, gold, and land, were unwilling to exist peacefully side-by-side with the indigenous. The indigenous continued to be enslaved on the *encomienda* with no rights or recourse to justice.

Las Casas then asked permission for a second project of pacifistic evangelization in Venezuela (Cumaná). The Spaniards, while colonizing, would peacefully co-exist with the indigenous in a sort of "business contract" in which both Spaniard and indigenous would be autonomous. Evangelization would not happen through forced baptism, as had been the practice among many non-Dominican congregations, but through conversion and persuasion—much as in ancient Christianity. The indigenous, in turn, would be given exclusive rights to tracts of land that would be untouched by the Spanish *encomenderos* and colonists. In these areas, the indigenous would have total autonomy and would be taught useful European skills while retaining their own culture. The friars would be the religious "leaders" of the project, and evangelize only through preaching the gospel and freely allowing the indigenous to convert or not as they chose, in this precursor to the Paraguay Jesuit reductions. This was also doomed to failure because of colonial practices. As long as the colonists saw themselves as dominators and perpetrated violence, control of land, and slavery, they were unwanted invaders. All of these Lascasian efforts and later similar projects by others—as predicted by Pedro de Córdoba—were ill-conceived from the start. These *encomenderos*, like colonizers throughout history, were not invited by the indigenous but forced themselves and their culture upon a sovereign people.

Around 1521, Bartolomé returned from Venezuela to Spain and later La Española, perhaps with the sense that pacifistic evangelization

---

6. Camorlinga Alcaraz, *Dos Religiones*, 84.

and colonization would never work. Shortly he received the devastating news that the indigenous in Venezuela had revolted against the Spanish colonists. He entered a period of depression and uncertainty, unsure how to live his new-found gospel commitment to the indigenous poor. In the same year, his long-time friend and collaborator, Pedro de Córdoba, died from tuberculosis because of his commitment to the *Taíno*. What to do now, Bartolomé asked?

During this time he engaged in a number of dialogs with Domingo de Betanzos, the director of novices of *Santa Cruz*. Isacio Pérez Fernández, OP, a Lascasian scholar, reconstructs one of these conversations. Domingo listens patiently to Las Casas' disappointments. He observes that Bartolomé has sincerely tried every avenue of accompanying the indigenous to no avail. Pacifistic colonization was especially ill-conceived. There is only one thing left, suggests Domingo in this imaginary dialog—the way of preaching. Why not simply preach the good news of Jesus and God's justice for the poor?[7]

Bartolomé found his answer. The year following Pedro's death, Las Casas joined the Dominicans of *Santa Cruz* and became a novice. Perhaps he was convinced, through conversation with Domingo de Betanzos—and the example of Pedro de Córdoba—that *The Only Way*[8] was preaching. Little would be heard of him for the next four years. The *encomenderos* were elated. They would no longer be bothered by Las Casas and his insistence about justice for the indigenous.

It was during these years that Bartolomé de Las Casas became *dux verbi*—a "Master of the Word," according to Pérez Fernández.[9] As a diocesan cleric of the early sixteenth century, Bartolomé would have had only a minimum of theological preparation. The four "silent" years of Dominican formation in theology were at the priory of La Española, where he would be immersed in Dominican charism of the word and become *dux verbi*. For Dominicans, the purpose of seminary was not to become doctors of theology who would teach only at the university. The sole reason for Dominican preparation was to become *dux verbi*, master and conductor of the word who, through prayer and study, would proclaim the good news of Jesus within a living context—contextual hermeneutics at its best. Bartolomé de Las Casas would, during this formation, be immersed in

7. Pérez Fernández, *El Itinerario Espiritual*, 16.

8. *De Unico Modo*, the name of a major Lascasian treatise.

9. Pérez Fernández, *El Itinerario Espiritual*, 21.

Scripture and theology. He became, in the style of Paul, a *doctor gentium*.[10] Here he acquired his love for Thomas Aquinas and theology. Later Las Casas would argue vehemently against Juan Ginés de Sepúlveda, a leading "humanist," who maintained that the indigenous were "slaves by nature" according to Aristotle. But no one was able to refute Bartolomé's recourse to Aquinas. Even Francisco de Vitoria, who readily agreed with Las Casas that the indigenous were suffering at the hands of the Spaniards, could not refute Las Casas when Vitoria took the side of the *encomenderos* and argued for a "just war" against the indigenous.

During the time of his preparation with the Dominicans, Bartolomé may have written *De Unico Modo*, so they were hardly the "silent years" the Spaniards had hoped for. Las Casas had already experienced his first conversion to the poor indigenous, and the *Santa Cruz* Dominicans who taught him had, in turn, learned well from Pedro de Córdoba. Thus Las Casas would have been specially disposed to see contemplation and study, two indispensible aspects of Dominican charism, in the light of the good news to the poor.

The "silent years" ended for Las Casas in 1526 with his solemn perpetual profession as a Dominican friar. From then on, he would become tireless *dux verbi* on behalf of the indigenous poor. Immediately upon completing his formation, he was assigned prior to a new friary which was opened to the north of La Española at Puerto de Plata.[11] In 1529 Juan de Zumárraga, the Franciscan Archbishop of Mexico City, and Julián Garcés, the Dominican bishop of Tlaxcala, wrote to the royal court in Spain asking for friars to help reform the mendicant orders in Mexico. They requested several by name, including Antonio de Montesinos, Tomás de Berlanga, and Bartolomé de Las Casas.[12] By 1531, Las Casas was back in Puerto de Plata, where he spent the next three years preaching against the abuses of the Spaniards and the colonial authorities of La Española.

In 1534 he left the island with a group that included Tomás de Berlanga, the recently named bishop of Panamá. The ultimate destination of Las Casas and a number of the friars was Perú, where they were intended for a new mission.[13] However, they suffered a shipwreck in Nicaragua and remained there for a time. In 1536, he was assigned to

10. Ibid.

11. Pérez Fernández, *El Itinerario Espiritual*, 23.

12. Ibid.

13. O'Gorman, "Prólogo," *Los Indios de México*, xxvi.

open a new friary in Santiago de Guatemala, where he would stay for the next few years.[14] Soon he would travel to Spain to defend the rights of the indigenous before the royal court. He was later instrumental in the passage of the *Leyes Nuevas* (New Laws, 1542) that, on paper, suppressed the system of *encomienda* as it had been practiced. But the tide of colonial greed for gold, land, and wealth persisted. Bartolomé, for his part, continued efforts on behalf of the indigenous.

Finally—after the third request—he became the first bishop of Chiapas in 1544.[15] There he would suffer even more for being *dux verbi* and *doctor gentium* on behalf of the indigenous. Las Casas resolved to assure that the *Leyes Nuevas* were observed by the colonists of Chiapas. His principal means of doing so were the same used by Pedro de Córdoba and the Dominicans of *Santa Cruz* over thirty years before—the refusal of sacramental absolution to colonists who, in spite of the law, would not give up their *encomiendas*. He wrote a *Confesionario* that instructed the priests of the diocese about when absolution should be withheld from the colonists.[16] He was accused by the Spaniards of many "abuses," from insensitivity to the pastoral needs of the colonists to being a Lutheran! When he left Chiapas for a bishop's conference in Mexico City in 1546 and tried to return, he was greeted by a group of colonists who refused him entrance.

Perhaps it was primarily from these years of bitter conflict with the *encomenderos* of Mexico, Chiapas, and Guatemala that the campaign to smear Bartolomé de Las Casas' reputation began. For the last centuries, Lascasian students have been divided into two schools. The first springs from these attempts to taint the reputation of Las Casas. His name unjustly became associated with the *Leyenda Negra*—the "Black Legend" of the Spanish support of African slavery. In fact at one point after his conversion (two years later in 1516), he advocated the importation of African slaves to work in the Spanish colonies in a futile attempt to undo the system of *encomienda*. This line of thought he came to regret bitterly—only a few years later. It unfortunately became the historical basis of the attempt to malign his name. He was painted as schizophrenic, and his strong-willed character was exaggerated beyond proportion. The most

14. Ibid. This was the same friary that, some twenty years later, would support a war against the indigenous.

15. Pérez Fernández, *El Itinerario Espiritual*, 30.

16. Camorlinga Alcaraz, *Dos Religiones*, 88–89.

concerted modern effort at defamation was a study by Spaniard Ramón Menéndez Pidal.[17]

The second school, based in an entirely positive view of Lascasian thought, has been reborn through the scholarly work of primarily five people, among others: Isacio Pérez Fernández, OP, Henry R. Wagner, Lewis Hanke, Helen Rand Parish, and Gustavo Gutiérrez, OP. They have deconstructed the false image in an effort to arrive at a more accurate portrayal of Las Casas. The meticulous historical study done by these scholars is rooted in early documents concerning the life of Las Casas, his writings, and the testimony of Dominican friars and indigenous people. Historical theology owes them a great debt, and I have relied heavily on their research and the forthrightness with which they portray this great Dominican defender of indigenous rights.

Finally, about 1547, Las Casas returned to Spain a last time. It was not because of the opposition of the colonists, the first "defamers," that he returned. They did, in fact, make the resumption of his pastoral duties as bishop practically impossible; but the resignation of his see in 1550 allowed him to dedicate the rest of his life to the defense of the indigenous at the court of Spain. Between then and his death in 1566, he engaged in tireless polemic with Juan Ginés de Sepúlveda, representatives of the colonists, and Toribio Motolinía and others who had evangelized Mexico.[18] These years were both challenging and productive for Las Casas and among his most important regarding the defense of indigenous rights. Ginés de Sepúlveda was a leading humanist who had been enlisted by the colonists to support their cause. He proposed an argument "by nature" from Aristotle. The indigenous, he actually conjectured, were hardly human, and, because of idolatry and human sacrifice, a just war could be morally waged against them. Once vanquished, they could rightly be enslaved because their character was such that they were

---

17. Menéndez Pidal, *El Padre Las Casas*.

18. Although there are exceptions, the Dominicans stood alone in their objections to forced baptism. Generally, colonial evangelization supported a pastoral theology that advocated minimal preparation for baptism. According to Camorlinga Alcaraz, this resulted in a radical clash of two distinct views of Christianity. The Dominicans advocated baptism only after sincere conversion and a catechumenate reminiscent of the early Church. This, for Camorlinga, went straight to the philosophical essence of Christianity. Would baptism be forced or free? One represented a "conquering Christianity," the other a "conquered Christianity." See *Dos Religiones*.

"slaves" by the natural law.[19] Las Casas' argument against slavery *a natura* was nothing less than brilliant. He began from the gospel. Since the God of Jesus did not claim a territorial lordship but a universal Reign, the indigenous were not under the territorial lordship of Jesus. The Spaniards could not claim what Jesus himself did not claim. *Encomienda* enslavement was consequently immoral. In fact, the indigenous had the right to defend themselves against the Spaniards in what would be considered a classic just war![20] The argument was fierce, and the attitudes underlying the Sepúlveda polemic, unfortunately, prevailed. But no one was able to refute Las Casas. He was never brought before the Inquisition.

During these years at court, Bartolomé de Las Casas deepened his theological reflection regarding the indigenous poor. This thinking revolved around three key points:

1. There is no such thing as a "just war" against the indigenous, because violence directed against them is always the result of greed (Bartolomé even taught, using Aquinas as a source, that the Spaniards owed restitution for what had been robbed from the indigenous).

2. Baptism should never be forced and should always be the result of a process of evangelization.

3. The system of *encomienda* is deeply immoral and should be abolished.[21]

On these pillars, Bartolomé developed his defense of the indigenous and his polemic against Juan Ginés de Sepúldeva and the *encomenderos* who argued against him at the Spanish court.

First, war could never be justified against the indigenous because it was always contrary to the natural law. According to a number of theologians—including Francisco de Vitoria—war could be justified against the indigenous under certain conditions. Among them was supposed recalcitrance regarding idolatry and human sacrifice. Even if these were the sole reasons, war against the indigenous was always unjustifiable for Las Casas (contemporary Latin American indigenous theologians posit that pre-Columbian cultures were *not* polytheistic and did *not* practice human sacrifice). Furthermore, the real reason the Spaniards waged war against the indigenous was the greed for gold, territory, and wealth. It was

19. Camorlinga Alcaraz, *Dos Religiones*, 89.
20. Ibid., 90.
21. Ibid., 81.

an unjust war of aggression. Following the teaching of Aquinas, Las Casas said a just war could only be undertaken in the case of direct attack for reasons of defense.[22]

Second, baptism could never be forced. To do so was to invalidate the sacrament. In this, Bartolomé de Las Casas followed the teaching of the friars of *Santa Cruz*. For Las Casas and the Dominicans, the sacraments were not magical superstitions but celebrations of the Paschal Mystery of Jesus lived in the people. To force the indigenous population to be baptized was to cater to the wishes of the *encomenderos*, who wanted a passive people controlled by civil religion. If the colonists appealed to faith, they stood on firm ground. The more indigenous who were baptized by the friars, the easier things would be for the *encomenderos*. They would invoke the name of God, and the indigenous could morally be enslaved— or if not, pacified through violence. For Las Casas and the community of the Sacred Preaching, baptism could not be forced. It was always to be the result of sincere conversion.[23]

Third, the system of *encomienda* necessitated unilateral condemnation. On this point, the Spaniards were intransigent because of colonial economics that demanded enslavement of the indigenous. The injustice of the *encomienda* was central to the theology of Pedro de Córdoba and the early Dominicans. Bartolomé, through the many years of collaboration with the *Santa Cruz* Dominicans, struggled sorely against the *encomienda*.[24] The "only way" was conversion through evangelical preaching and the dismantling of the system of *encomienda*.

Bartolomé de Las Casas died in 1566 in the Spanish city of Valladolid, faithful to Dominican *dux verbi* and the indigenous poor. Although he was responsible for the formal defense of the indigenous before the Spanish court, the dedication of the Sacred Preaching of *Santa Cruz* to the justice of God inspired his struggle. Pedro de Córdoba, Antonio de Montesinos, Bernardo de Santo Domingo, Tomás de Berlanga, and others who gave their lives to the Word made flesh in the oppressed *Taíno* of La Española were present in the voice of Bartolomé de Las Casas as he pleaded the cause of the poor before the powerful.

22. Gutiérrez, *En Busca de los Pobres*, 219–69.
23. Ibid., 139–75.
24. Ibid., 384–96.

3

What Does the Sacred Preaching
Say to Preachers?

Early on, Pedro de Córdoba and the Dominican community developed seven key characteristics of "apostolic activity" and preaching within the particular context of *Taíno* indigenous reality.[1] These principles are equally valid today for preaching with indigenous poor communities and from their imagination. When combined with David Buttrick's "moves in consciousness" and contemporary narrative preaching, this seven step methodology can also be helpful to the preacher who does not work directly with the indigenous poor. I propose, in fact, that narrative and inductive preaching that accounts for these seven steps can be effective in any context—much as African-American preacher Henry Mitchell uses the "moves in consciousness" methodology along with traditional African-American preaching.[2] The preacher can use Córdoba's principles—albeit contextually adjusted—in a middle-class or wealthy community as a source for solidarity with the imagination of the poor.

Pedro de Córdoba's seven steps, as enumerated by Miguel A. Medina, OP, are:

1. The need to learn the language of the people;

2. The importance of the story to preaching;

---

1. Medina, *Doctrina Cristiana*, 50. The following discussion is based on Miguel A. Medina's excellent presentation of these "characteristics" of Dominican preaching on La Española. I am entirely indebted to the creative scholarship done by him in his enumeration of these seven principles.

2. See Mitchell, *Celebration and Experience*.

3. The conviction that preaching should occur frequently;

4. The notion that the preacher should live a life of faith in solidarity with the poor;

5. The importance of a preaching prepared communally and contextually;

6. The belief that neither preaching nor preacher should be a "burden" to the indigenous poor;

7. The liberal use of dramatization, illustrations, and short narrations from Scripture.

These seven principles are equally at home in theology, in the imagination of the poor, and in contemporary narrative-inductive approaches to preaching advocated by David Buttrick, Barbara Brown Taylor, Fred Craddock, Henry Mitchell, Anna Carter Florence, and many others.[3] I will expound on each of these principles in terms of what preaching within a poor community in the United States—specifically Mexican—might look like. The preacher should take these principles and apply them to his or her context.

First, the preacher must have a working knowledge of the language. This is, of course, not a challenge for the pastoral agent or preacher who is a member of the indigenous group in question. But it is all too often overlooked by preachers from a First World, non-indigenous background who minister with the poor. This is of particular importance for preachers ministering within Hispanic-Latino communities in the United States. Language learning is a challenge at best. But if the preacher is to spend any significant time in his or her role as pastor within a predominantly Hispanic-Latino context, knowledge of Spanish is essential. However, knowledge of language goes much deeper than the spoken word; a preacher also should learn the language of the *culture*. Immersion within a cultural reality, leaving behind any excess baggage from the dominant perspective, is what solidarity with the poor calls for in this context. It is a challenge for the pastor who comes from a colonizing culture for he or she must strive, with a spirit of gospel justice, to move from "the colonizer who accepts" to "the colonizer who rejects" and beyond.[4] This was the

---

3. The literature in contemporary homiletics is too vast to be properly cited. Some of the works of these authors are included in the bibliography of this book.

4. See Memmi, *The Colonizer and the Colonized*.

situation that confronted the Dominicans in La Española and requires particularly disciplined and committed evangelizers who, while retaining their own cultural roots, enter into their host culture so deeply that they "feel with" (Oscar Romero's episcopal motto) the people and the local Church. Complete transcultural change is neither desirable nor possible, but it can be approached in the area of language by the pastoral agent who believes that God has made an option for the poor.

What if a preacher does not know the spoken language of the people? This is true of many sincere North American preachers ministering in immigrant communities. The imagination of the poor can help, even if the preacher does not speak the actual language; for in any context a preacher can speak the language of . . . *images*! Powerful images and metaphors have always been used in preaching. A preacher, particularly one ministering in a First World context, must be careful with the imagination, for it can easily become what Ivone Gebara has called a "metaphysical imagination" disconnected from the concrete reality of the poor.[5] The Fathers and Mothers of the first centuries, such as Basil the Great, Gregory of Nazianzus, John Chrysostom, and Augustine, painted homiletic discourse with graphic imagery. These theological homilies, full of the imagination of the poor, became the basis of much of the Church's later reflection. If preachers are to be effective in any context, they must use vivid images:

> In a sermon from 1932 (Dietrich Bonhoeffer) formulated in a striking image the high-spun ideal to which he wanted to measure preaching up to the end. "One cannot understand and preach the gospel tangibly enough. A truly evangelical sermon must be like offering a child a red apple or a thirsty person a glass of cool water and asking, 'Do you want it?' We should talk about matters of faith in such a manner that people would stretch out their hands for it faster than we can fill them."[6]

The images may be tender. The preacher can use imagery like Paul's "nursing" of the people with mother's milk (1 Cor 3:2), a "maternal nurturing" of the communities he founded.[7] Scripture is full of such tender images, which should be liberally exploited by the preacher. We are borne

5. Keynote address, Northwest Catholic Women's Conference, Bellevue, Washington, 2 May 2009.

6. De Lange, *Waiting for the Word*, 91.

7. See Gaventa, *Our Mother St. Paul*.

in times of trouble "on eagles' wings" (Exod 19:4), we are never forgotten by our maternally tender God (Isa 49:15) who nurtures and comforts us in the holy city (Isa 66:10–13), we fear no evil even in the "darkest valley" (Ps 23:4), we are like sated children in the lap of our mothers (Ps 131:2), we are infinitely loved by the Shepherd who "lays down his life for the sheep" (John 10:11) and knows us through and through (John 10:14). Or the images may be stark and prophetic. In a recent preaching with our Mexican community on Matthew's text about paying taxes to Caesar (Matt 22:15–22), I asked for a coin from the congregation and was given a dime. Reading the inscription on the coin, "In God We Trust," I said, ¡Mentira!—"That is a lie!" Dr. Jeremiah Wright, the African-American United Church of Christ pastor from Chicago who unjustly came into the limelight during the recent presidential elections in the United States, stood in biblical prophetic tradition when he preached, "God damn America!" It was not an easy message for many, but it was a powerful image that proclaimed the gospel of the oppressed. Images speak to people in any context. Andrew Carl Wisdom, OP, has recently written that the preacher should use the language of all cultures represented in the congregation—including "generational" cultures.[8]

Second, the preacher needs to learn how to "tell the story." Stories are important to every culture. Poor indigenous culture relies on the story for the transmission of cultural values. The *Mexica* creation account is important to the cultural identity of the Mexican people.[9] *Mexica* tradition during the tumultuous years following the Spanish invasion would not have survived if not for the story-telling skills of the elders. In indigenous culture, story plays a key role in the identity of the people. For the Mexican immigrant community in the United States, it is crucial that the people know their story for in the story is found, in linguistic symbol, who they are and who they are called to be. The stories may be told over and over—for example, the story of Our Lady of Guadalupe or the story of Cuauhtémoc—because the people never tire of hearing them. The stories are told by parents to children, by children to their children. The stories are told at *fiestas* and in the market-place. And the stories need to be told by the preacher. This is particularly true in the context of an indigenous people living within a dominant culture, like the Mexican people in the United States. Mexican children go to school in the United

8. Wisdom, *Preaching*.

9. See Guerrero, *Flor y Canto*, 317–35.

States, and not only do they *not* hear their stories, but other stories—the jaded stories of the dominant culture—are told them in a language that is not their own. Business is negotiated in a foreign language with foreign symbols, purchases are made in a different context, and life is lived out of different values. If the people can go to church and hear their stories according to their linguistic and cultural heritage, a sacred space is created. Arturo Pérez Rodríguez, a liturgist and priest, tells of presiding at a Guadalupe liturgy in a Mexican parish in Chicago, closing his eyes, and being mystically transported to Tepeyac. Good liturgy and preaching, he says, give the people a strong experience of their cultural identity.[10] This is facilitated through the creative use of story.

Third, preaching should be frequent. Many preachers do not want to hear this. "It is so difficult to prepare homilies," is a cry often heard in rectories, convents, and parsonages. Yet preaching is an indispensable part of accompanying the indigenous poor—and any people. At least every Sunday and on major feast days—such as Our Lady of Guadalupe—the people of the Mexican Church in the United States have the right to expect a well-prepared and articulate homily from the stance of their imagination. This means the preacher must dedicate the necessary time, in spite of constraints, to homily preparation. David Buttrick writes with special sympathy for pastors who are constantly barraged by the ministerial clock—meetings, pastoral visits, administration, pastoral counseling, and the like. But he reminds us: "Brothers and sisters, we are not mere functionaries. We are ministers of Word and Sacrament."[11] Preaching in poor indigenous communities, or any community, should occur often and be well-prepared.

Fourth, the preacher should be a person of faith and live in solidarity with the poor. These two realities are unified in what the preacher attempts to live faithfully if tentatively. Faith and solidarity are never mere ideas. Faith is a living person—the person of Jesus crucified and risen, alive in, and "conformed to" (*conformitas*) a living Church community, in the words of Dietrich Bonhoeffer. Solidarity is with living, breathing people, the poor who "die before their time" and suffer innumerable injustices.[12] The presence of Jesus crucified and risen is especially discerned

10. Workshop on Hispanic-Latino liturgy at Seattle University, June 1998.

11. A point put forward by David Buttrick in *Homiletic*.

12. This is Gustavo Gutiérrez' definition of poverty and is found throughout his writings.

in the poor whom the preacher accompanies in solidarity: "This topic (the presence of Christ in the oppressed), which has not usually been dealt with by christology, but has been relegated to spirituality, is taken up again by *Medellín*. Its premise is that Christ must be found today in history, but not where human beings would like to meet him, but where he is, even if this place is scandalous."[13] A conscientious preacher as a person of faith lives in solidarity with the least. Solidarity in faith with the poor also means a deep respect for the *religiosidad popular*, the popular faith of the people. Mexican parishes in the United States will have a strong presence of Mexican religious devotions and customs, particularly *Nuestra Señora de Guadalupe* (Our Lady of Guadalupe) but also local customs such as, for instance, *El Señor del Rescate* (The Lord of the Rescue) for the people of Tzintzuntzan, Michoacán. There is no room in preaching the imagination of the poor for those who lack respect for the deepest convictions of the *pueblo*.

Fifth, Pedro de Córdoba says that preaching is a communal action. When Antonio de Montesinos preached his cry against the abuses of the *encomenderos* on 21 December 1511, his was not a lone voice. The homily was prepared—and signed—by the entire Dominican community of La Española, who had been analyzing the system of *encomienda* for over a year. This was the *sacra praedicatio*—the Sacred Preaching—in the best Dominican sense. It was a communal announcing of the Baptist's "voice in the desert" and denouncing of the enslavement of the *Taíno* by the *encomenderos*. In the same way today's preacher, in accompaniment of the indigenous poor (or in solidarity with the poor from a different context), never works in a vacuum. He or she accompanies, and is accompanied by, an historical group of people. Those with whom the preacher is in special solidarity are the *pueblo*—religious communities, parishioners, friends, family, and the poor. Many Dominican communities of women and men still practice the "Sacred Preaching"—a communal approach to preaching by sisters and brothers gathered together in the name of Jesus and the Spirit especially present in the poor.

Some preachers, regardless of whether they belong to a religious community such as the Dominicans, practice the *sacra praedicatio* through homiletic preparation groups that meet on a regular basis to share the Sunday Scriptures. These groups often are comprised of parishioners who represent a cross-section of the community. In poor indigenous parishes,

13. Sobrino, *Jesus the Liberator*, 19.

their membership reflects the socio-economic-racial reality. In a Mexican parish in the United States, the homiletic preparation group will represent the Mexican people and may even take on aspects of the *comunidad eclesial de base*—the base ecclesial community. The *sacra praedicatio* is especially important to the imagination of the poor, which is communal by nature.

Sixth, neither the preacher nor the preaching should be a "burden" to the indigenous poor. Medina, in speaking of this specific Cordobian principle, uses the Spanish verb *gravar*, which is translated "to burden." "To burden" also means "to offend." Neither preacher nor preaching should be burdensome or offensive to the indigenous poor. This means that homilies will be read and re-read, practiced and re-practiced, until the preacher is certain there is nothing offensive or burdensome to the *pueblo*. Here "offensive" does not mean that which does not homiletically challenge; "offensive" is, rather, that which is pejorative toward race, class, or culture. There is no place for cultural chauvinism from the preacher who chooses to accompany a poor indigenous community. This is especially important in parishes with Hispanic-Latino presence in the United States, where too often the people receive the preacher's own cultural insecurities in what is disguised as gospel proclamation. Concretely, this means recognition on the part of the preacher of the way he or she participates in the structural sin of the dominant culture.

Perhaps Pedro was also referring to the gospel passage of the scribes and Pharisees placing *burdens* on people's shoulders, which can especially point to preaching: "The scribes and the Pharisees sit on Moses' seat; therefore, do whatever they teach you and follow it; but do not do as they do, for they do not practice what they *preach*. They tie up *heavy burdens*, hard to bear, and lay them on the shoulders of others; but they themselves are unwilling to lift a finger to move them" (Matt 23:2–4, italics mine). There are two things in this passage pertinent to the preacher—heavy and unjust burdens are *not* to be placed on people, and the preacher should live what is preached (this refers back to point four).

Finally, the preacher should not be afraid to use scriptural narrative and dramatization, spiced with copious illustrations and examples, in homiletic delivery. Why not experiment with different styles of oratory? The importance of story-telling has already been mentioned. Here Pedro de Córdoba is calling, I think, for rhetorical flair in service of the gospel. Unfortunately, rhetoric has a bad name these days. But among preachers, the *art* is slowly being recovered. This is not rhetoric for rhetoric's sake, but expresses the Augustinian tradition of "teaching, delighting, and persuading" in preaching the good news of Jesus for the poor. When explaining a Pauline passage, why not play the part of Paul himself?!—or some other biblical personality which fits the Sunday scriptural narratives.

All of us preachers go through "dry spells" or times when, no matter how much we prepare, we feel ill-suited to the task of preaching on a particularly Sunday. Or perhaps we want to accompany an immigrant community in the preaching but do not speak the language well. The preacher should not be afraid, occasionally, to fall back on Chrysostom's classic advice—there is nothing wrong with reading the great homilies of the Patristics/Matristics during homiletic time. In a Mexican context, perhaps this means parts of the *Nican Mopohua* (the indigenous narrative of the Guadalupe story written in *Náhautl* and translated into Spanish) during the preaching time for the feast of the *Guadalupana*. Or a pastoral agent who knows the language and culture well is invited to preach, while the pastor takes an accompanying role. Is not all good preaching, after all, *acompañamiento*—accompaniment of the *pueblo*?

We do not know the results of Pedro de Córdoba's first homily to the indigenous poor in Concepción. Like Pedro himself who died at thirty-eight of tuberculosis, most would die before their time. This, as Gustavo Gutiérrez says time and again, is the lot of the poor. Whether there were any "converts" from that first homily is not recorded. It would not have mattered to Pedro. What slowly became apparent to him—and to his faithful friend, Bartolomé de Las Casas, and to Antonio de Montesinos, and Tomás de Berlanga, and Bernardo de Santo Domingo, and the other friars who formed the community of *Santa Cruz* on La Española—was that the indigenous poor were human beings who, like themselves, were created in the image and likeness of the God of Jesus who takes an option for the poor and asks the disciple to do likewise. Their fidelity to the Dominican charism of preaching and *dux verbi*, grounded in the love of Domingo de Guzmán for the Word, graced them with compassion for the suffering.

With the ravages of time, the Dominicans who built around the ruins of the first priory have lost track of where Pedro is buried. But the ground is hallowed by the blood of the *Taíno* and sanctified by the commitment of Pedro de Córdoba, Bartolomé de Las Casas, and the Holy Dominicans of

La Española. The imagination of the poor and God's option for the exiled continue to be preached today, in the spirit of Pedro and the Dominicans and in the context of the poor indigenous. In their faces, the modern-day follower of Jesus discerns the Holy Face. It is, at core, a mystical experience of the mysterious God who wishes to be revealed in the poor other. This contemplative experience is lived in praxis and preached in solidarity with the *pueblo*. Its corner stone is the theological imagination rooted in mystical-indigenous experience and in the God whose option is for the poor of the earth.

Preaching Practicum One

One of the most important purposes of theology is to serve the pastoral practice of the Church community. For the theology of preaching, *the* pastoral question is the Sacred Preaching itself. I will end each part of this book, therefore, with two homilies that try to put flesh on what has been spoken of in the section. Part One has dealt with the preaching of the Dominicans in La Española, so the preaching presented will attempt to follow Pedro de Córdoba's methodology from the last chapter as well as recuperate, for a contemporary context, the lasting values of the Sacred Preaching of the Dominicans of *Santa Cruz.*

The first homily was preached in both English and Spanish on the Twenty-Fifth Sunday of Ordinary Time, Cycle A (*Roman Catholic Lectionary*). The gospel text was Matt 20:1–16, the parable of the landowner. The preaching was prompted by a number of workers from the parish community—all Hispanic-Latino—who had been adversely affected by "clean-up" of an environmentally contaminated area. A deacon in a neighboring parish and I agreed to preach about the issue on this particular weekend because of the gospel reading and its temporal proximity to the event. The decision was the result of an ecumenical gathering concerning the rights of the workers in question. It was agreed that specifics would be vague—some of the undocumented workers had been threatened and negotiations with the employer were pending. The following is a synopsis of the preaching, which, as other homilies presented in this book, will use narrative and inductive style and be constructed around David Buttrick's "moves in consciousness."[1]

---

1. Like most preachers, I use a wide variety of resources for homily preparation. They vary from week to week, depending on the preaching. Some, however, are used regularly. There are a number of very good Bible commentaries and dictionaries—for instance, Harper's, Eerdmans, or the *New Jerome Biblical Commentary*. The introductory and

Introduction: Orthodox bishop and theologian Kallistos Ware tells the story of a Russian "fool," a "holy person." His name was Nicolas. Now, we've all heard the stories of Ivan the Terrible. One day Nicolas marched into the imperial palace and placed in Ivan's hands a fresh piece of meat still dripping with blood—an act that said Nicolas was no "fool" at all but a courageous prophet of God's justice and God's holiness. He symbolically proclaimed to Ivan, "This meat represents the blood of all the innocent you have shed."

Move One: We've often thought the owner of the vineyard in today's parable "foolish," or even worse, "heavy-handed"—that's the way he's described by a well-known theologian who comments on this gospel. I remember a homily a priest gave years ago when I was growing up. He said that the grumbling workers were right—the vineyard owner was "unfair"! We really don't "get" this story at all, do we? We shouldn't feel bad—not even those who have studied the parable for years "get" it. I wonder—have any of us ever thought that the vineyard owner was simply being "just"? We've compared the parable to God's mercy and generosity. God's mercy is not human justice, we've said. That's true. But have we ever tried to look at the parable through the lens of *God's* justice? The daily wage paid to all the workers by the landowner—without exception—was so that each worker and their families would have *enough* to eat and to live, as one theologian puts it, *for a day*. "Give us this day our daily bread . . ." That is God's desire—our daily bread, daily bread for everyone in the world, rich and poor. Everyone, the parable says, has a right to basic

---

textual notes of many Bibles are scholarly and thorough—the *New American Bible* or the *Biblia Latinoamérica* are examples. There are also fine commentaries on the weekly lectionary readings available from various theologians such as Gustavo Gutiérrez or Gerard Sloyan. For a more in-depth study of a particular point or issue, the Anchor dictionary and commentaries are among the best. For exegetical word study, a good Bible computer program, such as *Bible Works* or *Logos* (Libronix), is a wise investment. There are also computer programs available for free on the Internet. Among them are *E-Sword* (www.e-sword.net) and *Interlinear Scripture Analyzer* (www.scripture4all.org), which Gregory Heille suggests. The Internet can be the biblical "blessing or curse" for preachers, so use it well but wisely! I have three favorite Web sites: *The Center for Liturgy* at St. Louis University (http://www.liturgy.slu.edu/); *Servicios Koinonia* (http://www.servicioskoinonia.org/); and Jude Siciliano's *Preacher's Exchange* (http://www.judeop.org/). I will deal with the challenges of weekly homily preparation in chapter 9.

dignity and humanity. The vineyard owner is not "foolish" at all—just like the "fool" Nicolas!

Move Two: God's justice gives to each according to their need, not by the hours they have worked or their status. Recently, an abusive employer—this is a true story that involves workers from our parish—hired people to clean up an area that was chemically contaminated with arsenic and, consequently, very dangerous. The first group was trained in "Hazmat"—the removal of contaminated material from a site. But they all quit within days because the work was too dangerous. Just not worth it, they said. The second group—this time thirty to forty undocumented Hispanic-Latinos—was brought in to do the clean up without proper training. Some became sick.[2] A number complained about headaches and nausea. A few went "public" and, as a result, have been threatened. The company hired a new group of workers who have been "properly trained." But as for the others, they have been offered little. Now, if the parable of Jesus is used here, equal justice will be given to all these workers simply because of the dignity due all human beings—our "daily bread." God's justice measures according to *need*.

Conclusion: I recently attended an ecumenical meeting. We were asked to define "justice." There was the "usual stuff," including my own poor attempt—something about Thomas Aquinas and justice! Finally, a visiting Latin American priest spoke. He said, "Justice in the Bible is the *holiness* of God." (*Pause*) This is a parable of God's holiness, God's justice. I ask, after hearing it so many times, "Do I *really* get it?"

The second homily was preached in English on the Thirtieth Sunday in Ordinary Time, Cycle A (*Roman Catholic Lectionary*). The texts were Exod 22:20–26, 1 Thess 1:5–10, and Matt 22:24–30. The preaching is a study in how Cordobian methodology can be applied to an English-speaking context. The congregation was predominantly pluri-cultural, with a mixture of middle-class North Americans and a few wealthier people. Three particulars struck me during the preparation:

1. A "hermeneutic of suspicion" that led me to base the preaching almost entirely on the Exodus text. The suspicion was aroused through

2. One worker has since died.

a computer search of the digitized version of Karl Barth's *Church Dogmatics* (all fifteen volumes!) that turned up not a *single* reference to the text! Why? Later, the suspicion deepened when a word study on the Hebrew *ger* gave the translations "alien," "stranger," "foreigner," or "sojourner." But "immigrant" or "migrant" was seldom used.

2. A reflection on a recent anthology on abstention from voting from the Christian perspective, particularly the thoughtful essay by theologian Todd David Whitmore;[3]

3. A commentary by Gustavo Gutiérrez, OP, on the readings for the Thirtieth Sunday, Cycle A, in which he asks the simple question, "Where do the poor sleep"?[4]

Introduction: On this last weekend of October, we remember, as we do every year, parish stewardship—how we share our time, talent, and treasure with the community. Let's begin these three weekends with a reflection on the biblical idea of stewardship. Stewardship is *caring for* God's creation, the gifts with which we've been entrusted. Maybe the best description of the word is its use in Spanish with regards to the stewardship program—"co-responsibility." In stewardship, we are responsible for creation, for the world, and for one another. Scripture tells us that stewardship is about *life* and *love*. It is love of God and love of neighbor—the widow, the orphan, and the immigrant.

Move One: We're getting ready to vote—or perhaps we already have, if we filled out our absentee ballot. Now, an important question is: how do we express love for God and neighbor, how do we nurture life, through the vote? Is there a "stewardship" of voting? How do we care for life and love by the vote? Catholic moral theologians talk about voting as a "limited responsibility." It is not "absolute." There *are* people in the Christian tradition that opt *not* to vote for reasons of conscience—some of our Mennonite sisters and brothers, for instance, have chosen that path. Or perhaps you don't vote because you are not a citizen of the United States, or because the choices are really not "choices." Those things "limit" the responsibility to vote. But what is most important, as in most Catholic

---

3. Whitmore, "When the Lesser Evil," 62–80.

4. Gutiérrez, *Compartir la Palabra*, 341–42.

moral teaching, is what is called the "common good." The Christian community concerns itself, in voting as in all things, with life issues that are important *to the community*, to the well-being of the community. That is *stewardship* of life. It has been called the "seamless garment" approach by Cardinal Bernadine. Abortion and assisted suicide, of course—it's hard to believe that I-1000 (*a "death with dignity" initiative on the Washington state ballot in 2008*) is even on the ballot! I suppose it says something for our culture's view of life. But I'm talking today about *all* life issues. Scripture says "choose life" (Deut 30:19). They don't give us the option of choosing *which* life issues. So for the Christian the war in Iraq, the economic situation, capital punishment, immigration rights and justice for the poor, *all* are life issues and *all* are important. The Christian community chooses life. I just read about a local physician who went to Iraq with some medical colleagues. He says that the civilian deaths there have exceeded the half-million mark. That's the size of the city of Seattle! A recent essay by a Catholic theologian condemns the war in Iraq not because it does not meet the traditional "just war" criteria (it does not), but because it is against the first commandment, which prohibits *idolatry*. The Christian call is to bring *life* to the voting booth.

Move Two: Is there a "stewardship of voting"? Can we really love God, neighbor, and life through voting? Here's a suggestion—why not use Exod 22:20–26 as an "examination of conscience" for voting—a "litmus test" for issues and candidates? In fact, maybe we should just photocopy it from our Bibles and bring it along with us into the voting booth! The words should probably be inscribed on our hearts anyway. Let's look at what it says (*the scriptural text is in quotes, my commentary in italics*): "You shall not wrong or oppress a resident alien, for you were aliens in the land of Egypt." *Now, usually I hear "alien" as the translation here (like an "extraterrestrial"?!), or sometimes "stranger" or "foreigner." But one translation that really struck me is "immigrant." Let's listen to the text again with the word "immigrant." You shall not wrong or oppress an* immigrant . . . "You shall not abuse any widow or orphan." *Or "immigrant"—these three groups represent those for whom God has a special compassion in Scripture; they are also the ones for whom we, the Christian community, are called to care—remember stewardship?* "If you do abuse them, when they cry out to me, I will surely heed their cry; my wrath will burn, and I will kill you with the sword . . ." (*after a long pause*) *Now that's a sobering thought . . .*

"and your wives shall become widows and your children orphans. If you lend money to my people, to the poor among you, you shall not deal with them as a creditor" ("extortionist" in NAB used in Catholic liturgy); "you shall not exact interest from them." *Does that remind us of the financial crisis? Some of you are directly suffering the results—foreclosures on homes worth 150,000 dollars but artificially "upped" to 400,000 or even 500, 000 dollars in the mortgage, in money that was "created out of nothing." Isn't that idolatry? Isn't God the only one who can "create out of nothing"?* "If you take your neighbor's cloak in pawn, you shall restore it before the sun goes down; for it may be your neighbor's only clothing to use as cover; in what else shall that person sleep?" *Peruvian theologian Fr. Gustavo Gutiérrez asks simply, when commenting on this reading, "Where do the poor sleep?"* "And if your neighbor cries out to me, I will listen, for I am compassionate." *Our God is a compassionate God, a God who has a passion for justice, for life, for love. The passion for the widow, the orphan, and the immigrant must be reflected in who we are as Church community, in how we follow Jesus, in what we do to the widow, the orphan, and the immigrant. That's the stewardship of voting!*

Conclusion: When you go into the voting booth this November, remember life. Take these words of Exodus with you. Remember God and neighbor—the widow, the orphan, and the immigrant. Amen.

Part Two

Where Are We Now?

Theology is, at core, a profound reflection on *Church community*. All good theology is ecclesiology, Christology, and pneumatology—theology of the Triune God. The question is not academic, something that can be "known" and "understood" through the study of theology at the university. That is, of course, helpful and has its place. But theology is defined at its most profound level, Jean Corbon, OP, says, by John 17:3—"And this is eternal life, that they may know you, the only true God, and Jesus Christ whom you have sent." This "knowledge" is a question of *who we are*, as Church, *right now*, at this moment, *hic et nunc*—a "being known" by the Triune God. Theology is the "contemplation of the Holy Trinity" through which *we are known*. And the Church is the "icon," the image, of the Holy Trinity, manifested in its structure of communion.[1] The theologian's task, then, is to "contemplate" that icon.

Dietrich Bonhoeffer says that the Church is visible. It "occupies space." He tells his students in Nazi Germany that this ecclesial visibility is, in fact, the core issue of *all* theology.[2] But how are we to speak of this visibility? Bonhoeffer says that the visible Church is not an institution but a *person*—the incarnate Word.[3] The Church is *not* the "prolongation" of the Incarnation,

1. Forte, *La Iglesia*, 29.

2. Bonhoeffer, *Discipleship*, 225, especially n2.

3. Ibid., 218.

47

as in the *societas perfecta* model of the Counter-Reformation. It *is* the Incarnation, in the deepest sense for Bonhoeffer, the incarnate Word itself—"Christ existing as Church community." The community as incarnate person can be *seen*. It occupies space. Who is the Church now? How is the Holy Trinity contemplated in the Church community? Precisely where it is visible—in the body of Christ, the *pueblo*; in its *martyrion*, the witness of the martyrs; and in its *kerygma*, its proclamation—of which the most visible sign is its *preaching*.

The Church is the living temple of the Spirit of God, the "living community of the living Jesus Christ," says Karl Barth. All theological reflection must begin—and end—with the Church community. The Church is the living Person of Jesus Christ, a people God's very own, brought to life by the Spirit of God. It is the body of Christ (1 Cor 12:27) made visible through its preaching and its witness—word and sacrament. Jesus Christ is Word and Sacrament—the Sacramental Word, says Karl Rahner. The proclamation of the Sacramental Word, who is Jesus, is part of the Church's very identity. By this witness and proclamation, the Church is the visible *pueblo*, the visible body of Christ brought to continual birth by the Spirit of the living God. It has no real meaning outside of this witness, outside of the preaching of the Sacramental Word. In this *hic* it is visible, in this *nunc* it occupies space. Here, and only here, is the Holy Trinity contemplated.

4

Word of Life, Sacrament of Grace

I long ago read that theology can be divided into two metaphors. First, there is "get the job done" theology. The great majority of theology—especially pastoral—occurs within this framework. It is methodological, precise, and knows what task it wishes to accomplish. "Get the job done" theology generally views the theological task as a choosing of the proper tool for the job, the distinguishing between the claw and the ball peen hammer, between the monkey and the crescent wrench. All of us have done theology within this framework, and it is perhaps the most popular way to do pastoral theology—including preaching. We say to ourselves, "I think I need a Gutiérrez hammer to connect these two pieces of wood," or, "I'd like a Schillebeeckx wrench to tighten this nut." In the preparation of the homily, preachers are constantly doing this without thinking—and that is good. All of us have our operative theologies, all of us have our favorite methods of biblical exegesis, and all of us have our hermeneutical approach to Scripture and to our congregations. Pastoral theology—and homily preparation—generally take the approach of "get the job done" theology. After all, there seem to be a million and one tasks in weekly ministry, and, of course, there is the all-important preparation of the homily through which, hopefully, God touches people's lives in a way that makes sense to them.

The second approach to the theological task, less employed, is "blueprint" theology. Blueprint theology sees the necessity of not only the proper tool for the task but an overall plan in which the task is accomplished and viewed as wider than "just one more homily to prepare" or "just one more pastoral visit to make." Blueprint theology has been

49

rarer in the history of the Church. Perhaps that is why busy pastoral agents are reticent to use it. A true blueprint theologian is something of an oddity in the history of theology. They are what Hans Küng refers to as "paradigm change" theologians.[1] Historical examples of blueprint theologians would include the Cappadocians,[2] Augustine of Hippo, Thomas Aquinas, and Martin Luther. Outstanding modern-day examples include Dietrich Bonhoeffer, Karl Barth, Edward Schillebeeckx, OP, Karl Rahner, SJ, Otto Semmelroth, SJ, and, in my opinion, Latin American theology as a whole with outstanding spokespeople such as Gustavo Gutiérrez, OP, Jon Sobrino, SJ, Ivone Gebara, Leonardo Boff, Elsa Tamez, José Marins, Víctor Codina, SJ, and José Comblin, among innumerable others.

This chapter will not deal with "get the job done" theology. Rather, it will deal with blueprint theologies and blueprint theologians. For all Christian blueprint theology has one thing in common—it is, at core, Christological ecclesiology, Trinitarian through-and-through, centered in Jesus Christ crucified and risen from the dead and his presence in his communal body, sustained by the living Spirit of God. Christian theology within any context must begin with "Christ existing as community," the blueprint for all blueprint theologies. This is the starting point for all theology—systematic, biblical, sacramental, ethical, historical, and pastoral—and, most especially, the theology of preaching.

Word and sacrament have been two important categories of Christian reflection since the beginning, continually present in all blueprint theologies. Unfortunately, they became more and more separated over the centuries. A perceived rupture, for many, was the Protestant Reformation. Protestantism, in its predominantly dialectical manifestation, has been identified with a *sola scriptura* emphasis on the sovereign word of God, while Catholicism, in its predominantly sacramental manifestation, has been identified with an emphasis on the sacrament—as that which primarily "effects" the grace of God. Western Christianity has, unfortunately, largely left the Orthodox communions on the periphery of the dialog. But as our Orthodox sisters and brothers have always known, the "rupture" between word and sacrament is illusory. Thoughtful Protestants and

1. See Küng, *Great Christian Thinkers.*

2. Sts. Basil the Great, Gregory of Nyssa, Macrina the Younger, and Gregory of Nazianzus.

Catholics are beginning to make their way through the illusion to a theology founded upon the Sacramental Word.

The early Church Fathers and Mothers maintained an integral unity between word and sacrament (*logos* and *mysterion*³). The word arose from the sacrament and the sacrament from the word. Both were indispensable to the faith. Contemporary theology has, by and large, attempted a return to the integral unity of word and sacrament in the theologies of Karl Barth, Karl Rahner, Edward Schillebeeckx, Otto Semmelroth, and Latin American theology in general. But the "rupture" mentality continues, unwittingly, to dominate North Atlantic theology and ecclesial imagination.

The imagination of the poor is different. It sees word and sacrament in an integral unity that yet retains their distinctive characteristics. Word and sacrament, in the imagination of the poor, have the strong Christological center articulated by North Atlantic theology. But they are contemplated on another level, more communally and less individualistically. In the imagination of the poor, word and sacrament are *nepantla*,⁴ a radical unity in the midst of a rich multiplicity. Jesus is Word *and* Sacrament—the Sacramental Word.

Perhaps Hans Küng is right when he maintains that the starting point of postmodern theology is Karl Barth and his Christological perspective. Küng says, "[I]n 1934 he (Barth) inspired the Barmen Synod with its clear confession of Jesus Christ as the 'one Word of God,' alongside which no 'other events and powers, figures and truths [might be acknowledged] as God's revelation."⁵ All contemporary theology, in one way or another, has had to come to terms with Barth's relentless Christocentric theology of the word.

However, Barth's genius lay not so much in what was unique to him. Rather, his theological revolution was a rediscovery buried over the last centuries by Protestant liberalism and Catholic neo-scholasticism but by and large preserved by the East—the historical propensity of theology to

3. Aquinas, like the patristics/matristics, often used *sacramentum* and *mysterium* interchangeably. See Schillebeeckx, *Christ the Sacrament*, 16.

4. I am entirely indebted to Javier Garibay Gómez, SJ, for the creative theology he has developed around *nepantla*, a *Náhuatl* word meaning "situated in the middle" or "in the midst of." See *Nepantla*.

5. Küng, *Theology for the Third Millennium*, 190.

begin from the Christological Word. The author of the Prologue to John's gospel says, "In the beginning was the Word . . . " (John 1:1). The Fathers and the Mothers of the Church reflected extensively on Jesus, the eternally begotten Word of God. The scriptural word, in those early centuries, is integrally connected to the Incarnation of the *Logos*. Ignatius of Antioch sees the word in Scripture as "flesh and blood of the incarnate *Logos*.[6] Augustine speaks of the "inverbation" of Jesus. Jesus is the incarnate Word, and the word of God is "wholesome food," "divine banquet," "the bread of angels," and "the voice of the Spirit" for Augustine. There is a strong equation of word and sacrament through which we are "born in the spirit."[7] These patristic/matristic themes were picked up in medieval Western theology and continued through the Scholastic period, culminating in Thomas Aquinas' affirmation about Jesus the Word: "The Father utters himself and all creatures in the word which he begets, in as much as the begotten word is an adequate representation of the Father and of all creatures."[8] Aquinas begins his theological summary of the *Summa*—the *Compendium* he wrote at the request of his friend Reginald—with the following words: "To restore man [*sic*], who had been laid low by sin, to the heights of divine glory, the Word of the eternal Father, though containing all things within His immensity, willed to become small. This He did, not by putting aside His greatness, but by taking to Himself our littleness."[9] For Aquinas, all comes forth from God in the creative love of the Trinity (*exitus*), and all returns to God (*reditus*) in the humanity of the incarnate Word.

Reformation theology was strongly Christocentric, as was some Counter-Reformation reflection. But the biblical-patristic/matristic image of Jesus the Word would suffer at the hands of post-Reformation Protestantism and Catholic neo-scholasticism. The twentieth century rediscovery came through a Reformed pastor-theologian strongly affected by the horrors of two world wars—namely, Karl Barth. On the Catholic side, three theologians were key—Otto Semmelroth, Karl Rahner, and Edward Schillebeeckx.[10] They developed theologies which sprang from Jesus as the incarnate Word and were highly influenced by modern scrip-

---

6. Scheffczyk, "Word of God," 364.

7. Ibid.

8. Aquinas, *Summa Theologiae* I, q. 37, a 2, quoted by Semmelroth, *The Preaching Word*, 20.

9. Aquinas, *Aquinas's Shorter Summa*, 9.

10. See Janowiak, *The Holy Preaching*.

tural, theological, and patristic/matristic studies. More will be said about these North Atlantic theologians later.

The Letter to the Ephesians, written many centuries ago, reminds all generations who follow Jesus of the centrality of the Word: "There is one body and one Spirit, just as you were called to the one hope of your calling, one Lord, one faith, one baptism, one God and Father of all, who is above all and through all and in all" (Eph 4:4–6). Like this passage from Ephesians, and perhaps more than any contemporary Western theology, Latin American theology unites Christology, ecclesiology, pneumatology, sacramental theology, and the theology of the word—all in the contemplation of the Holy Trinity. The source of all words is the incarnate Sacramental Word, Jesus Christ, the *Logos* of the Holy Trinity. Jesus the Word is the source—word of God as Scripture, word of God as preached by the ecclesial community and inspired by the Spirit, word of God as lived by the *pueblo*, "Christ existing as Church community." The Church is the body of Christ. This ecclesial community sees the Word not just as an "object of faith," but as the absolute ground of faith for the believer.[11] Jesus the Word is the "fidelity of God,'" the ground of faith for the Latin American poor sustained by the Spirit of life.

For Jon Sobrino and many Latin American theologians, the poor followers of Jesus the incarnate Word in Latin America are, literally, Jesus in the crucified body of Christ—the "crucified people." The *pueblo*, in the light of the word of God, reflects on the Paschal Mystery and lives it. Gustavo Gutiérrez, in commenting on Matthew's account of the sending of the Twelve (Matt 9:38—10:6), says that the Church is "people of God" and "sacrament of salvation." Its mission is nothing less than the mission of Jesus the Word—proclamation of the reign of God. In this proclamation, the poor occupy a central place. Like Jesus, the disciple is called to make an "option for the poor."[12]

Ecclesiology from Latin America is integrally connected with the Word. Víctor Codina mentions three names from European Protestant theology cited time and again by the Latin Americans: Karl Barth, Dietrich Bonhoeffer, and Jürgen Moltmann.[13] Their theology sees Jesus as a center with two strong radials—the word of God and the Church. As

11. See discussion on Jesus as "object of faith" vs. "ground of faith" in Rahner, *Foundations*, 238ff.

12. Gutiérrez, *Compartir la Palabra*, 228.

13. Codina, *Para Comprender la Eclesiología*, 67.

Barth says, "Theology must begin with Jesus Christ . . . the very Word of God himself . . . [and] theology must also end with him."[14] The greatest contribution of the dialectical imagination to Latin American theology is, in fact, its Christocentric focus. Dutch Dominican Boniface Willems, some forty years ago, encouraged Catholic theologians to examine closely the persistent Christocentrism of Karl Barth.[15] Latin American theology has taken up this challenge, and among the best known Christologies are those by Jon Sobrino and Leonardo Boff. But there are many others. It can rightly be said, in fact, that all Latin American theology is, like Dietrich Bonhoeffer's, Christology with a decidedly ecclesial bent. Leonardo Boff actually refers to a "liberation Christology."[16]

Latin American Christology is always done from the stance of the poor. The God of life, in God's unconditional love, takes an option for the poor, and the incarnate Word of God becomes the depth expression of that option. The Word of God, incarnate within human history, is a liberating Word that not only takes on human flesh but does so as poor *pueblo*. The incarnate and saving Word assumes weakness, smallness, and poverty: "[T]hough he was in the form of God, [Jesus] did not regard equality with God as something to be exploited, but emptied himself, taking the form of a slave, being born in human likeness" (Phil 2:6–7). Martin Luther was fond of such Christological expressions and developed his *theologia crucis* as opposed to the *theologia gloriae* prevalent at the time. This, according to Víctor Codina, is one of the primary ways classic Protestant theology has affected Latin American liberation theology.[17] Jesus the Word of God is Jesus the *poor* Word of God.

Leonardo Boff, in his Christology, speaks of what he calls "christic structure."[18] This refers to the dialectic between "divine proposal" and "human response." The divine proposal is always first and based in God's love. The human response can have varying degrees, good and bad. The One who lived this out perfectly, in whom divine proposal and human response were one and the same, is Jesus Christ. This christic structure of divine initiative and human response is incarnated in the Word who invites us, in turn, to live that same christic structure in praxis. This is

14. Barth, *Church Dogmatics* II/2, 4.
15. Willems, *Karl Barth*.
16. Boff, *Jesus Christ Liberator*, 255.
17. Codina, *Para Comprender la Eclesiología*, 69.
18. Boff, *Jesus Christ Liberator*, 252.

reminiscent of the *Wort* and *Antwort* sacramental theology developed by Otto Semmelroth a few decades before Boff's writing. Semmelroth speaks of Christ as "principal liturgist" within the Eucharistic liturgy. Jesus is the incarnate Word of God (*Wort*) who comes forth from God and takes on our humanity. Jesus is also the saving Word (*Antwort*) who returns in "answer," offering himself to the God of life on our behalf. In this scheme, *Wort* is the "divine initiative" in the Incarnation, and *Antwort* is the "human response" in the Redemption.[19] This, like Boff's christic structure, is paradigmatic for all divine initiative and human response.

When this Christology is viewed from the stance of the *pueblo*, radical insights result. Jesus is the incarnate liberating Word "uttered" by God from before all ages in the *Logos*. But this Word is uttered on behalf of humanity, whom God loves with a relentless passion. The Word is incarnate because, in its time, it is uttered, through the breath of the Spirit, in the depths of the human experience. This liberating Word is uttered by the God of life, the God who remembers the covenant—"I will be your God, you will be my people"—and definitively speaks that covenant in an irrevocable way (Barth and Rahner) in Jesus. This Word is uttered within history to the *pueblo*. It is then heard by the *pueblo* as incarnate liberating Word. In the very hearing of the liberating Word is salvation itself, for the hearing becomes the human response—*Antwort*—to God's graciousness. The response can only occur because of the self-communication of God—grace (Rahner). But grace effects the response and consequently, following the logic of Semmelroth and Boff, effects salvation in the incarnate Word uttered by the God of life in the Spirit. The incarnate Word is the body of Christ, "existing as Church community" (Bonhoeffer), the locus of salvation. This is the root meaning of *extra ecclesiam nulla salus*.

Boff speaks of two liberation Christologies. The first, which he calls "sacramental," is roughly equivalent to what North Atlantic theology associates with the sacramental imagination. Boff sees this Christology as necessary but inadequate. The second is called "socio-analytic." It attempts to analyze, from the Christological perspective, the social structures of sin. The first is good because it sees Christ as Sacrament (Boff refers the reader to Schillebeeckx). It is in this Sacrament that we come to know God. However, it does not sufficiently account for the social structure of sin. Perhaps Boff would say that divine initiative in the Incarnation is

19. Paul Janowiak offers a cogent explanation of Semmelroth's *Wort* and *Antwort* theology in *The Holy Preaching*. See especially 20–27.

present, but human response with its intrinsic sinfulness is not sufficiently considered. Sinfulness within structure is human response gone awry. By becoming the liberating Word that actually effects human salvation in the perfect response of *Antwort*, Jesus is effectively our only hope.[20]

The cross of Jesus occupies a privileged place in Latin American theology. It is lived out in a unique way through the indigenous poor who suffer at the hands of the powerful. José María González Ruiz writes of the ecclesial call to live a *theologia crucis* instead of a *theologia gloriae*. This call is consistent, he maintains, throughout the Pauline corpus. In *kenosis*, Jesus empties himself in the womb of the *pueblo*.[21] The Church can do no less. In a similar vein, Manuel Arias Montes writes that the word *kenosis*, in the context of the indigenous poor of Latin America, is best translated "self-marginalization." The word used by Arias Montes is *automarginarse*, a powerful double reflexive that expresses what Jesus really did in *kenosis*—and what we, as his body, are called to do.[22] Thus Christology, the Paschal Mystery, ecclesiology, theology of the word, and the contemplation of the Trinity come full circle. Jesus the incarnate Word of God sends the disciple community forth, by the power of the Spirit, to proclaim the reign of God by proclaiming that with which they have been entrusted—the holy word of God.

Around the period of the Second Vatican Council and shortly before, theologians began to speak of Jesus as the "Sacrament of God." The universal Church is deeply indebted to Edward Schillebeeckx, who wrote the ground-breaking *Christ the Sacrament of the Encounter with God* in 1960, two years before the beginning of the Council. Schillebeeckx, like Aquinas, maintains that while natural theology can give the human person a sense of the divine, it is only through grace that a personal encounter with the God of life can be experienced. But humans need this divine encounter mediated. This is the primary reason for the Church and the sacraments. Schillebeeckx relies on Aquinas' theology of the sacraments of nature and the sacraments of Israel to develop his notion of Christ as primordial Sacrament.[23] With the coming of Jesus, revelation was fulfilled. God's

20. Boff, *Jesus Christ Liberator*, 255.

21. González Ruiz, *La Teología de la Cruz.*

22. Arias Montes, *Y la Palabra de Dios*, 119.

23. Schillebeeckx, *Christ the Sacrament*, 13–17.

love is irrevocably expressed through this one primordial Sacrament. Jesus is Sacrament precisely because in his humanity, he signifies God's love for the human person through Jesus' deeply human actions of love, compassion, justice, and tenderness. This is crucial, for Schillebeeckx cites Aquinas to say that in his very humanity, Jesus is the Son of God.[24] God's saving will for humankind is accomplished definitively in history through the person of Jesus. The human presence of Jesus makes divinity a sacrament, and the divinity of Jesus makes humanity a sacrament. As primordial Sacrament, Jesus once and for all effects what is signified.

In his humanity, in his very body, Jesus is the Sacrament of our salvation.[25] In developing this theology, Schillebeeckx relies on the Thomistic notion of sacrament as efficacious sign. The Incarnation is central. In his humanity Jesus effects, through the infinite grace of God, our salvation in his human body. His "bodiliness" is the *visible* sign of our salvation:

> Because the saving acts of the man Jesus are performed by a divine person, they have a divine power to save, but because this divine power to save appears to us in visible form, the saving activity of Jesus is *sacramental*. For a sacrament is a divine bestowal of salvation in an outwardly perceptible form which makes the bestowal manifest; a bestowal of salvation in historical visibility. The Son of God really did become true man—become, that is to say, a human spirit which through its own proper bodiliness dwelt visibly in our world. The incarnation of the divine life therefore involves bodily aspects. Together with this we must remember that every human exchange . . . proceeds in and through man's [sic] bodiliness. Human encounter proceeds through the visible obviousness of the body, which is a sign that reveals and at the same time veils the human interiority.
>
> Consequently if the human love and all the human acts of Jesus possess a divine saving power, then the realization in human shape of this saving power necessarily includes as one of its aspects the manifestation of salvation: includes, in other words, sacramentality. The man Jesus, as the personal visible realization of the divine grace of redemption, is *the* sacrament, the primordial sacrament, because this man, the Son of God himself, is intended by the Father to be in his humanity the only way to

24. Ibid., 14, especially n10.

25. See Janowiak, *The Holy Preaching*, 44–46, 48–51, for a discussion of Schillebeeckx's "bodiliness" and sacramentality.

the actuality of redemption . . . Human encounter with Jesus is therefore the sacrament of the encounter with God.[26]

This persuasive connection of the visible body with sacramentality is revisited, a number of years later, by Louis-Marie Chauvet, OP.[27]

Latin American theology deepens the sacramentality of Jesus. "If you want to know something about God, look to Jesus Christ," maintains Carlos Mesters in a succinct summary of sacramental Christology.[28] Jon Sobrino says, "The fundamental witness that Jesus bore to his God is therefore expressed . . . primarily in a sacramental way by making the true God present."[29] He calls Jesus the "perennial sacrament in this world of a liberator God."[30] Leonardo Boff says Jesus is "the basic sacrament of martyrdom."[31] Liberation theologians see the Incarnation as crucial to this understanding. Jesus, in taking on our humanity, "empties" himself and takes on our *bodies*. This is significant in Latin America because the body of the poor has been devastated by the dominant culture. The poor are simply disregarded—the experience of the poor in the First World—or even tortured and killed, as recent history in El Salvador and Chiapas has proven. The body of the poor comes, most often, to an early death. This is how Gustavo Gutiérrez consistently defines poverty. The body of the poor has little access to nutrition, to dignified living conditions, to medicine, and to all the other things to which the wealthy have regular access. Latin Americans speak of the "crucified people": the body of Christ, in the poor, scourged and beaten "not once but thousands of times," as Bartolomé de Las Casas so often said. The body of Christ, in the poor, is sacrament.

The strong communality of Latin American imagination maintains that, in the Incarnation, God in Jesus takes on flesh in the *pueblo*. The body of Christ is the community. Latin American theologians refer to the Church and the reign of God as sacrament. In order to know Jesus the Sacrament of God in Latin American theology, the encounter with neighbor and *pueblo* is essential.[32] Christ is the Sacrament of God, and the

26. Schillebeeckx, *Christ the Sacrament*, 15.

27. Chauvet, *The Sacraments*.

28. Mesters, *La Persona de Jesucristo*, 73.

29. Sobrino, *Jesus the Liberator*, 268–69.

30. Ibid., 273.

31. Ibid., 266. Sobrino cites an essay by Boff.

32. Ibid., 74.

neighbor is the sacrament of Christ. Whether the historical sacrament is the Church as for Gustavo Gutiérrez,[33] or the reign of God and the poor as for Víctor Codina,[34] Jesus, the Church, the reign of God, and the poor are all referred to in sacramental terms with Christ as the foundation. Jesus is the visible sign of God, the Sacrament *par excellence*: "God manifests himself visibly in the humanity of Christ, the God-Man, irreversibly committed to human history."[35]

Jesus is the primordial sacrament in Latin American theology. Víctor Codina maintains that rather than speaking of Jesus as the *founder* of an ecclesial community, it is much better to say that he is the *foundation* of the Church.[36] Jesus Christ is the firm foundation—the foundational sacrament—of the disciple community. If the believer wishes to know who God is, he or she simply looks to Jesus, who is the "visible sign" of God's incarnate love:

> For John the glory of God [Jesus], the visible sign of his presence among men [*sic*], was the manifestation of his boundless love and his total self-surrender. And since this life has passed to us through our love inspired work of building, Paul can say that we ourselves are "God's temple" (1 Cor. 3:16). In the new Israel God is not present in some sacred place or time. He has established his dwelling among us in the fullest sense . . . He has pinpointed the locale of this encounter. It is [the presence of Jesus] in every human being who needs our love.[37]

If the believer wishes to know Jesus, the human being is the "locale" of encounter. Jesus is the Sacrament of God, and the Church is the sacrament of Jesus—the very body of Christ: "The risen Christ is the new Adam, who incorporates to his glorified body the new humanity, the new people of God, the Church. Christ is the individual person, but [he] is also collective, his body is his glorified body and the Church. The Church is the living Christ in the form of community, it is his total body."[38] The sacramentality of Jesus Christ is inseparable from his body in the Church and from his face in the neighbor (Matthew 25).

33. Gutiérrez, *A Theology of Liberation*, 255–79.

34. Codina, "Sacraments," 219.

35. Gutiérrez, *A Theology of Liberation*, 192.

36. Codina, *Para Comprender la Eclesiología*, 27.

37. Segundo, *The Sacraments Today*, 150.

38. Codina, *Para Comprender la Eclesiología*, 30.

Juan Luis Segundo, SJ, maintains that the sacraments are integral to faith in Jesus and to the community. Traditional Catholic theology, he says, has often compared and contrasted the Christian sacraments with non-Christian rituals. This has its place and is rooted in the theology of Aquinas. However, it runs the risk of over-identifying the sacrament with rite and gesture. The sacraments, in such a view, risk becoming magical. Segundo maintains that the Jesus of the gospels united gesture and faith. Using the example of Jesus' healings, he refers to the gesture of the laying on of hands. The gesture, for Jesus, was integrally connected with faith. Jesus could not perform his healing signs without the faith of the person.[39]

Likewise, the community who follows Jesus combines ritual *and* faith in the celebration of the sacraments. The sacraments are not ritually magical gestures. The gestures are the *materia* in traditional sacramental theology. However, it is the *forma* that makes the sacrament Christian. That *forma* is, for Segundo, faith. The sacraments we celebrate as Church are not sacred rites only; they are radically accompanied by faith in the person of Jesus. Jesus is the foundation and the primordial Sacrament.

Segundo says that sacramental language can be too ritualized in traditional Catholic theology. This is also true of the language of sacrifice.[40] Sacrifice is seen as cultic, particularly the Eucharistic sacrifice. However, with the Incarnation, faith in the person of Jesus—the one sacrifice and the one Sacrament—becomes essential. Segundo refers to the Letter to the Hebrews when speaking of the one sacrifice of Christ.[41] In this light, the Eucharistic notion of cultic sacrifice is in dire need of renewal. The overly ritualized view of sacrifice, popular in traditional Catholicism, was not present in the early Christian community. Segundo stresses that the word "sacrifice" is by no means outdated. But it requires radical transformation. The one efficacious sacrifice was the sacrifice of Jesus—not a cultic sacrifice but an offering of life as the ultimate act of love within human history.[42] This radically Christocentric view of sacrament and sacrifice is paralleled in the way the Christian community lives. Sacrificial love in the community moves from ritual to historical when it is not just done for the sake of penitential practice, but when it is concretely tied to the sacrificial love and mercy of Jesus on behalf of the suffering other. We

39. Segundo, *The Sacraments Today*, 21–27.

40. Ibid., 36–37.

41. Ibid., 23.

42. Ibid., 36.

thus "sacrifice" ourselves as community, according to the attitude of Jesus (cf. Phil 2:5–11), in acts of love, in praxis, on behalf of the concrete other. Faith and sacrificial obedience, as for Bonhoeffer, are inseparable.

Perhaps the contemporary crisis in sacramental theology does not have to do so much with the sacraments themselves, suggests Segundo, but with the community.[43] Liturgy is essential. But there is grave danger in divorcing the sacraments from the community. They then become magical acts "dispensed" to individuals and not faith-expressions of the community rooted in Jesus crucified and risen. Jesus, the foundational Sacrament, shows us the way to historical love through the one sacrifice efficacious for all humanity. It is in this sense that Jesus is the primordial sacrament. We, as community, are sacraments of Jesus.[44]

Liberation theology seeks "a new sacramental horizon," according to Víctor Codina, intimately connected with Jesus and God's reign.[45] "[T]he Church is sacrament of the Kingdom and must continually undergo conversion to the Kingdom, if it seeks to be church of the poor and historical sacrament of liberation."[46] The Church's primary task is fidelity to Jesus and, through him, to the proclamation of God's reign, which is its evangelical demand. Liberation theologians invite us to return to the patristic/matristic notion of sacrament as *mysterion*. The sacraments, at their roots, are mystery. Codina says, "The Kingdom of God . . . which comes near to us in Christ . . . is the primordial *mystery* of the faith, the original sacrament." [47] He insightfully observes that "to ask soldiers at a Eucharist to stop the repression, as Archbishop Romero ordered 'in the name of God' on the eve of his assassination . . . is not an injection of politics into the liturgy, but a clear prophetic orientation of sacramentality to the Kingdom of God."[48] The person of Jesus and the reign of God are associated to the point of identification in the gospels.[49] This is true for both the Synoptics and John. The word "kingdom" is not mentioned in the fourth gospel because it is personified in Jesus. For Codina, the sacramentality of the reign of God, Jesus, and the Church are all integrally

43. Ibid., 38.

44. Ibid., 15.

45. Codina, "Sacraments," 219.

46. Ibid., 220.

47. Ibid., 221, emphasis mine.

48. Ibid.

49. Codina, *Para Comprender la Eclesiología*, 37.

connected. The poor are seen as sacraments of the primordial mysteries of Jesus and the Reign, and the seven sacraments are "prophetic symbols of the Kingdom" that *announce* and *proclaim* the good news of God's reign in the midst of the bad news of poverty, oppression, and injustice—what Jon Sobrino calls "anti-Kingdom." *Announcement* and *proclamation* are normally associated with the Word. The sacraments, in Latin American theology, are not seen as items to be "confected" and "dispensed." Rather, using Schillebeeckx's terminology, they are events intimately related to the word. They demand an announcement—a proclamation directed especially to the poor.

The theology of Jesus as Sacrament, for the Latin Americans, is associated with praxis. Theology is defined as a critical reflection on praxis in the light of the word of God.[50] José Comblin refers to Jesus—and the Spirit—as "the action of God."[51] He uses Irenaeus' image of the Son and the Spirit as "the hands of God."[52] They are the "action" of God, manifested through Jesus' proclamation of the reign of God in the Spirit. The disciple community—the Church—becomes, in turn, the action of the Spirit through acts of love and the proclamation of the reign of God.

Comblin maintains that Christology has concentrated too exclusively on the identity of Jesus. Another essential question is: what does Jesus do? "Christology tries to know who Jesus is and not what Jesus does," Comblin says.[53] The person of Jesus became separated from his roots in the New Testament early in the history of Christology. The famous Christological debates dealt primarily with the question of identity to the neglect of historical action, and the Chalcedonian formulas were the result. Medieval Christology likewise divorced Jesus' being from his action, culminating in the satisfaction theory of atonement in which Jesus was sacrificed to "placate" an angry God. The most negative effect of this theology was the rupture of the action—and humanity—of Jesus from the efficacy of his death and resurrection. Modern Christology, though it attempted a return to the historical Jesus, fared no better. The real question, maintains Comblin, is not the scientific approach of the modern era to the humanity of the historical Jesus. The question is not which scientific method is available for knowing the "real" Jesus, but what the

50. Gutiérrez, *A Theology of Liberation*, 11–15.

51. Comblin, *Tiempo de Acción*, 67–68.

52. Ibid., 29.

53. Ibid., 124.

historical Jesus *did* in his actions—and more importantly what the risen Jesus does today. How is his action manifested today in the *pueblo*?[54] Combin aptly summarizes the "state of Christology": "The starting point for the knowledge of Jesus is Christian action today. It is from there that all theological methods go searching for Jesus . . . [T]his . . . does not mean a deformation [of Christology], but [it is] a true knowledge of Christ through the Spirit. Christ cannot be separated from his people. It would be of no service to know a Christ isolated and separated from his present action in his total body."[55]

If Christology is divorced from the action of Jesus, it remains "orthodox" but has little to do with "orthopraxis." Right belief is one thing, and it is important. But right practice—orthopraxis—flows from right belief. One is not possible without the other. Faith and obedience were likewise intimately united for Dietrich Bonhoeffer, who says that the most important question for theology is not, "Who was Jesus Christ for us in the past?" but rather, "Who is Jesus Christ for us *today*?" This is what Comblin means by the *action* of God in the Church community, the body of Christ impelled by the Holy Spirit. Comblin and others decry the Christological confusion that has arisen because of the rupture between orthodoxy and orthopraxis. The result has been a destructive dichotomy between Christology and ecclesiology—the dualism that has hounded North Atlantic theology for centuries. Rather, the sacramentality of Jesus deals not only with who Jesus is but also, and more especially, with what Jesus *does* in his historical body—the *pueblo*. *That* leads to the reflection on who Jesus is today. As sacraments are actions of the ecclesial community, so Jesus the Sacrament of God is the action of God, with the Spirit, in the people.

In a small chapel in Yanhuitlán in Oaxaca, Mexico, there is an image of the *patrón* of the town—*El Señor de Ayuxi*. The image of the Crucified, enclosed in glass, is worn by centuries of the touches and kisses of thousands of pilgrims—the indigenous poor of the *Mixteca Alta* culture. The image is Sacrament, the sacred Word of tender mercy for the *pueblo* uttered by the One who makes the option for the poor divine in the tortured and

54. Ibid., 122–29. These pages are an excellent synthesis of the history of Christology and the contemporary contribution of Latin American theology.

55. Ibid., 128.

crucified body of the Nazarene. The people of the town, in turn, tenderly care for *El Señor de Ayuxi*, whose feast day is celebrated annually on the fourth Sunday of May. At the bottom of the hill is the colonial church of Santo Domingo. Is it possible that Bartolomé de Las Casas passed through, perhaps sojourning for a week or so at the Dominican priory that was here in Yanhuitlán? Was he resting from his weariness at seeing Christ crucified "not once, but a thousand times" in the indigenous poor he so loved and defended? Did he meditate on Christ's passion in the *pueblo* made sacrament in the image?

El Señor de Ayuxi* bows his head from the weight of the sin he bears. He guards the town, protecting the indigenous poor, abiding not the suffering of those he loves. His holy word of promise to the *pueblo* is, "Come to me, all you that are weary and are carrying heavy burdens, and I will give you rest" (Matt 11:28). The word of rest is a word of justice: "May he judge your people with righteousness, and your poor with justice" (Ps 72:2). But the crucified One who is risen, *El Señor de Ayuxi*, protects more than Yanhuitlán. *Ayuxi*, in the indigenous language, means "poor." The Lord of the Poor guards the exiled of all times and places, for the poor are the word of God and the sacrament of Jesus Christ crucified and risen. Their imagination is his. It lives in the word of life and the sacrament of grace proclaimed by the Church community that witnesses and preaches the thirst for justice.[56]

---

56. See Codina, *No Extingáis el Espíritu*, 243–46, for a similar reflection from the imagination of the Bolivian indigenous.

5

Jesus Christ Sacramental Word
of the God of the Poor

Jesus is Word of God from before all ages. Jesus is Sacrament of God who effects what is signified in the Word of grace to the poor. Karl Rahner, in a stroke of theological genius, unites the two in one powerful phrase. Jesus is the "primal sacramental word of God": "Christ is the *primal sacramental word of God*, uttered in the one history of mankind [*sic*], in which God made known his irrevocable mercy that cannot be annulled by God or man, and did this by effecting it in Christ, and effected it by making it known . . . The Church is the abiding presence of that *primal sacramental word* of definitive grace, which is Christ in the world, effecting what is uttered by uttering it in sign."[1] Rahner makes a profound theological statement about God, Christ, and the Church here. It would be fascinating to see how this "primal sacramental word" takes flesh in Rahner's theology, for in these words we have *in nuce* the entire Rahnerian corpus. A careful reading of *Hearer of the Word*, I believe, would be helpful in developing further what *exactly* Rahner means through this insightful phrase (any doctoral student specializing in Rahner who is reading these words and looking for a dissertation topic—enlighten us, please!). In the chapter that follows, I will revisit Rahner's theology of "hearing the word" primarily through the ecclesial ears of the poor.

---

1. Rahner, *The Church and the Sacraments*, 18, emphasis mine. See Janowiak, *The Holy Preaching*, 27–31, for a discussion of Jesus as the primal sacramental word in the Rahnerian sense.

But I am not particularly interested, at this point, in developing what Rahner meant by "primal sacramental word," or how this is seen in Rahner's theology. I am interested, rather, in a "contextual hermeneutic" of the phrase—particularly the question: How is the Sacramental Word seen from a Latin American perspective? What are the consequences for the indigenous poor and their imagination? What does the Sacramental Word mean for the preacher who accompanies the indigenous poor in solidarity?

Perhaps we can begin with a few verses from the resurrection narratives in the twentieth chapter of John's gospel. The first is the risen One's proto-appearance to Mary Magdalene; the second is his breathing of the Spirit upon the disciples; and the third is his word to Thomas. All these episodes occur within verses of one another. I see them as a unified whole through which the mystery of the Sacramental Word can be approached—however, only after removing our sandals (Exod 3:5):

> Jesus said to her (Mary Magdalene), "Do not hold on to me ('touch me'), because I have not yet ascended to the Father." (John 20:17)

> Jesus said to them (the disciples) again, "Peace be with you. As the Father has sent me, so I send you." When he had said this, he breathed on them and said to them, "Receive the Holy Spirit." (John 20:21–22)

> Then he said to Thomas, "Put your finger here and see my hands. Reach out your hand and put it in my side. Do not doubt but believe." (John 20:27)

Within just ten verses, the Johannine community is told: 1) do not "touch" the risen One; 2) "receive the Holy Spirit"; and 3) "touch" the risen Jesus and believe.

The Sacramental Word is not to be "touched." He is mystery. And yet, he is "touchable"—by the power of the Holy Spirit. Luke already assumes the presence of the Spirit when the risen Jesus tells the disciples: "Touch me and see; for a ghost does not have flesh and bones as you see that I have" (Luke 24:39). This explains why the Eastern Church has retained, from the earliest times, the sense that the sacraments are *mysterion*. The sacraments are "touchable"—water, bread, wine, oil, hands—but they are mystery. The ancient teaching of the Church is that the risen Jesus has a *body*. It is "touchable," but it is mystery. The human body of the risen Jesus eats (Luke 24:42–43) and speaks (Matt 28:9–10, 18–20) yet appears and

disappears (Luke 24:31, 36, John 20:19). It has the wounds of the crucifixion (Luke 24:39–40, John 20:20, 27) yet passes through closed doors
(John 20:19). It is human *and* divine—a "touchable mystery."

The Sacramental Word is made *touchable* by the gift of the Holy
Spirit. After Mary's proclamation of the risen One's presence, all of the
disciples are gathered "behind closed doors" in fear. The risen Jesus appears "in their midst" and gives them the gift of Easter peace. The disciples
are incredulous with joy. The risen Jesus shares the Johannine Pentecost,
breathing on them the gift of the Spirit so that they might make present
his reconciling love and justice in the world.

It is only *after* the risen Jesus shares the gift of the Spirit that Thomas
is told to "touch" him. The Holy Spirit makes the risen body of Jesus palpable, touchable, and human. What could not be "held to" can now be
touched. A hand can enter deeply into the wounded side. The wound can
be *felt*. Was Tertullian reflecting on the touchable, mysteriously wounded,
Sacramental Word when he said, "The seed of the Church is the blood of
the martyrs"? The power of the Spirit makes the body of Christ "touchable" and *visible*. It makes Christ's risen body a human body that can
be touched—the "body of Christ." Is this not Luke's central concern, as
well, in Acts, when he writes about Pentecost? The Spirit, for Luke and
for John, takes this group of fearful disciples and makes them *Church*
through an *epiclesis* of the Spirit.

A sacrament is mystery, but it can be touched. It is concrete and tangi-
ble. That is why the Catholic Church relies so strongly on Thomas Aquinas
and *causality* when it speaks about the sacraments. The sacraments bring
about, they "effect." What is "effected" through the Sacramental Word?
That this incarnate Word *can be touched*; that it is *concrete* and *human*;
and that this very humanity of Jesus, as Aquinas says, is the *reditus*, the
"return," to the God who is the source of all life. *Reditus* in the humanity
of Jesus is the only way the transcendent God can be "approached." We
must do so in a human—a *sacramental*—way. The incarnate Word is eternal *Logos* from before all ages, a mystery *par excellence*; but the mystery
can be *touched* by the gift of the Spirit. It can be grasped through the
human body of the risen Jesus, the incarnate Word. This is the mystery,
in my opinion, that the Fathers and Mothers meant when they referred
to the *disciplina arcani*, the guarding of the sacred mysteries by the early
Church community; why, perhaps, Dietrich Bonhoeffer uses the term so
carefully and yet with so much meaning. "Do not touch me" and "touch

me" must both be respected; they are commands of the risen Jesus. The bridge is the gift of the Spirit in sacramental *epiclesis.*

Jean Corbon speaks of ordained ministers in the Church community as "servants of sacramental *epiclesis.*"[2] This is precisely what makes "liturgical preaching" a sacrament and an *epiclesis.* By the power of the Holy Spirit, the words of the preacher, pronounced in *epiclesis* over the assembly, "make" this group of disciples the *body* of Christ. Preaching is so deeply connected with the ecclesial community that this sacramental *epiclesis* (Martin Luther and many others considered preaching to be sacramental activity) is the task of the ecclesial community itself—the baptized. The "ordination" to the sacramental ministry of preaching is not through the sacrament of holy orders but through the sacrament of *baptism.* Preaching is a gift of the Spirit, a charism, imparted to the baptized. *All* of the baptized are called to proclaim the Sacramental Word. That is the task entrusted to the Church community by the Holy Spirit. Perhaps this is why the Second Vatican Council says that preaching is the "primary duty" of the presbyter. It calls the ordained to take preaching seriously. But the presbyter, the pastor, the minister, is "ordained" to preaching through baptism. This is precisely what makes preaching "sacramental." The preacher is enflamed by the Sacramental Word through the gift of the Holy Spirit, much as John Wesley's famous statement, "When I preach, I set myself on fire, and the people watch me burn." We do not "set ourselves on fire"; it is, rather, the Spirit of God who enflames us with the Sacramental Word as we preach. That Sacramental Word is the risen Jesus, who becomes the preaching ecclesial community *in his body* through the *epiclesis* of the Holy Spirit.

With these preliminaries remarks, I can now continue toward a contextual reading of "the Sacramental Word" in a Latin American context.

Like North Atlantic thinking on word and sacrament, the theology that springs from the Latin American experience of poverty and injustice is deeply Christological and ecclesiological. Jesus is the primal Sacramental Word. Everything in the created world—especially humankind—has its source in him. Scripture and all human words begin with the one definitive Word of God, Jesus Christ. This Word is a Sacramental Word because it is the *Logos* who, in the words of Jon Sobrino, reveals in his flesh the

2. Corbon, *The Wellspring of Worship,* 174.

presence of God.[3] Jesus, in all that he is, does, and says, reveals God's glory as *Logos*, as Word. For Sobrino, the word *Logos* bridges the gap between Hebrew and Hellenistic thinking about Jesus. It unifies the two testaments with the later patristic/matristic categories the Church used when speaking about Jesus.[4] Sobrino bases his reflections about Jesus as the *Logos*-Word on the Prologue of John's gospel, where the *Logos* is seen not only from the Greek perspective of reason and meaning, but in the Hebrew light of God's creative Word (*dabar YHWH*) and Holy Wisdom.[5] Creation is brought into being *through the word*. The *dabar YHWH* is later personified in the Hebrew Scriptures as Wisdom and exists before creation itself. Sobrino points out that the God of the Hebrew Scriptures has no image, but only *voice*.[6] This pre-existent Wisdom who speaks is ever present within history as the recreating Word of God and will be definitive for later Christological reflection on Jesus as the *Logos*-Word and Holy Wisdom.[7]

In John's gospel, maintains Sobrino, the words of Jesus are integrally identified with him and are part of his being, and John invites the reader to see not just the words but Jesus himself as the Word enfleshed. In John, the word in Jesus becomes history, "humaniz[ing] and sav[ing] it, and also remain[ing] at its mercy."[8] This Johannine theology of Incarnation is entirely new. The Word takes on flesh in the midst of human history with all that that entails and is, in a special way, identified with the poor and the oppressed. The Word—that which is God—now becomes what is "not-God": "The invisible, inaccessible mystery of God has become accessible in what is not-God . . . Glory is faithful love, love situated in history and in the midst of a conflict that reaches to death."[9] This is the root meaning of Jesus as the Sacramental Word of God. The *Logos* is poured out in sacrificial love. The Word becomes human, sacramental, poor. All of God's being is identified in this manner—and not just God's being, but God's "being for": "God . . . has provided the means of annulling his radical otherness in relation to us and of doing so without ceasing to be God and

3. Sobrino, *Christ the Liberator*, 191.

4. Ibid.

5. Ibid., 192.

6. Ibid., 193.

7. Ibid., 192.

8. Ibid., 194.

9. Ibid., 196.

therefore mystery. In words that everyone can understand, when Jesus welcomes poor people and sinners, God welcomes them; when Jesus castigates oppressors, God castigates them; when Jesus rejoices in eating with publicans and prostitutes, God rejoices; when Jesus suffers on the cross, God suffers on the cross."[10] The work of Jesus is continued by the Spirit. Sobrino develops a pneumatology that makes his reflections thoroughly Trinitarian. The Spirit, in turn, animates the work of the Church, and the work of the Church as sacrament becomes the very mission of Jesus the Sacramental Word: proclamation of the good news of God's reign to the poor. Víctor Codina takes pneumatology and makes it even more central. He and José Comblin rightly maintain that the Holy Spirit has largely been neglected by the West, which should learn from the theology of the Eastern Churches.

Jesus the Sacramental Word of God is incarnate in the reality of the poor *pueblo*. All theological reflection on praxis in Latin America is done in the light of this Sacramental Word who identifies himself with the poor and the Church. For base communities that lack regular access to the sacraments, the Word becomes the icon of *Jesús Sacramentado*, the sacramental presence of Jesus in the Eucharist. Juan Luis Segundo speaks of the "hermeneutical circle," which further "sacramentalizes" the word of God:

> [T]here must . . . be four decisive factors in our circle. *Firstly* there is our way of experiencing reality, which leads us to ideological suspicion. *Secondly* there is the application of our ideological suspicion to the whole ideological superstructure in general and to theology in particular. *Thirdly* there comes a new way of experiencing theological reality that leads us to exegetical suspicion, that is, to the suspicion that the prevailing interpretation of the Bible has not taken important pieces of data into account. *Fourthly* we have our new hermeneutic, that is, our new way of interpreting the fountainhead of our faith (i.e., Scripture) with the new elements at our disposal.[11]

This is the way the base ecclesial communities read the Bible. The word of God is necessary in order that judgment be passed on the reality of poverty and injustice. The word is sacrament because it effects what it signifies. Reality is *seen* in its light, and it is judged. The Sacramental Word

10. Ibid., 199.

11. Segundo, *The Liberation of Theology*, 9.

is present in the word of Scripture and in the suffering of the poor. The Church *acts* in favor of gospel justice by the power of the Spirit. Segundo's hermeneutical circle is pastorally lived in Latin America—and many other parts of the world—through the methodology of *ver, juzgar, actuar* (see, judge, and act).

We now turn to Edward Schillebeeckx to set further the table of sacramental dialog with Latin American theology. If God wants to communicate with us through the grace of our body, and if all of God's communication with us must happen bodily—"bodiliness" for Schillebeeckx—then all encounter with the divine happens through the human body. This is a basic principle of sacramental theology.

Schillebeeckx speaks of four stages of redemption.[12] The first is the graciously loving decision of God, from before all time in the Trinity, to send the divine person of Jesus so that we might be liberated from sin and death in all its forms. The second stage, as the third, is exemplified by Phil 2:5–11 with the kenotic response of Jesus to God's love. Jesus "emptied himself" (2:7) and takes on who we are with all that that entails, "even death on a cross" (2:8). Third, in continuation of the kenotic process, Jesus is exalted by the God of life. Finally, the Spirit is sent forth by the exalted Christ to be the presence of God forever, in eternal covenant, with the people.

Now, if all encounter with God is bodily, and if Jesus has been exalted to God's right hand; and if the Incarnation is not simply an act of God in the historical past, but it is the ever-present reality of the human body of the glorified Christ; then Jesus' presence continues with us—Jesus' very bodily presence, not now the historical Jesus, but the risen and exalted Christ who is nevertheless "historical" because the Incarnation is perpetually related to bodiliness in history. However, the exalted Christ is not "visible" to the human eye (Bonhoeffer says the "visibility" of the body of Christ is the Church community itself). There must be a way for God to continue bodily communication with us in Jesus, who is the visible sacramental presence of God with the people. This is the radical reason for the sacraments, which become the way that our God bodily communicates with us in the glorified Christ, through the gift of the Spirit.[13]

12. Schillebeeckx, *Christ the Sacrament*, 20–21.

13. Ibid., 43–45.

Now the glorified Christ becomes the historical Sacramental Word of the God of the poor. The eternal *Logos* of God, in Jesus, is "transverbized" in the Sacramental Word and becomes the real historical presence of the God of the poor among God's beloved people. If the reader will graciously permit a word invention, "transverbation" is similar to Augustine's "inverbation," Aquinas' "transubstantiation," and Schillebeeckx's "transignification." It attempts to express fidelity to Catholic sacramental tradition by echoing categories referring to the fundamental change wherein the Eucharistic elements become the sacramental presence of Jesus while applying these ideas to the change in the word brought about "sacramentally," in dialog with the people, through the act of proclamation.

However transverbation (the term "transecclesiation" might likewise express the sacramental presence of the body of Christ in the community), while occurring formally and materially—a "sacramentizing" (Schillebeeckx) of the word—in the act of the Church's liturgical proclamation, is also the perpetual act of God in the Incarnation of Jesus in what Otto Semmelroth refers to, in the person of Jesus, as "God's own sermon."[14] The eternal *Logos* of God becomes the Sacramental Word of the God of the poor. God, in the glorified Jesus, is transverbized into the very body of the *pueblo*. It is the eternal presence of the Word through the Incarnation, and the sacramental presence of the Word through transverbation, that occurs in liturgical proclamation but practically—as Augustine's "we become what we receive" in the body of Christ—is brought about in the historical stuff of the life of the poor. Jesus the Word sacramentally becomes his bodily presence in the poor in what happens in the act of the Church's liturgical proclamation.

Transverbation, in this model, follows a four-step sacramental Christology of the word: 1) Through transverbation, Jesus the Word is made present in the act of liturgical proclamation; 2) through the hearing of the proclamation, the glorified Jesus, the Sacramental Word, is made present in the hearer of the word;[15] 3) the Word becomes "bodified" in the human hearer—that is, the word and the body are intimately united; and 4) the poor as hearer, in turn, speaks the Word.

First, transverbation means that Jesus the Word, through the power of the Spirit, is made present in the act of liturgical proclamation. The

14. Semmelroth, *The Preaching Word*, 222.

15. The poor as hearer of the word, in the Rahnerian sense, will be treated in the following chapter.

Second Vatican Council, in the *Constitution on the Sacred Liturgy* (paragraph 7), speaks of four presences of Jesus in the liturgy: the sacramental bread and wine, the word, the people, and the ministers.[16] Theologically and historically, the presence of Jesus given the most importance in the Catholic tradition is that manifested in the consecrated bread and wine. This real presence has been spoken of since the patristics/matristics, but it was not until early in the second millennium that the word used to describe the reality was proposed by Thomas Aquinas: transubstantiation. This word refers to the change in the "substance" of the Eucharistic bread and wine such that they are no longer substantially bread and wine but the body and blood of Jesus. The teaching was officially adopted as Catholic doctrine by the Council of Trent. But contemporary sacramental theologians stress that the reference is not to the real presence of the "historical" Jesus as he walked the earth two thousand years ago, but to the exalted Christ as explicated by Edward Schillebeeckx. In fact, Schillebeeckx popularized the term "transignification" to describe this sacramental change, stressing that our contemporary notion of substance is different from the medieval view. "Transignification" (also spelled with a double "s") avoids the contemporary confusion over substance, respects both contemporary anthropology and the traditional doctrine, and stresses the sacramental change itself.[17] For Schillebeeckx, the real presence of Christ in the Eucharist cannot be separated from his presence in the people, for the Eucharist is the "bond of unity" in community that brings about the "consecration of the covenant."[18]

The presence of Jesus, in the teaching of the Second Vatican Council, is likewise manifested in the people, in the ministers, and—the concern of this discussion—in the word. This means that when the word of God is proclaimed and preached within the liturgy, Jesus the Sacramental Word is truly present within the word as proclaimed and preached. Bonhoeffer says that "the proclaimed word . . . is the Christ himself walking through his congregation as the Word."[19] Over the centuries, this real presence of Jesus in the word—as well as in the ministers and the people—has been largely obscured in Catholic theological and pastoral practice. Recently contemporary sacramental theologians, beginning with Otto Semmelroth,

16. Schillebeeckx, *The Eucharist*, 103; and Janowiak, *The Holy Preaching*, xiv.

17. See Schillebeeckx, *The Eucharist*, 89–151.

18. Schillebeeckx, *Christ the Sacrament*, 175.

19. Fant, *Worldly Preaching*, 126.

have turned their attention to the presence of Jesus in the act of liturgical proclamation. The discussion has revolved around how, in fact, the proclamation of the word itself can be sacramental. Schillebeeckx says that the bodily, human presence of the exalted Christ is manifested primarily through the celebration of the sacraments. This must also be true of the proclamation of the word, since the human word is so important to our bodily, historical being. The proclamation of the word is *sacramental.*

Second, the presence of Jesus the Word, through the transverbation of the word in proclamation, is manifested in the hearer of the word. As the body of Christ is made present in the community of believers who partake in the Eucharist, so the word of Jesus is made present in the hearer through liturgical proclamation and preaching. The hearer— that is, the community of hearers—becomes the real presence of Jesus the Sacramental Word. By partaking in the Eucharist, we become body of Christ for one another and the world; by attentiveness to the liturgical word, we become Jesus the Word for the other. In Latin American theology, the Church is the "sacrament of history" and—with *Lumen Gentium*—the "universal sacrament of salvation."[20] The Church becomes the body of Christ so that the poor might experience the presence of the exalted Jesus in the human search for justice. Similarly the Church in transverbation, through the act of liturgical proclamation, becomes the sacramental presence of Jesus the Word to the poor.

Third, the word is "bodified" in the hearer. For Schillebeeckx, the sacraments deal primarily with the human encounter with God. God is made present sacramentally, through the bodily humanity of Jesus, to the believer. This sacramental presence is manifested through the word. The word anthropologically "sets us apart" in creation. God has graced us with the gift of verbal communication and symbolic meaning through words.[21] In the context of ecclesial faith, word symbols have a decidedly sacramental dimension. Our human words *become* the bodily sacramental presence of the crucified and risen One.

Fourth, the poor as hearer, who through transverbation become the presence of Jesus the Word, *speak* the Word. In our contemporary world, full of systemic sin, the powerful steal the word from the poor. This has

20. Gutiérrez, *A Theology of Liberation*, 255–85.

21. Webb, *Preaching and the Challenge*, discusses word and language as conveyor of symbolic meaning in preaching. See 17–29 for what he calls "symbolocity" and 47–61 for a discussion of "hub symbols."

happened countless times throughout history when the poor are perse-
cuted—and martyred—and the word is taken from them. But through
transverbation, the word of the poor is changed into the Sacramental
Word who is Jesus the Christ. No longer do the "voiceless" feebly cry out
for justice. The Word is enfleshed in the poor through transverbation so
that the poor as *pueblo* cry out in one powerful voice through the Word,
who not only "gives voice" but is, in fact, transverbized into the very voice
of the poor.

This four-step process of transverbation has become real in our
time through the preaching of Dietrich Bonhoeffer, Archbishop Oscar
Romero, and many others martyrs. Archbishop Romero did not so much
give "voice to the voiceless" but, as representative of the poor in the celebration of the sacraments and the proclamation of the word, actually
became the *voice* of Jesus. The act of liturgical proclamation *is* the presence of Jesus the Sacramental Word of the God of the poor.

The poor in Latin America are the "crucified people," and liberation theology is the theology of the cross. Citing Jürgen Moltmann, Jon Sobrino
speaks of the cross as the crucifixion of God.[22] On the cross, we see God's
presence and absence.[23] The cross of Jesus is the paradigm for the suffering of the poor. It is God's once and for all "no" to the suffering of the
poor, God's word of justice and mercy to a people passionately loved. But
theology has side-stepped the cross of Jesus, giving primary emphasis to
the resurrection:

> The history of Jesus does not end with the cross, since God
> raised him from among the dead. The cross is not, therefore, the
> last word on Jesus, nor is the cross of the crucified peoples God's
> final word to them. But I do not think that we should thereby
> make the liberative aspects of Jesus' life depend only on his res-
> urrection. This, in effect, cannot be understood simply as a happy
> ending, but must be seen as the intrinsic consummation of his
> life. It is not just an exaltation of Jesus, but also a confirmation
> of the truth of his life . . . The divine confirmation that this life is
> the true life is the resurrection, but the historical confirmation

22. See Sobrino, *Christology at the Crossroads*, 179–235. In this chapter on the death
of Jesus and liberation in history, he presents fourteen theses on the cross and liberation.

23. Ibid., 225.

that Jesus' life is liberating and good news is—paradoxically—
the cross . . . [T]hrough the cross, Jesus' life is liberation and
good news today.[24]

On the cross, God is present in a word of love for the suffering poor
and a definitive "no" to their oppression, and God is absent in Jesus' cry,
"My God, my God, why have you abandoned me" (Matt 27:46)? On the
cross, all natural theology is meaningless. Theodicy, not theology, becomes here the primary question. Sobrino echoes what Karl Barth and
the North Atlantic dialectical theologians have stressed: there is no such
thing as "natural theology."[25] In his twelfth thesis on the cross, Sobrino
says: "The cross calls into question all knowledge of God based on natural theology. Knowing God means abiding with God in the passion. The
question of knowing God must be posed in terms of theodicy, in terms
of our experience of evil in the world."[26] God's presence cannot be found
here in the "beauty of nature." The cross is ugliness at its worst as the poor
suffer death at the hands of the powerful. Sobrino refers the reader to
Barth's mistrust of natural theology:

> By "natural theology" I mean here every attempt to gain access
> to God on the basis of what is *positive* in existence . . . [A]ll natu-
> ral theology operates by way of analogy. On the cross, however,
> we find nothing similar to what is usually regarded as divine. If
> there is some knowledge of God to be found on the cross, then
> some other principle of knowledge must be operative because
> the deity appears totally unlike anything we know . . . The first
> thing that the cross reveals about God is human *hubris*: People
> fashion images of God that are in direct contradiction to the real
> God. As a mechanism for our approach to God, natural theology
> is nothing else but a way for us to justify ourselves in the face of
> the true God, to turn aside so that we need not confront the true
> God (Barth).[27]

At the same time, the cross is sacramental. In it we see the sacrament
par excellence of the suffering of Jesus for the sake of the world. Sobrino
speaks on behalf of the imagination of the poor. A theology that seeks to
encounter God through what is positive in nature—natural theology in

24. Sobrino, *Jesus the Liberator*, 272.

25. Sobrino, *Christology at the Crossroads*, 221–22. He quotes from Bonhoeffer.

26. Ibid., 221.

27. Ibid.

the traditional sense—is not possible. Rather, God is found in *absence* and from the underside of humanity—in the suffering of the poor. This is like Schillebeeckx's "negative contrast experience," where God's presence is encountered in absence.[28] The cross is that place where the presence of God—*Deus crucifixus*—is found at its deepest level. There is no better place than the cross for finding the sacramental presence of Jesus. The crucified Jesus is the visible sign of God's presence, the sacrament of God for the suffering poor. "Jesus . . . faithful to his death on the cross . . . [is] the perennial sacrament in this world of a liberator God."[29] On the cross, God-for-us is enfleshed in death. This presence *and* absence of God—the primary paradox for the believer— is the "dual unity" (*nepantla*) of divine passion for the poor.

If Jesus is the Sacrament of the mysterious presence and absence of God on the cross, then the crucified *pueblo* are the sacrament of the crucified Jesus. Quoting Martin Luther, Sobrino says that the cross is "no one against God except God." He continues, "God 'bifurcates' himself on the cross, so that transcendence (the Father) is in conflict with history (the Son)."[30] God takes on, in the cross of Jesus, the suffering of the poor in history. In this terrible instrument of torture and death, we see at once the negative contrast of the suffering of the innocent and the passionate love of the God whose transcendence is made historical immanence in the poor. It is they who are the sacrament of Jesus. It is they who, through God's mysterious love on the cross, become the crucified *pueblo*. Sobrino relies on the theology of Moltmann, but he goes much further. Jesus is the crucified God; but more important—and this distinguishes North Atlantic from Latin American theology—*Jesus is the crucified people.* The crucified people are the "crucified body of Christ in history."[31] The primary theological question does not concern the *being* of God, as in natural theology, but rather *language* about God—how are the poor *told* of God's love, which Gutiérrez says is *the* theological question. How does one speak about God in the crucifixion and death of the *pueblo*?

Latin American theology and pastoral practice regarding the death of Jesus is communal. On the cross of Jesus, the Latin American poor are crucified again and yet again—"not just once, but thousands

28. Schillebeeckx, *The Church*, 5–6.
29. Sobrino, *Jesus the Liberator*, 273.
30. Sobrino, *Christology at the Crossroads*, 225.
31. Sobrino, *Jesus the Liberator*, 254.

of times." The crucified *pueblo* becomes the historical presence of the crucified body of Christ. The poor, in the deepest Christological sense, "save." Aware of theological and doctrinal raised eyebrows, Sobrino says: "Of course, my presentation of the crucified people here may be open to question. But we must be aware of the fundamental issue, which is much more important: it would be idle to say that Christ crucified has a body in history and not identify it in some way."[32] The crucified people save because they are identified with the crucified body of Christ. Acknowledged as the crucified suffering Servant, they "bear the sins of the world"—systemic, structural, social sin—and enlighten the darkness of the wealthy and powerful. They take structural sin upon their shoulders, though innocent, and in so doing reveal sinfulness to the sinner. Bonhoeffer would call this the "vicarious representation" of Christ and the Church community (*Stellvertretung*). Sobrino quotes Rahner: "[O]nly the sinner can know forgiveness."[33] Jesus the Sacramental Word is present in the crucified people. This saving presence, says Sobrino, is the "basic Christological datum" of liberation theology.[34]

Mexican indigenous theology is "nepantlic," and Jesus is the *Nepantla* of God (Garibay). I refer to *nepantla* often in this book. A word from the *Náhuatl* language, it means "situated in the midst of" and expresses indigenous "dual unity" (*unidad dual*).[35] Though it has been used in Hispanic-Latino theology in the United States to refer to the Chicano(a) experience as "in the midst of" Mexican reality and the oppression of the dominant culture in the United States,[36] its most systematic theological use to date of which I am aware is by Mexican theologian Javier Garibay, SJ. The idea speaks to the radical unity of contraries—sun and moon, night and day, male and female—and is integral to the cosmology of the *Mexica* culture. For now, I will deal with its Christological flavor in Garibay's theology.

   Nepantla, which cuts through Western theological dualism like a surgeon's scalpel, gives theology a methodology, planted firmly in the person of Jesus and in the Triune God, for approaching the transcendent

32. Ibid., 264.
33. Ibid.
34. Ibid., 254.
35. Garibay, *Nepantla*, 31.
36. Busto, "Chicano(a) Religions," 238–49.

and the historical. *Nepantla* is manifested in the love shared in the communal life of the Trinity through Jesus and in the Spirit.[37] For Garibay, the Trinity and the Incarnation are intimately related. The Triune God's communal love is incarnated in Jesus, the *Nepantla* of God. "Nepantlism is reciprocity, dual unity, and complimentary relationship of contraries . . . [W]ithout the Trinitarian aspect, the nepantlism [of Jesus] remains incomplete, as does the Christian interpretation of the transcendence of God in history. This Trinitarian dimension cannot be separated from the Christological dimension; to the contrary, it presupposes an historical and divine nepantlism of the person [of Jesus]."[38] The passionate love of the Triune God for the poor is revealed in the historical praxis of Jesus on the cross.[39] This praxis of Jesus expresses the essential unity of the economic and the immanent Trinity (Garibay refers the reader to Rahner's doctoral thesis).[40] Jesus is the *Nepantla* of the Triune God in two ways among others—the Incarnation (divinity-humanity) and the Paschal Mystery (crucifixion-resurrection).[41] He takes on our humanity—flesh, culture, history, poverty, victimization. The *nepantla* of the Incarnation is the divine answer to bridging the gap between transcendence and history. It makes these two "opposites" a radical unity in the person of Jesus. The God who is *totaliter aliter*, in Jesus Christ the Sacramental Word of the poor, is the God who is Emmanuel, "God-with-us" (Matt 1:23). Jesus the *Nepantla* of God *is* the Christological imagination of the poor.

Philippians 2:5–11 is central to Garibay's liberation Christology. In the kenotic emptying of Jesus, God takes on our nothingness, our weakness, our poverty, our slavery, our littleness. Jesus, "though in the form of God" and "not regard[ing] equality with God as something to be exploited" (2:6), "emptied himself" and took the "form of a slave" (2:7).[42] Jesus not only becomes human. He becomes *poor*. He takes on the condition of poverty. He assumes, in his humanity, what it means to be despised and exiled. He suffers "even death on a cross" (2:8). Jesus becomes nothing, a thing "despised" and "rejected" (Isa 53:3). He is crucified between two criminals on a hill outside the city walls, on the periphery. He dies aban-

37. For Garibay's discussion of the Trinity, see *Nepantla*, 332–45.

38. Ibid., 332.

39. Ibid., 337.

40. Ibid., 336.

41. Ibid., 322–25.

42. Ibid., 322.

doned by God (Matt 27:46) but commends his emptied body and spirit into the hands of God (Luke 23:46).

"Therefore God also highly exalted him" (Phil 2:9). Garibay mentions the importance not just of Pauline theology—emptying and exaltation—but also of Johannine cross and resurrection. Jesus is "lifted up" (John 3:14) as a sign to all people—crucifixion *and* exaltation for John—as the serpent was lifted up by Moses in the desert. The Son of Humanity is lifted up so that all might have life in abundance (John 3:15). Death is associated with life, lifting up with exaltation. Garibay says that Latin American theology never sees the crucifixion independently from the resurrection. The cross of Jesus is the cross of the risen One, and the resurrection is the exultation of the crucified One.[43] Life comes through death. Kenotic emptying finds its deepest meaning on the cross, through which Jesus is "lifted up."

The *Nepantla* of God is revealed in the *pueblo*.[44] The poor become the expression of the *Nepantla* of God in Jesus. In the imagination of the poor, the indigenous live *nepantla* in cross and resurrection, in death and life, in kenotic emptying and exaltation—or rather, *Jesus* lives it in them. Garibay cites Sobrino and Ellacuría, saying the poor are the "crucified people."[45] The crucifixion of Jesus is experienced daily in the suffering and death of the Latin American poor. They are the ones who "die before their time," crucified "not once, but thousands of times." The emptying of Jesus is the daily bread of the Latin American poor. They live in the multitude of shanty towns that surround large Latin American cities. Unemployed and underemployed, they are migrants in a strange and unfriendly context. They suffer sicknesses for which there is little recourse to medical care. Garibay speaks, from the perspective of *las víctimas* (the victims),[46] of the plight of this "crucified people" whose only "crime" is their very poverty. They are innocent, like Jesus, but suffer the radical injustice of mass crucifixion. Schillebeeckx speaks of "negative contrast," but when Latin Americans theologians write about the day-to-day existence of the poor, "negative contrast" is an understatement.

Many Latin American theologians have written about the double oppression of women in this situation of radical poverty. Ivone Gebara

43. Ibid., 326.
44. Ibid., 325–32.
45. Ibid., 327.
46. Ibid., 329. He cites Sobrino.

speaks of how interconnected creation, women, and the poor *really* are. Poor women are among the poorest of the poor because neither gender nor the poor are respected by the powerful. The poor suffer because creation has been abused, and poverty is a direct cause of the abuse of creation. Poor women who are single mothers are often forced into taking extremely low-paying jobs in order to make ends meet. Those abused by the capitalistic system often find themselves in situations of domestic violence, where they are also physically abused. Consuelo del Prado refers to the special suffering of women in Latin America: "Women of the poorer sectors suffer and weep much over their situation. They live in an estranged world. They are torn from their land; they are deprived of their schools, their language, and their traditional clothing as well as their children, spouses, and their place in the community. If poverty is death then poor women confront many deaths in their lifetime: the death from hunger, sickness, repression, the death of their traditions, and of their deepest femininity."[47]

Much of my pastoral experience has been with Mexican undocumented immigrant communities in the Puget Sound area of Washington State. Like all Latin American poor, Mexican people in the United States experience *kenosis* and crucifixion in their day-to-day existence. Immigration injustice, poverty, unjust working conditions, racism—these are just a few of their regular *kenosis* experiences. I see injustices daily, from the seemingly small—"I hope those 'Hispanics' don't move the flowers we've placed in the sanctuary"—to the hopelessly huge, such as the young Mexican woman I buried a number of years ago who died "before her time" because of complications from childbirth that would have been routinely treated for an Anglo woman in the same hospital. The *kenosis* of the *pueblo* is too vast to enumerate: a pregnant woman cursed at and emotionally abused by the police, a mother deported as an "illegal alien" without her children, a young man beaten by the police in a situation where he was literally "the innocent One," migrant workers who become sick, and even die, because they are improperly trained for "chemical cleanup," racism on the part of the dominant community, abuse in the work place, and discrimination in the parish from the minority but dominant Anglo community. Recently a young Mexican man brought a large crucifix to the parish to be blessed. The body of Jesus was vividly depicted in his suffering and *kenosis*—the crown of thorns on his bleeding head, the open side,

47. Tamez, ed., *Through Her Eyes*, 141–42.

the face set in agony. That same young man later asked why it was so easy to see the crucified Jesus suffering in an image of plaster, but not in the crucified *pueblo* of flesh and blood. *Kenosis* is no stranger to the Mexican *pueblo* in the Puget Sound area.

The people of Latin America live the *nepantla* of Jesus in death and *life*. Whether an indigenous woman in the slums on the periphery of a large Latin American city, a poor *campesino* in Guatemala or Honduras, or an undocumented Mexican recently arrived in the United States, the kenotic emptying of injustice mysteriously gives way to "lifting up," to exaltation, to new *life* in the midst of death, to resurrection from the tomb. What is the opposite of the kenotic emptying of suffering, injustice, and death? It is, very simply, the God of life—*El Dios de la vida*. Jesus is the resurrection and the life (John 11:25). He gives life to the *pueblo* through the Spirit of the risen One.[48] The positive force of life is diametrically opposed to the negative force of death, and "death before its time" is nullified by the Sacramental Word and taken up into the great *nepantla* of life: "Where, O death, is your victory? Where, O death, is your sting" (1 Cor 15:55)? The *pueblo*, in the midst of death, chooses *life* in the depth expression of *nepantla*: "I have set before you life and death . . . Choose life so that you and your descendants may live" (Deut 30:19).

During Lent in Perú in the 1980s, the Episcopal Conference would select a reflection theme for the entire country. This was combined with a colorful poster displayed in every parish church. The one I most remember was from the mid-eighties. The caption was: *Pasamos con Jesús de la muerte a la vida*—"we pass with Jesus from death to life." The poster was blue with a cross in the background that overshadowed one of the many *pueblos jóvenes* of Lima.[49] For the poor, life is consistently affirmed in the face of death. Though the *pueblo* live as "crucified people" in the emptying *kenosis* of their daily existence, they also hope in new life and resurrection.

The *fiesta* is a testimony to the life of the *pueblo*. Some years ago, I witnessed the marriage of two Mexican parishioners in a hospital chapel and baptized their newly born baby. Shortly after the woman gave birth

48. Garibay, *Nepantla*, 330.

49. A *pueblo joven* (literally "young town") is a new neighborhood in larger Peruvian cities populated by recently arrived poor from the *campo* areas. The people arrive *en masse* and set up make-shift shacks (*chozas*) of straw mats, cardboard, and fiberglass on the unpopulated (but privately owned) outskirts of the city. Over the years, they attain the status of a certain "permanence."

to this infant some three months before, she was diagnosed with pancreatic cancer that advanced quickly to the terminal stage. The marriage and baptism were wonderful occasions, true *fiestas* of the *pueblo*. Afterwards, the couple shared food, story, and life with their guests in *fiesta* and celebration. Several days later, the same people who had been present at the *fiesta* gathered once again for her funeral. At the *velorio*,[50] pictures were displayed of the wedding and baptism. Life was affirmed in the face of death. Faith and hope in the God of life were professed by the *pueblo* despite the presence of death.

El Dios de la vida stands in diametric opposition to the *kenosis* of the poor. The *pueblo* in *fiesta* celebrate the God of life in contrast to the idols of death. Jesus, *el Dios de la vida* made flesh, is the Good Shepherd who "lays down his life for the sheep" (John 10:11). "I came that they might have life, and have it more abundantly" (John 10:10) has vivid meaning for the *pueblo*. Jesus stands against the death-dealing thief who "comes only to steal and kill and destroy." The life of the incarnate Jesus, manifested in the crucified *pueblo*, vanquishes death in all its forms and nurtures *nepantla*—a "dual unity," lived deep within the *pueblo*, of *kenosis* and exaltation, crucifixion and death, transcendence and history. It speaks of the deepest longings of the *pueblo* in their living imagination. Jesus Sacramental Word of the God of the poor, through the life-giving Spirit, *lives* in the *pueblo*.

Jesus is integrally identified with the *pueblo*, who are the body of Christ and the sacrament of Jesus. The *pueblo*, in transverbation, is word of the Sacramental Word. Otto Semmelroth says that Jesus, in the Incarnation, is "God's own sermon."

> The phenomenon of preaching itself and more especially the hint which the bible gives us by employing the term "word" for Christ makes us aware that the act of preaching in the church expresses symbolically that element in the incarnation and life of Christ which compliments and supplements that other act expressed in the administration of the sacrament. If the celebration of the sacrament points to Christ's sacrificial death, then the preaching of the sermon points to the climax of *God's own sermon*, the incarnation of his Son as the word of God to men [*sic*].

50 An all-night vigil of prayer and *fiesta* before the day of burial.

In the incarnation God has expressed himself fully and entirely
. . . All the words of the Old Testament prophets are a preparation directed to this *divine sermon* which was preached in the
sending of God's Son (Heb 1:1).[51]

Paul Janowiak, SJ, maintains that Jesus, the "very Sermon of God"
(Janowiak's phrase), is central to the theology of Semmelroth.[52] But how
are we to speak of Jesus as "the very Sermon of God"? The starting point
must be the good news—the gospel of Jesus. There we see the words of
him who is God's Sermon. "Blessed are you who are poor," Jesus says
(Luke 6:20). "Do not weep," Jesus tells the poor widow who has lost her
only son (Luke 7:13). "Daughter, your faith has made you well; go in
peace, and be healed of your disease," Jesus says to the hemorrhaging
woman impoverished economically and socially by her condition (Mark
5:34). "The Spirit of the Lord is upon me . . . to bring good news to the
poor . . . to let the oppressed go free," Jesus says to a poor people thirsting
for liberation from all that would hold them fast (Luke 4:18). These are
all words of the definitive and irrevocable Sermon God sent to a people
in need. But there are two special ways, I think, in which Jesus is the *very*
Sermon of God.

The first is the cross. Often, *theologia gloriae* will travel the path of
looking solely to the exalted Christ who "sits at the right hand of God."
This exalted Christ cannot be "dirtied" by the sordid business of a suffering humanity. He is the Christ of the powerful. On the contrary, Latin
American theology places the exalted Christ square in the shadow of the
cross, where the resurrection is only seen in the light of the death of Jesus.
It is a *theologia crucis* much starker than that made famous by Martin
Luther. The "right hand of God" is *not* spatial. Its "place" is the cross mys-
teriously at the heart of the *pueblo*.

The imagination of the poor sees Jesus, "God's own sermon," as the
crucified One who cries out in his most desperate hour, "My God, my
God, why have you forsaken me" (Matt 27:46)? That is the sermon of God
at its finest. For here, our God uses a moving pulpit—the cross (Sobrino).
The poor Jesus and through him, the crucified people, echoes the words
of *el Santo Job*—Holy Job, as he is known in Latin America—"Therefore I
will not restrain my mouth; I will speak in the anguish of my spirit; I will
complain in the bitterness of my soul" (Job 7:11). Job cries out to God, for

51. Semmelroth, *The Preaching Word*, 221–22; emphasis mine.

52. See Janowiak, *The Holy Preaching*, 20–27.

God has abandoned him. His friends tell him he has done something to "deserve" his suffering, but Holy Job knows that he is *tam*—upright, just, and innocent.[53] Jesus' cry on the cross is that of Job and all the innocent poor. It is the cry that will not be quieted: the cry of the victim, the cry of the exiled, the very sermon of God.

The second way in which Jesus is the *very* Sermon of God is found in the garden of the resurrection (John 20:11–18) where Mary Magdalene becomes the voice of the poor and takes on their imagination. It is she who weeps inconsolably by the tomb. It is she who does not leave after Peter and John go their puzzled ways. She sits and weeps—metaphor for the poor who wait by so many tombs: unemployment and racism, murder and injustice, hunger and homelessness, the death of poverty. She has seen the crucifixion in its horrors—as the *pueblo* has witnessed the crucifixion of the poor. But Mary will not leave. She waits, like Job, for an answer.

Two angels appear. "Woman, why are you weeping" (20:13), they ask?—words of consolation for those, like her, who grieve outside the tomb of injustice. She turns and sees one she thinks is the gardener. In desperation she cries, "Sir, if you have carried him away, tell me where you have laid him, and I will take him away" (20:15). Those who mourn with the crucified *pueblo* are inconsolable; they will go to any extreme to be close to their wounded body. But then, in unexpected *nepantla*, the gardener calls her name—"Mary!"—the voice of life amidst death. And in an instant, Mary recognizes her beloved. The tortured body has been transformed. The crucified One lives! Mary is filled with the joy that only those who have suffered understand.

The crucified *pueblo*—the body of the risen One—is recognized in the Gardener. The cross, icon of the imagination of the exiled, becomes the cross of the risen One.[54] The risen Jesus gently calls the name of the poor, and they recognize, in his wounded body, their own tortured body—the body of Christ. The Church of the poor is the body of Christ. "The Church is, in the first place, the Body of Christ; it forms, with him, a single entity, a single beneficiary of the good things of God . . . We are with Christ a single body, we are members of his body . . . St. Paul goes so far as to say that we are a single person in Christ."[55] The One who was

---

53. Gutiérrez, *Hablar de Dios*, 36.

54. A favorite image Louise-Marie Chauvet; see *The Sacraments*.

55. Congar, *The Mystery of the Church*, 68.

disfigured, the One who suffered the indignity of the cross, the One who, in his humanity, was made barely human—he is risen from the dead by the power of the Spirit and lives forever! The exiled poor, the crucified but risen body of Christ, cannot be held by sin, death, and injustice.

The very Sermon of God tells Mary what to do: "But go to my brothers and say to them, 'I am ascending to my Father and your Father, to my God and your God'" (20:17). She is sent—"go" and "say." In the name of the crucified and the risen One, she is to share the good news of life in abundance in the midst of—and in spite of—death. She is to proclaim that death could not bind the One meant for life. She is to preach that life—Jesus Sacramental Word of the God of the poor—is God's final word of living Spirit to the crucified *pueblo*. God's own sermon becomes the Sermon of God in Mary.

Mary represents the crucified *pueblo*. She—a woman—is sent to proclaim, as "Apostle of the Apostles," the Sacramental Word of life to her brothers. Mary, while representing the crucified people who weep at the tomb, represents, in a special way, poor women. It is they who hold poor families together and, at the same time, seek dignity and justice for the *pueblo*. Mary is the paradigm for poor women. She represents the poor who weep at the tomb but are sent forth, in the name of the risen One, to proclaim the good news of the justice that will never die. The crucified people, the body of Christ dead and risen, proclaim, in the Spirit, the sermon of the living God of Jesus in the face of oppression, violence, destruction, poverty, injustice, exile, and death. The *nepantla* of life and death, radical contraries, are mystically united in the proclamation of God's own sermon—the life of Jesus within the exiled *pueblo*.

This, then, is the role of the preacher who accompanies the *pueblo* —to proclaim the very Sermon of God, to be so filled with the Sacred Preaching of the living Spirit of the God of Jesus that it is really only "God's own sermon"—Jesus the Sacramental Word—who preaches. The *nepantla* of cross and resurrection, of the crucified and risen *pueblo*, is proclaimed by the preacher as the very Sermon of God. This means that the preacher turns everything over to the "Preaching Word" who is the Sacramental Word of the God of the poor—Jesus Christ. Robert Farrar Capon says that the Sunday homily should be carefully prepared. But after all preparation is finished and the preacher enters the pulpit, the mind is cleared. "Jesus Christ, and him crucified" is all the preacher brings, at that point, to the Sunday preaching.[56] The preacher is "transverbized" into the very Sermon of God. Karl Barth says the preacher becomes *vicarius Christi*.[57] Perhaps this is the true meaning of *alter Christus*, a theological phrase that is imprecise. There is, strictly speaking, no "other Christ." We, as preachers with the poor, stand in the place of Christ—*alter Christus*—so that the *pueblo*, through word and sacrament, are transverbized into the Sacramental Word of the God of the poor, the *one* body of Christ, *solus Christus*. The *pueblo*, in turn, becomes the body of the Word for one another and the world infinitely loved by God.

Jesus the Sacramental Word of the God of the poor and the imagination of the exiled are both central to the act of preaching. The preacher who accompanies the *pueblo* must insure that the preaching event, along with the preacher, is Christocentric and grounded in the imagination of the poor—the privileged path followed by those who choose to accompany the poor. But really, it is Jesus Christ Sacramental Word of the God of the poor who does the choosing: "It was not you who chose me, but I who chose you and appointed you to go and bear fruit that will remain" (John 15:16 NAB). To be chosen by Jesus for the ministry of preaching with an exiled community—or any community in solidarity with the poor—is a unique honor. The preacher bears fruit that remains by the tedious and joyful preparation entailed in the homily, but more importantly, by the cultivation of the imagination of the exiled and a life centered in Jesus and trusting of the Spirit of the living God. The nourishing fruit that is the result—the "fruit that remains"—is tilled in the rich soil of a life ever open to the imagination of the poor. It becomes part of the preacher, theology as the "contemplation of the Holy Trinity." The fruit that remains is not particularly anything *said*. The preacher must *listen* in the Spirit to the Sacramental Word in the *pueblo*—not just with the ears, but with the *heart*.

The call of Jesus is heard through the voice of the crucified *pueblo*. It is in listening with the entire "heart, soul, mind, and strength" (Mark 12:30) that one hears the "still, small voice" (1 Kgs 19:12–13) of the God

56. See Capon, *The Foolishness of Preaching*, 46–47: "[N]o preachers will hear Jesus until they refuse to see anything else. 'I determined not to know anything among you, save Jesus Christ, and him crucified' (1 Cor. 2:2; KJV)."

57. Barth, *Homiletics*, 67.

who is passionately in love with the poor. It is through the *pueblo*, and their imagination, that the preacher hears the voice of Jesus Christ Sacramental Word of the God of the poor, who wishes nothing more than to utter the Word heard by the *pueblo*. The preacher, in turn, *proclaims* the Sacramental Word of comfort and justice for those God loves. Through the "preaching Word," they are gathered tenderly to the bosom of Abraham and Sarah as the exiled poor, the chosen ones, of the God of Jesus.

6

The Church of the Poor,
Hearer of the Sacramental Word

> The Spirit
>
> has decided
>
> to administer
>
> the eighth sacrament:
>
> the voice of the People![1]

In Latin American theology, the word of God is "the voice of the People." The Bible has given voice to millions. God's word in Scripture has in this sense become a sacrament of salvation—a sign of God's liberating love acting among the people through the word, which is reflected upon weekly by thousands in Latin America and poor Hispanic-Latino communities in the United States. This theology of the word is associated with an integral ecclesiology that arises from the grassroots. In paraphrasing Henri de Lubac's phrase regarding the Church's first centuries—"the Eucharist makes the Church"—one could rightly say that "the word makes the Church."

Latin American theology and its methodology vitally depend on the creative proclamation of Scripture both in formal liturgies and at informal community gatherings. Theology has been defined in Latin America (Gutiérrez) as "a critical reflection on Christian praxis in the light of the word of God." This theology is ecumenical, uniting Catholic

---

1. Pedro Casadáliga, quoted by Codina, "Sacraments," 222.

and Protestant in Latin America around the word as perhaps no other has been capable of doing. The result has been a Christianity that is deeply committed to a contextual hermeneutical reading of Scripture enabling liberating action in favor of God's reign of justice. Special attention is given to the contextual word in indigenous and ecofeminist theologies. In these as well as classic liberation theologies of the 70s and 80s, the word is sacramental—an efficacious sign announcing God's love, justice, and grace. God's word is also dialectical, a two-edged sword (Heb 4:12) denouncing injustice, oppression, sin, and death. In either case, its source is Jesus the Word sacramentally enfleshed in the *pueblo*.

By and large Third-World theology has, until recently, been overlooked in the North Atlantic conversation between dialectical and sacramental imaginations. But the experience of thousands of *comunidades eclesiales de base* (base ecclesial communities) in Latin America who have heard the word within the context of poverty and exile suggest another way to imagine the theology of the word. In this context, where the theological endeavor has been viewed as critical reflection on praxis, the word itself is a powerfully creative force that dialectically denounces injustice and sacramentally announces a word of mercy springing from the depths of human experience. The strong communal sense lived by the poor, the mysticism of poverty, the nepantlic radical unity of contraries within indigenous reality, the contributions of ecofeminism to a holistic view of creation, sexuality, and gender, and the parabolic imagination that reverses the "normal," all of these mark this deeper "mystical-indigenous" imagination lived by the poor in relation to the word of God.

The word that proceeds from the "wholly other" God cannot be divorced from the subject of that word, namely, the historical human community with all its vicissitudes. While proceeding solely from the God who is "holy mystery" (Rahner), the word can nevertheless *only* be received in an historical context and exists *only* as a word to human beings as they are in the created world. In Latin America, that context is the extreme poverty lived by the majority of Christians. The poor who receive God's holy word within this specific historical context of injustice and poverty receive that word, Karl Rahner would say, as "Hearer of the Word."[2] The word is heard in a milieu of deep faith, believed in the context of ecclesial community, and acted upon in the radical commitment to announce God's reign and denounce the "anti-Reign" (Sobrino).

2. Rahner, "The Word and the Eucharist," 253. See also *Hearer of the Word*.

〜

> [T]heology . . . exists because God speaks, not because we think
> . . . Yet even in such a science humanity cannot simply be over-
> looked or eliminated, since there would exist no word of God, if
> there were not someone who would at least be capable of perceiv-
> ing it. Hence there exists a theological anthropology. Not simply
> in the proper and strict sense, that God, in the divine Logos,
> manifests to us the ultimate structure of our own human nature,
> so that a theological anthropology is part of the *content* of theo-
> logy. But there exists also a "theological" anthropology in the
> sense that some, albeit naïve, unreflective self-understanding of
> human beings is the condition for the possibility of theology.[3]

In Rahner's theology, the word as proclaimed is meant to be *heard*:
"[T]he word of God always comes as the word that is heard and believed,
the word that is preached and attested because believed."[4] Both word and
sacrament, for Rahner, are integrally connected, radically ecclesial, and
deeply touch the human person in his or her "transcendentality": "Word
and sacrament constitute the Church. Or to put it more exactly: the power
to preach the word of God by the authority of God and of his Christ, and
the power to administer the sacraments . . . are the two basic powers of
the Church which are constitutive of its essence."[5]

The human person, in the context of ecclesial community, is the privileged recipient of the word of God. The human person as "transcendental
subject" is the hearer of the message, the "hearer of the word." The holy
mystery who is God is absolute mystery. God is the transcendent "abyss"
before whom the human subject stands in awe. God is creator; the human
person is creature. However, God is the holy mystery who wishes nothing
more than to be revealed to the hearer in loving self-communication. For
Rahner, this is *grace*. God privileges the human person not as object but
as transcendental subject. The human being stands at the center of God's
gaze—the human being as "event" of God's revelation[6]—and all God's
actions are directed toward humanity in loving mercy and compassion.
The human subject is hearer of this message, which is communicated in

3. Rahner, *Hearer of the Word*, 146.
4. Rahner, "The Word and the Eucharist," 253.
5. Ibid., 254.
6. Rahner, *Foundations*, 120.

three primary modes of knowledge about God: natural, revealed, and historical.[7] The first is not purely possible (sometimes Barth and Rahner are more alike than theologians want to believe!). But the latter two are integrally connected. God's love is *revealed* in human history. The human being is the *subject* of that revelation, the "hearer of the word." But Rahner goes much deeper. This is not just communicated knowledge in the epistemological sense but the very *being* of God "self-communicated" in grace—the divine being *with* the human person.[8] We actually *hear* God's word of grace in our depths, because *we* are God's beloved.

Gustavo Gutiérrez relies on Rahner but adds his own unique perspective. For Gutiérrez, salvation must be seen (heard!) in its integral *unity*. There is no such thing as salvation only in the "afterlife." Salvation is shared with the entire person *within historical reality*. It is not "extra-historical." God wants communion with the human being in his or her historical context. God's unconditional and gratuitous love saves, Gutiérrez is fond of saying, and is integrally connected with God's gracious word heard in the *pueblo*. God's grace inspires us to express the love that has been freely shared through word and praxis. The faithful disciple feebly attempts to follow Jesus, the brother of the poor and the least. We are called, through committed action, to reflect the love of God, who always chooses the insignificant other. God's compassion is reflected in our actions as disciples, God's option in our solidarity with the poor. God's gratuitous and unmerited love in Jesus and in the Spirit is the center of everything. We are saved by *hearing* the word of love: "God is Love . . . This was Christ's revelation. To be saved is to reach the fullness of love; it is to enter into the circle of charity which unites the three persons of the Trinity; it is to love as God loves. The way to this fullness of love can be no other than love itself. . . ."[9] To be saved is to be a "hearer of the word," to live praxis love through which the insignificant other is approached "with melting heart."[10] Salvation begins with God and returns to God. God is love; through God's gratuitous love that takes the initiative, I love by making God's option for the poor mine; and it is through this love whose source is God's Sacramental Word that I am saved in the Church community.

7. Ibid., 57–61.

8. Karl Barth simply says, "We *are* known before we *know.*" *The Word of God,* 95–96.

9. Nickoloff, *Gustavo Gutiérrez,* 153.

10. Ibid., 154.

The human person hears the word of salvation in *community*. *Extra ecclesiam nulla salus* is an ancient theological principle. Communion with God, the goal of the human subject, happens in history amidst historical beings, within a specific historical context and a specific historical people, a *pueblo*. This *pueblo* hears the word of God's love *only* in community. This communal experience of *pueblo* as ecclesial hearer of the word in historical reality is, in the Latin American context, the communal experience of the word heard within the context of extreme poverty. Salvation is the *ecclesial hearing* of the word in the midst of oppression.

A proper theology of salvation, says Víctor Codina, is rooted in the Fathers and the Mothers of the first centuries. Jesus assumes our humanity so that we can share his divinity. Salvation is health (*salus*), "divinization" for the *whole* person in community (*koinonia*). The Fathers and Mothers call this *theosis*.[11] *Theosis* sees discipleship and salvation, faith and obedience, as *nepantla*. Discipleship is a call to hear the Word *now*, in *this* time and context. The call is more radical today than ever, addressed more clearly to us than the first disciples (Bonhoeffer), for it is now the risen Jesus, through the Spirit, who calls. It is *now* that the Word must be heard by the disciple community.[12] This is what Codina means by *koinonia* and *theosis* as salvation in Latin America today.

Latin American ecofeminist theology also sees salvation as the ecclesial hearing of the word. Ivone Gebara is critical of the "dualistic epistemology" of Western theology—including classic male-dominated liberation theology of the 1970s and 80s. Many theologians, she says, are simply incapable of moving beyond dualistic thinking because of their uncritical education primarily based on the Platonic-Aristotelian heritage. Gebara invites us to hear the word in the midst of the poor, the excluded, women, and all creation. Along with the poor, she says, women and creation have experienced the wound of male-dominated power, production, and oppression. Salvation directs us to the poor other—women, environment, creation, and humanity. She affirms in contextual theological language what the Fathers and Mothers meant by *apokatastasis*, the restoration of all creation through Jesus Christ in the Spirit.[13]

---

11. Codina, *Los Caminos*, 72–76.

12. See Preface to *Discipleship*, 37–40.

13. See Gebara, *Longing for Running Water*, especially 19–65 and 193–212. Also see *Out of the Depths*.

The poor are the privileged recipients of God's love and mercy. Yet this is not self-evident and cannot be deduced by natural means. Actually it seems the opposite; and, in fact, the "opposite" has predominated Christian history. The poor are the "accursed" of God. They suffer because they are "morally bad." God rewards the good with material riches and punishes evildoers (the poor) with the curse. Even though "retribution theology" was debunked once for all in the book of Job, it is, unfortunately, still all too popular. This worldview has been revisited at different times throughout history, and Scripture has been abused in its support. Many modern mega-churches—particularly in the United States—still cling stubbornly (and sinfully) to this reading of Scripture. If *I* am wealthy, God blesses *me*, and there is no obligation to share with the poor. If I am poor, I must have done something for God to "punish" me. Achievement and success count; failure is a result of "not working hard enough." God gives to achievers, those who look after themselves ("God helps those who help themselves"), an abundance of riches because of their "works." This amounts to idolatry and injustice, the two major biblical sins. It is nothing less than classic Pelagianism—a contemporary denial of grace.[14]

The poor hear Scripture on a completely different plain. God's word is judgment for the powerful and mercy for the poor. The poor ecclesial hearer experiences, in passage after passage of Scripture, that God has made an option for the poor. God acts on behalf of the exiled with "strong arm" and "mighty power" (Jer 32:21). God loves everyone unconditionally and without preference, but opts for, chooses, the poor. The poor are the chosen ecclesial hearers of the Sacramental Word. In this gracious hearing, the *pueblo* is saved and liberated.

One aspect of the Church of the poor as hearer often overlooked by North Atlantic theology is the role of the *Spirit*. Here, the poor and their imagination invite us to much deeper reflection. While Rahner gives the privileged place to the human subject as hearer and Barth to the God who is *totaliter aliter*, Latin American imagination gives the hearer centrality but only as *ecclesial* hearer *led by the Spirit* of the wholly other God. In its commentary on Matt 10:5–15 (the sending of the Twelve), the *Biblia Latinoamérica* says that the Twelve—sent forth to proclaim the word that the reign is at hand—can only share that word haltingly as "uneducated and inadequate" human beings. However, the Spirit of God inspires, in the poor hearer of the word, openness to God's message within that very

14. Byassee, "The Health and Wealth Gospel," 20–23.

human word.[15] Although this seems self-evident and is generally taken as such by North Atlantic theology, the poor, because of their poverty, are much more deeply aware of human inadequacy, injustice, and sinfulness and thus more conscious of the consequent need for the inspiration of the Spirit in openness to God's word—what Paul Janowiak calls the "parabolic imagination." In the parables, there is a radical reversal of the "usual." The powerful cannot understand this reversal and are violent in their rejection of it. But the poor understand it perfectly. They are not wealthy Dives but Lazarus outside the gates, dogs licking at their sores (Luke 16:19–31). The parable is heard from the underside.

The God who is totally other, the God who is absolute and holy mystery wishing to be revealed, the God who is definitively revealed in the Sacramental Word, the God who wishes to self-disclose to the *pueblo* in an abundance of grace, the God who is Holy Spirit, stands at the center—as does the ecclesial hearer of the word inspired by the Spirit. Latin American liberation theology in the Catholic tradition accepts Aquinas' notion of causality. All things are "caused" and "moved" by God. But Thomism is nuanced and contextualized in Latin America, because God "causes" the poor and their history to be placed at *God's own center*, at the very heart of God's being. This causing and moving God is "moved" by human misery, suffering, poverty, and injustice—"compassionate" in the biblical sense. The God whose word is heard and received ecclesially self-discloses to the hearer and is actually *moved* by the poor ecclesial hearer, even as the Spirit of the God of Jesus moves the Church community as hearer to action. The God who "hears the cry of the poor" and is moved with compassion makes an option for the poor and in turn moves the hearer of the word—the Church. This God who creates in the image of Christ "sees" the suffering of the poor. The Sacramental Word, in whose humanity the divine is compassionately moved, "judges" that suffering in mercy for the poor and judgment for the oppressor. The Holy Spirit "acts" by moving within the *pueblo* who hear the word and, in turn, put it into practice (see Luke 8:21).[16]

Latin American theological and pastoral methodology, Trinitarian at core, has its roots in a process first articulated by Belgian priest and

15. *Biblia Latinoamérica*, Edición 1995, 28.

16. Semmelroth, *The Preaching Word*, 14.

founder of the Young Christian Workers Movement, Joseph Cardijn, in the 1930s. The methodology was integrated by the *comunidades eclesiales de base* and pastorally tailored, through the lens of liberation theology, to the reality of the indigenous poor of Latin America by Brazilian Fr. José Marins and others. It is called *ver, juzgar,* and *actuar*—in English, see, judge, and act. Through the inspiration of Marins and his pastoral team, two extra stages have been added to this methodology: *evaluar* (evaluate) and *celebrar* (celebrate). These words will be used in Spanish because they convey a meaning not aptly communicated by the English.

Theology is a "reflection on praxis in the light of God's word." Often in the base communities or pastoral catechesis an *hecho de vida*, an "example from life," is chosen as a starting point for reflection. The Bible is the primary text for catechesis and the ecclesial communities. The readings can be taken from the Sunday liturgy or chosen in a variety of other ways. The *hecho de vida* is most often the equivalent of the "negative contrast experience" proposed by Edward Schillebeeckx—an experience of injustice or oppression resulting in extreme human suffering. It is paradoxically these contrast experiences that contain within the mysterious revelation of God: "Although there are many experiences of meaning in any human life, nevertheless it is above all experiences of meaninglessness, of injustice, and of innocent suffering that have a revelatory significance *par excellence.*"[17] The negative contrast coincides with the first stage of the Latin American methodology of the word, the *ver* (see). An experience from the life of the poor is chosen for reflection. Perhaps it is a world event, something that has recently occurred in the neighborhood, or an individual experience. It could be an assigned *hecho de vida* for educational purposes—as was the case with *Catequesis Familiar* (Family Catechesis) when I was working in Perú. But more likely, it is a negative contrast experienced by the entire community. The *hecho de vida* is then shared with the community.

The next stage is the *juzgar* (judge). This can be compared to the "dangerous memory" of German theologian Johannes Baptist Metz. It is based on a personal experience that he had as a sixteen-year-old soldier forced into service at the end of World War II. He describes it to a friend who was a prisoner of war. The young Metz was sent on a mission to battalion headquarters. He says, "The entire night I wandered about through burning villages in ruins and farm yards." He returned to his company the

17. Schillebeeckx, *The Church,* 5–6.

next day only to find all his comrades dead: "I found only dead people . . . destroyed by a combined attack of bombers and tanks . . . [O]nly the day before I had shared children's fears and youthful laughter with them . . . I remember nothing but a soundless cry . . . [B]ehind this memory all my childhood memories have crumbled. I was never able to reconcile myself to this memory."[18] Metz asks, "What would happen if one took this sort of remembrance not to the psychologist but into the Church? and if one did not allow oneself to be talked out of such unreconciled memories even by theology . . . but rather . . . with them, speak about God?"[19]

Dangerous memory, in the context of poverty in Latin America or anywhere else, is a result of negative contrast. It is brought to the second stage of theological methodology for the word—the *juzgar*—by the ecclesial communities. There it is judged in the light of the word of God. What does God's word have to say in judgment pronounced, over negative contrast, about this dangerous memory? Whether the negative contrast and dangerous memory involve a life of desolate poverty in a *choza*,[20] the crossing of the desert Mexican *frontera* into the United States, or the death of a child,[21] it is taken up in faith and word and reflected upon by the communities (this is done with the larger parish community in the preaching, which is why it is so important for a preacher to *listen* to the communities). There a judgment is passed—God's daughters and sons cannot live like this; it is abhorrent to the God of mercy and justice and should likewise be abhorrent to God's people.

The third stage of word methodology is the *actuar*. This is an action decided upon by the community in the light of what has been seen in negative contrast (*ver*) and judged in dangerous memory (*juzgar*). The community always directs itself toward praxis in the light of the word (*actuar*): "What should we do" (Luke 3:10, Acts 2:37—in these verses, it is *preaching* that moves to action). The entire process is evaluated (*evaluar*):

18 Guenter, *Rahner and Metz*, 20–21.

19 Metz, *A Passion for God*, 2. James Hayes, in a fine essay called "Listen to My Sighing," relates the dangerous memory to preaching using this quote. See Heille, ed., *Theology of Preaching*, 65–66.

20. A shack made of *esteras* (straw mats made into walls) and covered with *Eternit* (corrugated fiberglass made into roofs). These landscape the outskirts of Lima (and all large Latin American cities in the form that they take in their particular country) and are the dwellings of the "poorest of the poor."

21. During the last weeks of 2008 at Holy Spirit Parish in Kent, WA, there were three children's funerals—all Mexican.

Was this disciple praxis? Did we as Church do justice? Did the "word make the Church" and motivate ecclesial action on behalf of the *pueblo*? Was the good news proclaimed to the poor? Did we "see, judge, and act" to proclaim liberation to the oppressed (Luke 4:18–19)? All is then summarized through celebration (*celebrar*), often in a liturgical context and always in *fiesta*.

This is the theological methodology of the poor. The process is lived communally in the holy transcendent Other who is the Triune God—or better, *the Triune God lives* in the people who see, judge, and act. The ecclesial community is a reflection of the passionate love of God who is *communion* of persons. The Triune God makes an option for the *pueblo* and for justice. The God who *sees* the suffering of the people (Exod 3:7) and *judges* (Exod 3:9) cannot stand idly by, but must *act* because of *who* God is (Exod 3:14). The Holy Trinity is *ver* in God's very being: "God always takes his stand unconditionally and passionately on this side and on this side alone: against the lofty and in behalf of the lowly."[22] The Holy Trinity is *juzgar* in the incarnate Word for the world so deeply loved by God (John 3:16) in Jesus. The "Just Word" proceeds from the "mouth" of the Trinity and judges negative contrast in what Metz calls *memoria passionis* (dangerous memory *par excellence*—the Paschal Mystery). Jesus lives *memoria passionis* deep within the suffering *pueblo*. The Holy Trinity is *actuar* in the Holy Spirit moving deep within the exiled *pueblo*. The Spirit inspires and acts within the poor ecclesial hearer of the word in praxis that bespeaks the most holy God at core. Latin American theology sees in Exod 3:14, the revelation of the divine name ("God said to Moses, "I AM WHO I AM"), a crucial passage. God *is who is* and *will be who will be* always on behalf of justice for the *pueblo* (Gutiérrez). God is eternally covenanted with the *pueblo* in *ḥesed, mishpaṭ,* and *ṣedeqah*—three of the most important words in the Hebrew Scriptures, integrally related to the covenant. *Ḥesed* is God's steadfast and covenantal love and mercy, and *mishpaṭ* and *ṣedeqah* (justice, righteousness) are practically interchangeable. Because of who God is, God can *never* forget the covenant, now forged through the *memoria passionis* of the One who is the definitive Sacramental Word inspiring the people to disciple praxis in the Spirit.

Evaluar and *celebrar* are essential tasks for the ecclesial community in fidelity to the Triune God of the covenant. These stages emphasize the *loci theologici* of Latin American theology, the poor and the Church

22. Míguez Bonino, *Doing Theology*, 113, quoting Barth.

(Gutiérrez). *Evaluar* is soul-searching appraisal on the part of the community, where the primary question is: how did this serve the cause of gospel justice and those for whom the Triune God opts, i.e., the poor? *Celebrar* is the great *fiesta* of the ecclesial community, the people of God—the reflection of the eschatological banquet of the poor in bread, wine, and word.

Gustavo Gutiérrez, in commenting on the story of the ten young women (Matt 25:1–13), stresses the radically ecclesial nature of this parable.[23] For Matthew, this is not so much a parable of readiness, for after all, all ten attendants fell asleep. Rather, this is a parable about the Church's role in going out to meet the spouse, Jesus, for his "marriage with humanity."[24] Can an evaluation (*evaluar*) on the "action" of meeting Jesus as *iglesia peregrina*, the "Church on pilgrimage"—be sure to bring sufficient lamp oil in the praxis of justice—be done by the "attendants," the ecclesial community? Then all would be ready to enter the great *fiesta*, the great celebration (*celebrar*) of the banquet.

This Trinitarian methodology of the liberating word is lived out in the *pueblo*, the poor hearer of the word, the Church community. In short, it can be summarized as follows: *Ver* (the God of Jesus), *juzgar* (Jesus the Sacramental Word), *actuar* (the Spirit of life), *evaluar* (the poor of the Triune God), and *celebrar* (the Church).

There is a more traditional theological methodology of the word appropriated by liberation theology and the imagination of the poor, first proposed by Peter Abelard and used by theology since scholastic times. It is called *sic et non*—"yes and no." In this methodology, a question is stated and followed by a *disputatio*—a systematic treatment of the pros and cons implicit in the question. Though *sic et non* was given a special place in theology by thirteenth century Thomas Aquinas, it is also eminently appropriate for twenty-first century theological reflection. Both dialectical and sacramental imaginations use this methodology. But the theological imagination of the poor continues—and deepens—its use. Specifically, in moving towards a mystical-indigenous theology of the word, the word as announcing and denouncing is seen as good news— the best news—for the poor ecclesial hearer. The word announces that

23. Gutiérrez, *Compartir la Palabra*, 353–54.

24. *Biblia Latinoamérica*, Edición 2004, 74–75.

the reign of God is at hand (Mark 1:15) and denounces what is contrary to that reign—Sobrino's "anti-Reign." In the *nepantla* of announcing and denouncing, a space is reserved for prophetic denouncing, seen by Latin American theology and the imagination of the poor as the neglected *non*. This task of denouncing and announcing is especially charged by Jesus to the Church community.

North Atlantic theology, particularly in its sacramental manifestations, has traditionally given the privileged space to the *sic*. But Boniface Willems and other Europeans, including Hans Küng, advise a strongly sympathetic ear toward the theology of Karl Barth. Latin American theologians agree with this assessment. Barth is cited in the works of José Míguez Bonino, Jon Sobrino, Víctor Codina, Julio de Santa Ana, and many others. Gustavo Gutiérrez has rightly been described as strongly influenced by Karl Rahner. But Gutiérrez' strong Dominican identity with the word gives him an affinity for Barth as well.

In 1934, Karl Barth and Emil Brunner engaged in a famous theological dispute over the question of "point of contact" between the "wholly other" God and "here and now" creation and humanity. Brunner argued that *some* point of contact should be admitted. After all, allowance needs to be made, Brunner felt, for "natural theology," albeit one irreversibly affected by the new theology of the word. Barth, expelled by the Nazis from his teaching post in Germany because of his role in the Barmen Confession, saw the necessity of a prophetic word that would unambiguously denounce Nazi totalitarianism. Thus, he felt compelled to respond with a strong *nein* to any point of contact between God and that which is human "unrighteousness"—"no" under any circumstance.

Latin American poor confront daily situations of systemic sin in which there is *no* possible "point of contact" with the God of life who cannot tolerate injustice. The *only* response of the *pueblo* as hearer of the Sacramental Word can be a resounding "no." And just what is it that the ecclesial community is called to denounce with its "no"? It is, very simply, situations of extreme poverty, exile, and injustice. The Latin American bishops summarize succinctly what is to be denounced by the ecclesial hearer of the word: "Latin America still seems to live under the tragic sign of sub-development, which not only deprives our brothers [and sisters] of the enjoyment of material goods, but takes away their very fulfillment as humans. In spite of the best efforts, hunger and misery, massive disease and infant mortality, illiteracy and marginalization, profound inequalities of income and tension between social classes, sprouts of violence and scarce participation of the people in the administration of the common good, [all of these injustices] are conjugated and multiplied."[25] Rolando Muñoz cites the above words from the Medellín conference of Latin American bishops in 1968, the second of five Latin American Episcopal gatherings over the last half century.[26] He compares the role of ecclesial denunciation in Latin America to the role exercised by the prophets of Israel during biblical times.[27] This task is impingent on the entire ecclesial community. The denunciation must extend to the oppressive structures within society *and* to the ecclesial institution when it dominates and does not serve. Denunciation is an essential part of the continuance of the mission of the risen Jesus, in the Spirit, through the Church community. It is proclaimed in faithfulness to the message of the reign of God entrusted to the community by Jesus: "He called the twelve and began to send them out two by two, and gave them authority over the unclean spirits" (Mark 6:7). In the synoptics, healings and exorcisms are signs of God's coming reign. Justice for the poor, mercy for the alienated, and the righteousness of God are its unmistakable hallmarks.

Jon Sobrino speaks of the "prophetic praxis" of Jesus. This praxis is not just a matter of announcing. That is better accomplished through what Sobrino calls the "signs" of Jesus associated with the word. Rather, prophetic praxis is associated with word *and* action. The actions of Jesus, not just his word, call the powerful to accountability. The prophetic praxis of Jesus denounces the religious and civil authorities. It denounces the religious practices of the Temple that are associated with the politics of the time. Scribes and Pharisees, Sadducees and priests, Roman authorities and the Empire itself—no one is spared. The denunciation is given because the justice of God's reign stands in dialectical opposition to the injustice of the anti-Reign. In order for the reign of God to be rightly announced, the oppression and greed of the idols of the anti-Reign must be denounced.[28]

25. Muñoz, *La Iglesia en el Pueblo*, 16. Quoted from *Medellín*, Paragraph 32.

26. The others are Rio de Janeiro in 1955, Puebla in 1979, Santo Domingo in 1992, and Aparecida in 2006. Medellín and Puebla are especially known for promulgating the teachings of the Second Vatican Council in the context of the extreme poverty of Latin America.

27. Muñoz, *La Iglesia en el Pueblo*, 17.

28. Sobrino, *Jesus the Liberator*, 160–79.

But Latin American theology and the imagination of the poor also see the word of God as an *announced* word, the great "Yes" of God (2 Cor 1:18–20) to a people passionately loved. And what is that announcement? It is the joyful proclamation of the good news to the poor ecclesial hearer of the Sacramental Word. It is the *kerygma* that announces the word of mercy. Barth succinctly states the message to be announced by the preacher: "There is mercy for you."[29] The joyful news of God's passionate love is for all people. This is the Yes—the *sic*—that God gives in a superabundance of grace and love. There is a definitive option, within that all-encompassing preference, for the poor. All people are God's preferred, but God *chooses* the poor.

"The Spirit of the Lord is upon me, because he has anointed me to bring glad tidings to the poor" (Luke 4:18). This is the starting point of the Church's announcement. Jesus, at the outset of his ministry, takes this passage from Isaiah and makes it constitutive of his announcing of the reign of God. The poor have a special place in this reign. They are the privileged recipients of "glad tidings," the good news of Jesus. Those who follow the One who announces good news to the poor find the meaning of discipleship in this passage. What the Master incarnates through announcing, the disciple attempts through preaching. This is an especially pressing task for the disciple in the United States, where injustice and oppression of the poor are no longer the exception but the norm: "[I]n our present world, a small portion of humankind, especially 'the powerful of this world', is doing fundamental injustice to the majority of humankind and oppressing it more than ever."[30] In the Incarnation, Jesus becomes human *and* poor. The Church community in the First World does not adequately stand in solidarity with the poor. Edward Schillebeeckx says that solidarity with the poor is indispensable to the *imago Dei*: "That human beings are the image of God means that humanity as such is God's representative. Human beings are God's image where and when they do justice, respect the integrity of creation, practice solidarity."[31] What is it that makes us human? What is it that makes us poor? This is the starting point—humanity and poverty as experienced by the preacher with the poor. The preacher tells the human story as Jesus lives it in the Incarnation with the *pueblo*. The "good news to the poor" is the good news of justice,

29. Barth, *Homiletics*, 109ff.

30 Schillebeeckx, *The Church*, xix.

31. Schillebeeckx, *I Am a Happy Theologian*, 54.

of God's compassion for the poor, of God's accompaniment of the exiled. The ecclesial hearer of the word *announces* this good news in following the Master. This announcing is only possible when the preacher is in solidarity with the *pueblo* and their imagination.

In Latin American indigenous culture, communication happens less on the epistemological level than on the ontological and communal level. Not only is an objective knowledge *about* something said. *The person* is actually communicated through the spoken word. In a poor indigenous context, something deeper happens. The word is now not just *any* story but *the* story of a people. It imparts community, culture, and *pueblo*. The word *is* person, it *is* people.

The people "hear the word of God and do it" (Luke 8:21). Otto Semmelroth insists that preaching is *this* presence and *this* action—the presence of the Sacramental Word, the action of the people. The Sacramental Word is uttered by the God of life. The utterance tells the story of God's justice, mercy, and consolation—God accompanies you in your suffering. But there is much more. The Sacramental Word is transverbized into the *hearer of the word*. The action of the Spirit of God now *becomes* the action of the *pueblo*. In this word that is preached, heard, and lived, the Sacramental Word, arms outstretched, invokes an *epiclesis* of the Spirit upon the ecclesial hearer. The God who thirsts for justice will not abide the oppression of the beloved. The hands of God—the Word and the Spirit—claim the poor as God's "very own and dear possession" (Exod 19:5). They "raise up the poor from the dust" and "lift the needy from the ash heap" (1 Sam 2:8). God, through the spoken Word, makes the Church of the poor into the people of God, the body of Christ, and the creation of the Spirit (Küng). The Church community, the presence of the Sacramental Word by the power of the Spirit, becomes Word for one another and for the world beloved by God.

Preaching Practicum Two

The following two homilies are examples of how one might preach what I have developed in the preceding three chapters. Where are we now? Are we the Church of the poor, the hearer of the word, and the presence of Jesus Christ Sacramental Word of the God of the poor? How our preaching unfolds every Sunday may help us to answer these crucial questions. Both of these homilies attempt to start from the Church community, the presence of the Sacramental Word. They try to get at the "expanded" meaning of poverty in the twenty-first century that I spoke of in the Introduction. They also attempt to deal with the "marks" of the Church that Christian communities have professed from the earliest times: disciples of Jesus are one, holy, catholic, and apostolic, whether Protestant, Orthodox, or Catholic.

The first homily was preached on the Third Sunday of Lent, Cycle A in the Catholic lectionary, on 24 February 2008 at Holy Spirit Church in Kent, Washington. It attempts to address a perennial ecclesial question in every Christian community—who are the "apostles"? Is our image of Church leadership based around the Twelve as the "only" apostles—the Jerusalem model? Or is apostleship something much more inclusive—the Pauline model? Paul is not chosen by the apostles in Jerusalem. He is an apostle "through Jesus Christ" (Gal 1:1). The New Testament suggests that there are other apostles: the Samaritan woman (John 4:29), Mary Magdalene (John 20:17), Junia (Rom 16:7), Prisca, (Acts 18:2, 18, 26; Rom 16:3; 1 Cor 16:19; 2 Tim 4:19) and Lydia (Acts 16:14, 40). Is there room in the institutional Church for a broader view? The text is John 4:5–42, the Samaritan woman. It was preached in both English and Spanish using David Buttrick's "moves in consciousness."

~

Introduction: Is there anyone here named "Photina"? I didn't think so! Would you believe there's a St. Photina? I've been Catholic all my life, and I didn't know about her until just five years ago. She was a saint, tradition says, who was martyred by Nero in the first century. We don't know much about her. In the Catholic Church, she's not much remembered. But in the Eastern Orthodox Church, she is well known as the Samaritan woman. They celebrate her feast day on February 26, just a few days from now. We Catholics "bury" her into one of a number of saints celebrated traditionally on March 20. That's probably because she is, well, *radical*! She's not at all the "immoral" woman we have been lead to believe. In the Orthodox Church, she's called "Equal to the Apostles."

Move One: Jesus asks for a drink. That's what start's it all. That's an important piece of this story—just a simple glass of water because Jesus is thirsty. It's a human need, so he reaches out to—a Samaritan woman. Now, we won't get into the history of the problems between the Jewish people and the Samaritans—we've talked about that before. What is interesting is that with this conversation between the Samaritan woman and Jesus begins one of the most dynamic dialogs about faith in all the gospels. And all because of a glass of water!

Move Two: At the end of the conversation—which goes almost a whole chapter—Photina leaves her water jar at the side of the well (she actually forgets about it—she's found the "living water"!) and rushes back into town to tell the people. The word used by St. John is "martyr." That's "testimony" in the gospels. John's gospel gives women disciples a primary role. In fact, it's Mary Magdalene who brings the good news of the resurrection to the men! Now, our Lenten theme is following Jesus as a Church community. I wonder if we can better reflect how it is that *women* of the Church invite us to share the good news. St. Photina is honored in the Orthodox Church for the testimony she gives to the risen Jesus, for she is traditionally thought to have been the first to proclaim the good news of Jesus in Northern Africa. It is for this commitment that she is martyred. But do you know why she just left that water jar on the edge of the well after hiking up in the hot sun all the way from town? The Spirit inspires her to be the "first witness" of the gospel in Sychar—a Samaritan town! She brings the good news of freedom in Jesus for the first time to foreigners, to outcasts, to exiles. Through Photina's apostle proclamation, the Spirit makes Church community!

Conclusion: This is a prayer used by the Orthodox Church on the feast day of St. Photina:

> You were illumined by the Holy Spirit,
>
> and refreshed by the streams of Christ the Savior.
>
> Having drunk the Water of Salvation,
>
> you gave copiously to the thirsty.
>
> O holy Great Martyr Photina,
>
> Equal-to-the-Apostles, entreat Christ our God that
> we may be saved.
>
> Amen.

The second homily was preached to an English-speaking Lutheran community. The occasion was the first Sunday of the Christian Unity Octave on 18 January 2009. Rev. Jane Prestbye, pastor of Kent Lutheran Church, and I did a "pulpit exchange" to begin the Octave. The text was John 1:35–42, from the Catholic Lectionary (Second Sunday in Ordinary Time, Cycle B). The preaching is organized in homiletic moves and inspired by Karl Barth, Paul Tillich, Douglas John Hall, Robert MacAfee Brown, and many others from our Christian tradition who have found so much meaning in the Issenheim altarpiece.

Introduction: It is with "fear and trembling" that I enter the sacred space of the Lutheran pulpit, for Lutheran fidelity to the word puts us Catholic preachers to shame! Two years before Martin Luther nailed the *Ninety-Five Theses* to the Castle Church door in Wittenberg, an obscure German artist named Matthias Grünewald was commission by the Antonite Friars in Issenheim to paint an altarpiece at the hospital where they cared for the victims of "St. Anthony's Fire." What is striking about the altarpiece is the crucifixion scene at its center. The crucified Jesus is gruesome—a dead Jesus with all the marks of St. Anthony's Fire, including the disfigured hands and the gaping mouth. John the Baptist stands in the painting, looking out at us and pointing his finger at Christ crucified. Behind John the Baptist is the caption, *Illum oportet crescere me autem minui*—"He must increase, but I must decrease" (John 3:30). It is, perhaps, Grünewald's most famous work. When he died around the year 1530, he died poor, as many artists do. By his bedside was Martin Luther's translation of Scripture and a Catholic rosary.

Move One: "Behold the Lamb of God." These are the simple words of the Baptist in today's gospel. It is by those words that we follow Jesus. John the Evangelist's discipleship is presented differently than discipleship in the other gospels. It points to the PERSON of Jesus, like the figure of the Baptist in Grünewald's painting. That is why we follow. Dietrich Bonhoeffer, the famous Lutheran pastor, theologian, and martyr, understood this well. Discipleship, "following after," or as Bonhoeffer starkly puts it, "simple obedience," cannot be separated from faith. "Behold the Lamb of God," the Baptist says to his disciples. We behold the Lamb, today, at Kent Lutheran Church and Holy Spirit Catholic Church, in the midst of twenty-first century Kent and the world, and we follow.

Move Two: Grünewald tells us about discipleship. When he dies, the rosary and Scripture are beside him as his most precious possessions. Really, the denomination, Lutheran or Catholic, does not matter. The *Church* does. The fact that my ecclesial institution will not permit me, in my official capacity as a Catholic priest, to share the Lord's Supper with you is a scandal. It is sinful. It is not an excuse to say like many, "It is a painful sign of disunity that we do not share the bread and cup." How can the Eucharist—which is a sacrament of *unity*, be a sign of *disunity*? It is, rather, a *sin* of disunity that we do not share the Eucharist. But it gives me great joy that we can share this pulpit, this preaching, which Martin Luther calls a sacrament. The sacrament unites in one Church. Discipleship is following the One who calls through his *person*, in the Spirit, *in Church community*. Grünewald says, "It is not a priority in the Christian life whether you are Catholic or Lutheran or Protestant or Orthodox. But it *is* that you *follow*. And we follow as one Church, though distinct denominations.

Conclusion: We are called to follow Jesus in community. May God bless this community, the holy Church of Kent Lutheran. Pray for your Catholic sisters and brothers, also the holy Church of Jesus, on the other side of the street. Blessed be God, through Jesus, in the Spirit, who calls us to be Church community. May God grant us the grace that one day soon we will be one in Jesus and in the Spirit. Amen.

Part Three

Where Are We Going?

Where have we been, and where are we now? These are two important questions for the theology of the word and preaching. The first deals with historical theology, the second, ecclesiology. But any substantive theology of the word poses a third question: where are we going? "Eschatology" is the name given to this endeavor, which traditionally deals with questions of the "last days" and the "end times." Unfortunately eschatology, too, like history and ecclesiology, has been placed on the North Atlantic theological block and chopped off into a small corner of the academic world, where specialists dissect it even further.

"I am the way, and the truth, and the life" (John 14:6). Theological truth *is* the Sacramental Word of the God of the poor. True Christian eschatology, much more than a "technical" word, says that the last times should not be "separated out" for special theological treatment; they have, rather, begun *now* in the Sacramental Word who is Jesus. "Christ has died, Christ is risen, Christ will come again," we proclaim in the liturgy. This is the Paschal Mystery that initiates the "last times." It casts us into the *present moment* and reminds us, "Now is the acceptable time . . . now is the day of salvation" (2 Cor 6:2). Jesus Christ Sacramental Word of the God of the poor is eschatology *hic et nunc*. In Jesus, the "last times" have begun here and now, lived in the present moment—not *kronos*, by which we measure out chronological seconds, minutes, hours, weeks, months, years, centuries, and eons, but *kairos*, in which the only measure is the Sacramental Word uttered in the *pueblo*. *Kairos* is the "mission" of the Holy Trinity *lived* by the disciple community.

Kairos is gift, the mission that belongs to the Church community, as Karl Barth reminds us, the time between the Ascension and the Parousia. It is the time of the Church, the *kairos* of Trinitarian mission, the time of the discipleship of Christian praxis—the *last* times that are really the *first* days of the new creation in Word and Spirit. The question "where are we going," then, is of utmost urgency to the theology of the word and the preacher.

7

A Latin American Theology of the Sacramental Word for the Twenty-First Century

I have referred to the classic liberation theologians of the 1970s and 1980s as they interpret the ecclesial hearer through the imagination of the poor. I have also spoken often of more recent Latin American theologies. In this chapter, however, I will focus exclusively on newer, "postmodern" voices for a Latin American twenty-first century theology of the Sacramental Word of the God of the poor. One thing immediately noted about these "new voices" is their integral connection with the pastoral life of the Church community. Classic liberation theology is also known for this. But these newer voices are connected in such a way that their primary concern is not the theological academy as such but discipleship as lived by the Church of the poor in concrete praxis. Many are not professors of theology in academic institutions, but pastors and pastoral agents involved in ministry. Perhaps we are on the verge of a new patristic and matristic era in which, once again, the great theologians like John Chrysostom, Gregory of Nazianzus, Macrina, Augustine, and Basil are also the great pastors of the Church community (Peter Chirico).

Classic liberation theologians who have been open to the newer Latin American theologies have acknowledged that theology as done in Latin America thirty to forty years ago no longer adequately addresses the context of the "new poor" of the twenty-first century. An example is the critique, written on the verge of the new millennium, by Brazilian theologian José Comblin.[1] He maintains that liberation theology must open

1. Comblin, *Called for Freedom.*

111

itself to the new paradigms of the twenty-first century if it is to remain meaningful to the contemporary poor. Similar critiques are proposed by Víctor Codina and Pablo Richard, among others (see Introduction). But the strongest criticism comes from Latin American theologies which, I believe, are the "liberation theologies" that move us globally into the twenty-first century. Of these, indigenous theology and ecofeminism are perhaps among the most vocal. I will also look at two additional voices that should be heard: The *comunidades eclesiales de base*, the base ecclesial communities; and contemporary Protestant theology in Latin America.

Ecofeminist theology has been an important voice for twenty-first century Latin American theology of the Sacramental Word. Its primary representative has been Ivone Gebara, a Brazilian theologian and Catholic religious woman who has done extensive pastoral work with communities of poor women in northeastern Brazil and has taught theology for many years in Recife. She is critical of the classic liberation theology of the 1970s and 80s and cites its innate inability to move towards the truly unified epistemology so necessary to twenty-first century theology. She feels that classic, male dominated liberation theology, in attempting to move from dualism, actually reaffirms what she calls the "dualistic epistemological perspective."[2]

Gebara reflects on the inadequacies of the traditional Platonic and Aristotelian categories utilized in past theological reflection. These affected theology as it was done during the Enlightenment and Modern eras. Contemporary theology—including classic liberation theology— has fared no better and has been unable to break its connection to the Western tradition.[3] She talks poignantly about the false hopes implanted in many Latin American pastoral agents and the *pueblo* by the theology of the 1970s and 1980s. It was a time of "optimism" in which the poor were supposed to organize and throw off their oppression through education, betterment of social conditions, and structural change. However, the situation of the poor was not improved significantly; in fact, it became worse with the advent of neo-liberal global economics. She invites Latin American theology to take up anew the challenges of the poor in the twenty-first century.

2. Gebara, *Longing for Running Water*, 46–47.

3. Ibid., 44–48.

Gebara calls Latin American theological discourse beyond the categories of traditional androcentric theological anthropology and epistemology in two ways. First, she invites her readers to see human reality as radically centered in the deeper context of all created reality. While humanity is central in the providential plan of God, the human being does not occupy an absolute place. Its privileged centrality can only be seen in the light of *all* creation. Everything is gift of a good and a gracious God. Oppression of the poor woman or man always occurs in the wider context of the abuse of the earth. Creation in its ecological context—what, for instance, is done by the oppressor to the rain forest in the name of capitalism—occupies a central focus in the theology of Gebara. The Trinitarian God is manifested in a divine word about creation, humanity, and the cosmos.[4] The human being—particularly the poor person—is caught up in this abuse of creation and the cosmos by the dominant. This is a theology that respects indigenous culture at its roots in the reverence for *pacha mama*, mother earth. It also integrates the best of the apostolic tradition as taught by the Fathers and Mothers of the early Church—particularly the theology of *apokatastasis*, the restoration and salvation (healing) of *all* creation and *all* humanity in Christ. Gebara alerts the Church community to the danger of idolatry, for the god most often worshipped in male-dominated Western society is *not* the God of revelation. Rather it is, she says, an idol created in *man's* (male) image *by man*.

Gebara has been sharply criticized by a number of her male colleagues in the academy. I read one who even accused her of "heresy" for the sentence: "We are one another's salvation."[5] But the statement, made in connection to the Eucharist, is not to be taken out of context. We are, Gebara says, body and blood of Christ for one another—what Augustine said centuries ago. When we receive the Eucharist, we "become what we receive." In fact, Gebara stands in the best of the Christian tradition, reminding us of Cyprian of Carthage and *extra ecclesiam nulla salus* (no salvation outside of the Church)—something insisted on by Dietrich Bonhoeffer as well, who warned the Confessing Church in Germany of the dangers of Nazism through his restatement of Cyprian's claim,[6] and Jon Sobrino, who recently responded to accusations of unorthodoxy with a paraphrase of Cyprian: *extra pauperes nulla salus* (no salvation outside

4. Gebara, *El Rostro Nuevo de Dios*, 49.
5. Gebara, *Longing for Running Water*, ix.
6. Bonhoeffer, "On the Question of Boundaries," 158–67.

of the poor). North American and European critiques of Gebara do not understand the deeply communal nature of Latin American theology—a contemplation, with the Eastern tradition, of salvation (*salus* is "health") in its deepest sense: *koinonia* (community) and *theosis* (divinization) in Jesus Christ and in the Holy Spirit. Gebara's theology, like Barth in the *Epistle to the Romans*, is a wake-up call to the dangers of idolatry in the halls of the academies and the cathedrals of our world, a criticism of so-cietal religion, and a call to communal faith. Her theology is a warning against "neo-Arianism." Centuries ago, Arius said Jesus was "created," a "creature" (that is why "begotten not made" became such an important part of the profession of the faith). Neo-Arianism is subtler. Jesus no lon-ger is called a "creature." But male-dominated Western neo-liberal global-ism, in which the religion of the privileged participates, "creates" Jesus in the image of a powerful *man* from the dominant culture (at least Arius said Jesus was *God's* creature!). Perhaps it is for this reason Gebara is more critical than many of some movements found in the contemporary Church, such as "a variety of Pentecostal groups" (charismatic renewal?) or recent devotional practices fostered by traditional Christian sectors and supported by the powerful. These, she warns, can anesthetize the poor and shield them from their reality, substituting illusory religious feelings for faith in the God of the poor.[7] Her critique of *religion* as opposed to *faith* is the same as that made many years ago by Dietrich Bonhoeffer and Karl Barth, but now in a Latin American ecofeminist key.

Second, Gebara challenges theologians to see how theological an-thropological reflection has become androcentric—a reflection on *man's* place in God's plan. Women, over 50 percent of the human race, are relegated to secondary status or even total alienation. Gebara says Latin American theology can learn much from women in the North Atlantic, specifically Rosemary Radford Ruether, Elizabeth Johnson, Sally McFague, and others. In turn, she invites her sisters in the North to learn from the experience of poor women in the South. If liberation theology wants to reflect on the praxis of the poor in the light of God's word, the neglected voices of poor women—and a creation that cries out to the heavens for justice—must be heard.

The androcentric roots of Western theology come from what Gebara calls a dualistic epistemology—her primary critique of all theol-ogy. Epistemology, or the study of how we know, is a word we should

7. Gebara, *Longing for Running Water*, 164.

not be afraid of. What is needed, she says, is not avoidance of the word, but rather a fresh approach to knowledge and the theological task—an approach that does not divide human knowledge, and theology, into the dualisms of a former age, but takes a unified, holistic stance to the mystery that is God and the cosmos.[8]

Another new voice for a twenty-first century theology of the Sacramental Word is indigenous theology, which comes primarily from Latin America, although there are outstanding examples in North America, Asia, Africa, and Australia.[9] I will mention several, some of whom I have already referred to, that have made a significant contribution to an indigenous theology of liberation in a Mexican context.

Javier Garibay is a Mexican systematic theologian presently involved in pastoral work in the diocese of Tabasco in southern Mexico. I have already referred to his use of *nepantla* regarding the Trinity, Christology, and the Incarnation. He has vast experience in both the academy (former professor of systematic theology at the *Centro de Reflexión Teológica* in Mexico City and the former editor of *Christus*, a Mexican theological journal) and as a pastor in the indigenous context (he presently works in a parish). His published doctoral thesis is a study of colonial Franciscan friar Gerónimo de Mendieta and *nepantla* applied to systematic theology. *Nepantla* has particular significance during the period of the sixteenth-century European incursion into Latin America, a situation in which the indigenous cultures found themselves "in the midst of" two distinct realities.

Anthropology has traditionally referred to *nepantla* as "dualism" expressed, for instance, through the *disfrasismo*—a Spanish word referring to the indigenous expression of two opposites.[10] This furthers the erroneous view, still adhered to in many circles, that Mexican indigenous reality is radically "dualistic." Garibay proposes an entirely different interpretation. Rather than dualism, indigenous reality is expressive of *nepantla*, an *integral unity* of two opposites both absolutely necessary

8. Ibid., 19–65.

9. See, for example, Wilson, *A Native American Liberation Theology*. Much work has also been done in Asian contexts by Samuel Rayan, SJ (India), Tissa Balasuriya, OMI (Sri Lanka), Kosuke Koyama (Japan), and Bishop Chito Tagle (Philippines), among many others.

10. Rodríguez, *Our Lady of Guadalupe*, 37.

but in complimentary relationship and communion. An example is the *Náhuatl* word for God—Ometéotl. This word sees God as both male and female in perfect unity—what Manuel Arias Montes calls *Dios Padre-Madre de la vida* (God Father-Mother of life).[11] If God is perceived only as Father, God cannot be "seen" rightly because an integral aspect of the divine being is neglected. But *nepantla*, whether in the Incarnation of Jesus or in life and culture in general, is a root expression of the mystical-indigenous imagination of the poor.[12] It is a basic stance toward God, Jesus, Spirit, human life, and the entire cosmos. Given the fact that dualism, which has plagued the Christian West throughout the centuries in various forms of Gnosticism, is so prevalent in North Atlantic theology, *nepantla* and indigenous theology can offer an alternative way of doing Christian theology. The Sacramental Word was never meant to be uttered in the dissonant tones of Gnostic dualisms that wrench body from soul and nature from grace.

Manuel Arias Montes offers another new voice from the perspective of Mexican indigenous theology. A theologian from Oaxaca, Mexico, he presently serves as pastor of the parish community of *Nuestra Señora de Juquila* in Oaxaca. After a number of years as a priest in indigenous communities, he began to develop a theology that addressed Mexican indigenous reality from his pastoral experience and his cultural heritage as *Mixteca Alta*. He later did his doctoral work at Tübingen in Germany with a dissertation on catechesis and the indigenous cultures in Mexico.

Like Ivone Gebara, Arias Montes has received criticism from his theological colleagues, including some classic liberation theologians. While it has done important analysis of the economic systems that oppress the Latin American poor, liberation theology has sometimes bypassed indigenous culture as an important factor in defining twenty-first century poverty. Arias Montes says that classic liberation theology has treated indigenous theology as second class, looking upon it as its "child" and correcting it for "dividing the poor." Rather, he says, indigenous theology is "sister and brother" to liberation theology and in dialog with it.[13]

In his book *Y la Palabra de Dios Se Hizo Indio*, Arias Montes develops an indigenous approach to catechetics that expresses the essence

11. Arias Montes, *Y la Palabra de Dios*, 133–38.

12. My discussion of Garibay is based on *Nepantla* and on a conversation with him on 15 June 2005.

13. Conference at Pacific Lutheran University, Tacoma, WA, 24 April 2008.

of the imagination of the poor. Unlike Garibay, he does not directly use the word *nepantla*. But his theology is deeply concerned with nepantlic imagination, both in his writing and in his pastoral practice. When he celebrates the Eucharistic liturgy, he prays to God as *Padre-Madre* (Father-Mother). His indigenous roots give him a deep sense of the presence of God that permeates all creation. Arias Montes believes that the catechetical task within poor indigenous communities can only be fulfilled by taking on the indigenous imagination and centering on the poor Jesus, the Sacramental Word inviting us to solidarity with the indigenous poor.

Arias Montes maintains that the three sources for theological reflection in an indigenous framework are Scripture, the magisterial documents, and the life and culture of the indigenous ecclesial communities.[14] Indigenous theology, he says, sees theological reflection and later systematization as a "second movement." This reflection can only happen within a living and indigenous *pueblo* and will account for all of the joys and challenges of life. He invites classic liberation theology to a more sensitive reflection on indigenous reality and a deeper immersion into indigenous culture and the "popular religiosity" (*religiosidad popular*) of the *pueblo*.[15] The primary catechetical text, he insists, is the word of God. This is interpreted from a thoroughly indigenous perspective. It is a challenge to maintain this priority in a culture where many are unable to read and write. But within this context, the pastoral agent is called to accompany the *pueblo* in making the word of God in Scripture a living part of their reality through reflection on indigenous culture[16]—including, and especially, the history of the *pueblo* and the presence of God in the *semillas del Verbo* (the seeds of the Word) manifested in the pre-Christian milieu before the Spanish incursion.

Alvaro Quiroz Magaña, SJ, is another systematic theologian who has reflected on indigenous reality and the poor. Though a great deal of his ministry has been in the academy, where he taught philosophy for many years to Jesuit scholastics and theology at the *Centro de Reflexión Teológica* in Mexico City, he recently finished a number of years of pastoral work with indigenous communities in Tabasco. He is presently engaged in pastoral ministry visiting ecclesial communities in Mexican urban settings. An example of his work in English is found in the anthology of

14. Arias Montes, *Y la Palabra de Dios*, 19–25.

15. Ibid., 222.

16. Ibid., 21.

liberation theology (*Mysterium Liberationis*) edited by Jon Sobrino and Ignacio Ellacuría. Quiroz Magaña did his doctoral work in ecclesiology under the direction of José Ignacio González Faus in Barcelona, Spain.

The theology of the word is critical to the thinking of Quiroz Magaña. He relates the word particularly to its importance for the ecclesial community. The community of those who follow Jesus, the community of the poor at the grassroots ecclesial level, is called to a special solidarity with the *pueblo*. The Church of the poor proclaims the reign of God through the word:

> When we speak of a church of the poor . . . we mean to testify to the rebirth of the people of God that is taking place on the outskirts of our cities, in rural areas, in native regions, in the places of socioeconomic marginalization and helplessness. The expression *church of the poor* connotes a church . . . in which the gospel is announced in solidarity with the exploited classes.[17]

He further clarifies the relation of indigenous ecclesial communities to the word of God. God's holy word is "actualized" through the praxis of the ecclesial community and can only be concretized through approaching Scripture as the *living* word of God—a "Sacramental Word"—that speaks to the reality of the poor and the indigenous.

> A concrete theology capable of giving answers to life and human necessities is not possible if it does not arise from the practice of love, justice, and mercy. In the same way, a theologically coherent and actualized word is not possible if it is not based and inspired by a coherent biblical deepening. The theological turning toward the bible as the living word of God, orientated from the Magisterium and guided by the mission of the Church, has been a primary source in the theology of liberation in the accompaniment of the poor and in the illumination of this accompaniment.[18]

The word of God in Scripture is crucial, says Quiroz Magaña, to the way in which the indigenous *pueblo* reflects on the reality in which they live.

Gonzalo Ituarte, OP, is a concrete example of how indigenous Mexican theology is lived out in a pastoral context. He has been involved, since his ordination in 1978, in pastoral work with indigenous communities in

17. Sobrino and Ellacuría, eds., *Mysterium Liberationis*, 204.
18. E-mail from Quiroz Magaña to the author, 11 July 2005.

Chiapas, where he was episcopal vicar to Don Samuel Ruíz, the retired bishop of San Cristóbal de Las Casas. He is presently provincial to the Mexican Dominicans (*Provincia de Santiago*). Ituarte believes that the imagination of the poor deeply affects how the word of God is interpreted in the context of poor indigenous reality. He makes special mention of the image of Our Lady of Guadalupe as an "indigenous codex" that expresses God's love and option for the poor in much the same way as Scripture. God "writes" justice for the poor in the word and in the image of the *Guadalupana*. Preaching occupies a special place for Ituarte as a Dominican, but preaching, he says, should not be seen in the traditional sense of "imparting" knowledge of Scripture to the poor. Rather, it is the indigenous poor themselves who are the preachers of God's word. Liturgical preaching, according to Ituarte, should most often be a conversation of the *pueblo* around the word led by the preacher. Even when traditional preaching is done, it is always a dialog with the *pueblo*, a homiletic conversation—the root meaning of "homily"—that accounts for the voice of the indigenous poor.[19]

Yet another new voice of the Sacramental Word for the twenty-first century is found in the theology of Brazilian ecclesiologist José Marins and his colleagues. Although the *comunidades eclesiales de base* and the Marins team have been part of the Latin American ecclesial landscape for years, their creative approach to pastoral life constantly keeps pace with the newer contexts of the poor. The base communities are still very active in Brazil, Argentina, Mexico, and other countries in Latin America. They are also attractive to Mexican undocumented immigrant communities in the United States as a supplement to the more formal and structured parishes commonly found in the First World. The base communities provide people with a more personalized experience of Church in which each person is valued and the experience of poverty and injustice is shared. Human rights and dignity for the undocumented poor in a dominant society such as the United States is a theme that is visited and revisited many times by Mexican immigrant base ecclesial communities. One of the base communities in the parish that I pastor, after sharing the scriptural word, has the person in charge of the *noticiero* (the news) go through the sig-

19. I formally interviewed Ituarte at the Dominican priory of Santa Rosa de Lima in Mexico City, Monday, 27 June 2005.

nificant local, national, and international events of the week. They discuss the situation of the undocumented Mexican workers in the country—particularly as it affects people in the Puget Sound area. In Latin America, the *comunidades eclesiales de base* (often abbreviated CEBs) reflect upon the common and everyday struggles of the poor in urban or rural settings in the light of the word. The communities "do" theology—a critical reflection on praxis in the light of the word (many pastoral agents working with the base communities have a strong theological background).

José Marins and his colleague, Teolide María Trevisan, ICM, are among the best known animators of the base communities in Latin America, with well over thirty years presenting workshops on the CEBs. "Marins," as José Marins is affectionately known by his friends, is a "classic" liberation theologian in the best sense. As a young priest and theologian, he was present at the sessions of the Second Vatican Council as an advisor to the Brazilian bishops. He was also a process coordinator for the Latin American bishops at the conferences of Medellín (1968) and Puebla (1979) and pastor to a large parish in his diocese. He has taught theology and ecclesiology at a number of theological schools and seminaries and developed an extensive text for the teaching of the patristics and matristics with contemporary Latin American "Fathers"—deceased bishops and martyrs who were instrumental at Vatican II, Medellín, and Puebla. Marins still actively travels throughout the world and animates the base communities through workshops. With Latin American theologians such as Leonardo Boff and José Comblin, Marins is among those who are most open, among classic Latin American theologians, to the new voices of theology in the twenty-first century.

From early involvement with the *Better World Movement* in Brazil, Marins began to work with smaller faith communities. He, and other pastors of his generation, found that traditional parish structures and sacramental practices were inadequate in dealing with the issues facing the contemporary poor and the working class. Making use of the methodology *ver*, *juzgar*, and *actuar*, he and his team applied the principles of liberation theology to pastoral practice in Brazil and encouraged establishment, within existing parish structures, of the *comunidades eclesiales de base*. Around the same time (late sixties and early seventies), pastoral agents in Panama begin working along similar lines. Eventually, the "movement" (Marins strongly discourages the use of the word when referring to the CEBs: "The base communities are not associations or clubs within the church; they *are* the church," he says[20]) spread to other parts of Latin America and the world—and to poor Hispanic-Latino communities in the United States. Marins recently finished several months of workshops on base communities in India and Korea. He has also given conferences in the Philippines. When one hears of the "small faith communities" or "faith-sharing groups" in English-speaking congregations in the United States or in Europe, they likely have their roots in the Marins ecclesiology and base ecclesial communities.

The Marins team relies heavily on Scripture in their workshops with the *pueblo*.[21] The theology of the word is integrally connected with a fundamental ecclesiology—that is, Scripture can only be seen in the light of its role as *the* book of the Church: "The word of God is neither a philosophy (in reference to the Greeks) nor a technical-religious outline (in reference to administrative and pastoral activism). It is in the experience of life itself that it exists and manifests all of its fruitfulness. We would stress that this is significant, especially in community life, because the project is the New People of God. Consequently the Base Ecclesial Communities are a privileged space of that ecclesial praxis."[22] The Bible is central to the life of the *comunidades eclesiales de base*. It is an integral "literacy tool" for the faith of the people:

> The most important thing, in my experience, has been to see the simple people of the Base Ecclesial Communities and also other ecclesial groups, do theological reflection and discover the continued presence of God in their individual lives, in their human history, and in their ecclesial journey. This has been possible because the Word became the "mark" of the literacy of their faith; even more, when [the poor] began to discover the presence of God in the Word that is also spoken in everyday experience and historical situations. The Word makes it possible that theological reflection is not reduced to a mere rational experience of the faith, but the Word transforms itself into a faith expression.[23]

The methodology is that of classic liberation theology—the experience of the people is looked at in the light of the word of God. The

20. Cleary, "A New Social Structure," quoting Marins.

21. See Marins, *De Todas las Razas*, 86–87, for the centrality of Scripture to the CEBs.

22. E-mail to the author from Marins, 16 September 2005.

23. E-mail to the author from Teolide María Trevisan, 19 September 2005.

Marins team bases its reflections primarily on the New Testament communities in the Acts of the Apostles and the Pauline corpus. These form the text for their workshops and are supplemented with materials they have developed over many years. After talking about the experiences of the early Christian communities—Jerusalem, Rome, Corinth, Caesarea, Antioch—they will "play act" specific characters from Scripture. These characters, in turn, will verbally reflect on the cultural, economic, and political realities that formed part of the milieu of the New Testament communities. This theology is then pastorally tailored for a contemporary hermeneutic—"reader context" methodology at its best. Later during the week, the participants are "assigned" to one of the early Christian communities. They learn all they can about that particular community and are then sent as "missioners" to another community, where they share the salient characteristics of their study.

The proposal of the Marins team is a return to an ecclesial context in which all members of the Christian communities had equal voice and an important ministerial task (Víctor Codina calls this the primary work of the pastoral agent—to accompany each member of the Christian community in discovering their charism). The base communities share two characteristics with the New Testament communities: they are the Church at its grassroots as lived by the poor; and they are not directed towards the Church in its *inner life*, but towards the reign of God.[24] The Church as institution in its hierarchical structure—or even in the reality of the local parish, which can be large and impersonal—is simply not adequate to meet the many needs of the indigenous poor in the twenty-first century. That is a primary reason that fundamentalist sects are making so many inroads in Latin America and with Latino(a)s in the United States. When institutional Church reality is made palatable and personal through the experience of the small *comunidades de base* (usually no more than fifteen or twenty members), Jesus the Sacramental Word in his Spirit is made present to the indigenous poor in a concrete way. These base communities, in turn, reflect on present day-challenges, much as early Christian communities reflected on their reality. Injustice, racism, sexism, economic inequality, and lack of human dignity can be taken up and reflected on at the local level.

At the same time, the identity and mission of the *comunidades eclesiales de base* must not be boiled down to one definition of, or one

24. Marins and Trevisan, ¿*Valió la Pena?*, 15.

way of viewing, the Church community. Marins rightly points out that many well-meaning descriptions of the CEBs are oversimplified. There is much more to the base community than just a weekly meeting of fifteen to twenty people. Rather, he says, the communities are a unification of two "processes" that are "complementary." There is the "heart" of the community that meets regularly, the committed ecclesial core of the base community. And then, there is the wider community of the baptized who consider themselves members of the Church institution and "little by little gain a sense of belonging" to the more deeply committed community.[25]

The preferred methodology of the base communities is *ver, juzgar, actuar, evaluar,* and *celebrar*. The *ver* is the reality upon which the group reflects in its gathering; the *juzgar* is the word of God used for reflection; the *actuar* is the action the community chooses to allow God's Spirit to work through them as the body of Christ on the local level; the *evaluar* is the appraisal of what has taken place in the light of gospel justice for the poor; and the *celebrar* is a joyous liturgical gathering or a *fiesta*.

I will now turn to another voice of twenty-first century Latin American theology of the sacramental Word—Protestant theological thought in Latin America. This has been too often ignored by dominant classic liberation theology done in the strictly "Catholic mode." But it is an important voice for Latin American theology in the twenty-first century. International theology is already well-acquainted with the work of José Míguez Bonino, Julio de Santa Ana, Elsa Tamez, and Rubem Alves—among many others. The Brazilian section of the International Bonhoeffer Society is, perhaps, one of the most creative new sources for Latin American Protestant theology from the stance of the poor. Luís Eduardo Cumaru, a pastor and professor of theology in Rio de Janeiro and president of the Portuguese-speaking section of the International Bonhoeffer Society, and Carlos Filho Caldas, professor of systematic theology at MacKenzie School of Theology in São Paulo, are fine examples, among many others, of Latin American Protestant theologians who have creatively applied the theology of Dietrich Bonhoeffer to the situation of the poor in Brazil.

Protestant theology in Latin America is marked by a wide-reaching ecumenism. It is also deeply rooted in the imagination of the poor. There are, of course, the classic names like José Míguez Bonino, the Argentinean

25. E-mail from Marins to the author, November 2005.

Methodist who has been so instrumental in the development of liberation theology. But the creative work of the women and men of the Brazilian section of the International Bonhoeffer Society, for instance, is full of dynamism with its youthful theologians and Church people. Cumaru recently served on a committee that organized a theological conference in Rio de Janeiro bringing together Leonardo Boff, Jürgen Moltmann, and Rubem Alves as the keynote speakers. That marks the creativity that gives Latin American Protestant theology two special characteristics making it a voice for twenty-first century theology of the Sacramental Word: 1) It takes sin and death realistically, but 2) intertwines this traditional Protestant insight into a "love motif" full of hope.

Recently, I had a conversation with a North Atlantic Catholic professor of theology. The topic was the Pauline theology of grace. I mentioned that what the Catholic Church in North America needed right now was a good infusion of the Lutheran theology of grace! The professor, disagreeing, responded, "I always thought we Catholics had a pretty good take on grace." Actually, in my opinion, neither Catholics nor Protestants in the North Atlantic have a "pretty good take on grace." North Atlantic Catholics are too glued to the neo-scholastic notion of "grace building on nature." It is a cookbook grace, a theology of recipes—"take nature, add a pinch of grace, and shake well." Rather, Thomas Aquinas and, more recently, Karl Rahner with his theology of "uncreated grace," are much more concerned with the grace that *transforms* nature. Both Catholic and Protestant in the North Atlantic can learn from Eastern Orthodox theology, which talks about the "uncreated divine energy" that permeates reality and, through Jesus and in the Spirit, transforms created nature so that there is no longer "sacred and profane" but only that which is real—*permeated* by the Spirit: "The ascension of the Lord, his going up to the Father, is the Trinitarian *epiclesis* of the Son who asks the Father to send down the Holy Spirit. This is the unleashing of Pentecost . . . over both cosmic and human nature."[26] North Atlantic Protestants (particularly "evangelicals") see grace, by and large, exclusively as a *personal* conversion, a "turning away" from *individual* sin. North Atlantic Catholics see grace similarly—look at the way the sacrament of reconciliation is treated, for instance, in many parish religious education programs; or how many "traditionalist" North Atlantic Catholics are so overly attached to rules and rubrics, the newest form of Pelagianism in the Catholic community in the United States. Western

26. Evdokimov, *In the World*, 93–94.

Catholics and Protestants alike lack a "good take" on grace, precisely because there is not a "good take" on sin and death.

Protestant Latin American theology is not a theology of "cheap grace" (nor is Latin American Catholic theology—José Marins calls Bonhoeffer's costly grace *la gracia que sangra*, "the grace that bleeds"). It takes evil, sin, and death seriously, seeing them through the eyes of what Julio de Santa Ana calls "hopeful realism."[27] This hopeful realism sees conversion—biblical *metanoia*—as a necessary ingredient to the gospel. But unlike many strains of North Atlantic Protestant fundamentalism, conversion is not just a cheap renunciation of individual "sin" and "acceptance of Jesus Christ as my *personal* Lord and Savior." Jesus can only be savior to a *community*. The individual is always saved *within the community*—the truest meaning of *extra ecclesiam nulla salus*. Conversion is not simply a *profession* of faith; it is a *lived* and costly faith that turns toward the "other" in praxis.[28] It is solidarity with the other, who is the concrete and real poor woman, man, or child.[29] Jesus crucified and risen is manifested in the *other*. The Spirit impels us, as the baptized Jesus is impelled—"driven" and "pushed"—into the wilderness (Mark 1:12), into the "desert" of the other. Contemporary ecumenism, Santa Ana maintains, has little to do with organized churches "getting together." It is that, but much more. Ecumenism is the Church moving toward the other, the poor, the *oikoumene*.[30] The option for the poor is nothing new, for it has been taken by many in the Christian tradition who had a deep sense of the *oikoumene*—Paul, Augustine, John Chrysostom, Thomas Aquinas, Martin Luther, John Calvin, Dietrich Bonhoeffer, and many others.[31] Santa Ana emphasizes the special challenge of the Church in all ages— the approval of Christianity as the "state religion" under Constantine and Theodosius. St. Basil the Great, and his option for the poor of Caesarea, is an outstanding example of a response to that challenge.[32] Contemporary poverty in Latin America, and other parts of the world, is an expression of evil, sin, and death. The Christian faithful are called to "hopeful realism"—hopeful, because through the death and resurrection of Jesus

27. De Santa Ana, *Beyond Idealism*, 211.

28. Ibid., 214.

29. Ibid., 219–20.

30. Ibid., 216–17.

31. Ibid., 55–87.

32. De Santa Ana, *Good News to the Poor*, 67.

and in the Spirit, sin and death has been once and for all destroyed; realism, because evil and death are still present in the world of structural idolatry, oppression, and injustice.

Latin American Protestant theology calls the Church to praxis of the "love motif," in the words of José Míguez Bonino.[33] This love motif is especially expressed through the *comunidades eclesiales de base*, which he calls a "concrete expression" of the praxis of love. There is a special word for Christian love in action—solidarity.[34] But it is a unique solidarity. Míguez Bonino explains that the word was used in traditional North Atlantic Catholic moral theology in an ontological sense. Latin American theology uses the word much more specifically. Solidarity is *love in praxis* that is strongly Christological and eschatological.[35] It is Christ-centered because the "love motif" *par excellence* is the very essence of God, by the power of the Spirit, incarnate in the person of Jesus. Allan Figueroa Deck, SJ, a North American Hispanic-Latino theologian, explains how we have traditionally fostered the message that the "mission" belongs to the Church. But in fact it belongs to the Holy Trinity—the mission of the Triune God, through Jesus and in the Spirit, is shared with the Church, which in turn "shares" the Trinitarian mission through its proclamation and its life. We have said that "the Church has a mission." Really, Figueroa Deck says, "The mission has a Church."[36] It is that very mission that makes solidarity Christological. The mission also makes solidarity *eschatological* because it is concerned with the "last times" as they are manifested *in community*. Traditional North Atlantic eschatology is overly centered in the individual. Latin American eschatology is directed toward the mission of the Trinity lived in the Church community in a global solidarity. *All* things, *all* creation, are reconciled to God by Jesus in the Spirit. Míguez Bonino says that perhaps the *apokatastatis* of the Fathers and Mothers, the restoration of everything in Christ, is the most appropriate expression of the way Christology and eschatology are lived in Latin America.[37] The love motif is a universal restoration, a *healing*, of all creation in Jesus.

33. Míguez Bonino, "Love and Social Transformation," 90.

34. Ibid., 96.

35. Ibid., 98.

36. Conference for "Preaching Paul," Bellevue, Washington, 4 February 2009.

37. Míguez Bonino, "Love and Social Transformation," 104.

Julio de Santa Ana calls attention to two phrases used often by Dom Hélder Câmara (1909–1999), the Catholic archbishop of Recife in Brazil so committed to the poor: "hidden discipleship," which Santa Ana likens to Dietrich Bonhoeffer's use of the *disciplina arcani* of the early Church, and "Abrahamic minorities," which are the *comunidades eclesiales de base*.[38] There is little doubt, in Santa Ana's observations, that Latin American theology is thoroughly affected by Dietrich Bonhoeffer—an ecclesiology of "hearing the Sacramental Word" that is inseparable from Christology, the unpredictable action of the Spirit, and the praxis of discipleship.

Dorothee Sölle, on the back book jacket for the collected works of Dietrich Bonhoeffer in English (Fortress Press), says that Bonhoeffer "is the one German theologian who will lead us into the third millennium." The only thing I would change regarding Sölle's insightful comment would be to take out the adjective "German." I believe that Dietrich Bonhoeffer is probably *the* theologian who will lead us into the third millennium. For this final section of the chapter, I will use Bonhoeffer's ecclesiology as a point of departure for some personal reflections.

In *Discipleship* (formerly *The Cost of Discipleship*), written over seventy years ago, Bonhoeffer presents us with a vision of Church community for the twenty-first century—now no longer a national or sociological institution of doctrines and beliefs, but a Church *community* that is a living Person and praxis. Ecclesial faith is inseparable from "obedience"— perhaps better rendered "praxis" for the twenty-first century. It revolves around three key notions in Bonhoeffer's ecclesiology: *conformitas, Stellvertretung*, and *disciplina arcani. Conformitas* is the crucified and risen Jesus "conforming" himself to the Church community, what Bonhoeffer calls the real presence of Christ in the community—"Christ existing as Church community." *Stellvertretung* is "vicarious representative action," as translated by the editors of the new English translation of Bonhoeffer's complete works. Jesus "represents" God in the world; his body, the Church community, represents Jesus. But where I believe that Latin American theology is especially attentive to a contextual reading of Bonhoeffer is in Julio de Santa Ana's observation about Dom Helder's "hidden discipleship" in the "Abrahamic minorities"—the *disciplina arcani*, the "hidden discipline." *Disciplina arcani* was concretely expressed in the early Church through the dismissal of catechumens from the Eucharistic celebration after the Liturgy of the Word and the preaching and *before* the profession

38. De Santa Ana, "Priest and Prophet," 9–21.

of faith and the celebration of the mysteries around the table. Those who were not yet baptized followers of Jesus could not share in the deeper mysteries of the faith. Matthew 7:6 was used as a rationale: "Do not give what is holy to dogs; and do not throw your pearls before swine, or they will trample them under foot and turn and maul you." After the time of Constantine and Theodosius, when the Church became the official "re-ligion" of the Roman Empire, these mysteries of the faith needed further protection from the profanation of the civil religion of the empire.

Catholics have a traditional prayer popularly ascribed to St. Ignatius of Loyola—the *Anima Christi*. It is a direct appeal to Christ for mercy: "Oh good Jesus, hear me. *Within your wounds, hide me.*" St. Catherine of Siena, in her *Dialog* predating Ignatius by almost two centuries, de-scribes a constant "battle" with the devil in prayer. I will take the liberty of paraphrasing Catherine. She says that the devil constantly tormented her—"You think, Catherine, you are so good. You're nothing but a hope-less sinner." She finally tired of the barrage and shouted, "You *are* stupid, aren't you? Of course I'm a sinner! But I am a sinner who *hides* in the wounds of Jesus."

I wonder if Catherine and Ignatius had the *disciplina arcani* in mind. We pray to the crucified and risen One, "Hide us in your wounds." We become hidden in the wounds of Jesus, like Luther's *Deus absconditus*, an *ecclesia abscondita*. The best place to be a "hidden" Church, in the world so loved by God (John 3:16), are the wounds of the risen Christ. Thomas the Apostle says to the disciples, "Unless I see the mark of the nails in his hands, and put my finger in the mark of the nails and my hand in his side, I will not believe" (John 20:25). When the risen Jesus appears again, he tells Thomas, "Put your finger here and see my hands. Reach out your hand and put it in my side. Do not doubt but believe" (John 20:27). What Jesus is *really* saying to Thomas, and the entire disciple community, is "Place yourself—your *entire self*—in my wounded hands, feet, and side. Let me become *you*. Church, be what you are—my risen body in the world." But it is, as Bonhoeffer says from prison, a hidden presence, a hidden discipleship, a hidden discipline—the body of Christ, conformed to the community, living the *disciplina arcani*. The wounds of the risen Jesus are the place of hiddenness. The gospels present these transformed wounds as an important—and mysterious—aspect of the resurrection. It is there that we "hide" as a Church community—*ecclesia abscondita*—so hidden that we, the *ekklesia, called out* of the world by Jesus, are only *thrown back* by the Spirit of Jesus into the world loved by God, a *hidden* presence like the mustard seed, like the yeast in the bread (Matt 13:31–33). "[I]t is only by living completely in this world that one learns to have faith . . . By this-worldliness I mean living in life's duties, problems, successes and failures, experiences and perplexities. In so doing we throw ourselves completely into the arms of God, taking seriously, not our own sufferings, but those of God in the world—watching with Christ in Gethsemane. That, I think, is faith; that is *metanoia*."[39]

The wounds of the risen Christ are the wounds of what Ivone Gebara calls "the sacred body of the earth." They are earth's polluted seas and rivers, they are undocumented Mexican immigrants in detention centers awaiting deportation, they are indigenous peoples denied access to culture and dignity of life, they are those marginalized by dominant society because of sexual orientation, they are women abused by alcoholic husbands, they are Latin American children huddled around a stove in their *choza*, they are the scorched earth and the undocumented Latino workers sickened and dying by "cleaning" it. These are the wounds of the risen Jesus today. Here the Church becomes *ecclesia abscondita* by the grace and mercy of the Master and the power of the Spirit. There the *ecclesia abscondita*, hidden deeply in the wounds of the risen Jesus, becomes the very body of Christ—the sacramental presence of the "preaching Word" in a new century, a new millennium.

---

39. Bonhoeffer, *Letters and Papers*, 369–70.

8

Life in Abundance: The Sacramental Word of Indigenous Culture

At the top of a high mountain where the heavens touch the earth, the Giver of life dwelt in a cave, according to the *Mixteca*[1] account of creation. God made a river spring forth in front of the cave. The river gave life to two trees. When the trees had grown strong, solid, and wise, God breathed on them and created man and woman, and love and sacrifice flowed from the Giver in the breath of creation.

In the *Mexica* creation story Quetzalcóatl, the great feathered serpent manifestation of the true God Ometéotl, "for whom all things live," allowed the creative blood of life to flow forth upon the dust of bones from a former humanity.[2] The dust, with the divine blood, was fashioned into the new humanity—woman and man. Then Quetzalcóatl gave *maíz* for nourishment, strengthening woman and man with fertile corn and blood in the creative gift of divine compassion and sacrifice.

Humanity is called to reflect this basic posture of creative love and sacrifice in a life of service to the community. The *Mexica* believed that male warriors who had given their lives for the defense of the people carried the sun, with an *anda*,[3] to its place in the noonday sky. Afterwards the warrior women who had died in childbirth carried the sun to its resting

1. Two major indigenous groups in Oaxaca, Mexico are the *Mixteca Alta* and the *Mixteca Baja*.

2. For a full account of the *Mexica* creation story, see Guerrero, *Flor y Canto*, 327–40.

3. An *anda* is a platform with poles that carries something sacred in indigenous ritual. They are used today to carry images of Jesus, Mary, and the saints.

place in the earth. They were then sent to protect the *pueblo* from every-thing that, during the dark of the night, could harm them. These warrior women and men were, in turn, examples for the *tlamatinime* (wise ones) of divine compassion and sacrifice. The *pueblo* go to the *tlamatinime* for help and advice, for these wise ones are reflections of the life-giving divine virtues. Creation is ordered on this integral harmony of women, men, nature, and the divine.[4]

During the first years of the Spanish incursion into Mexico, the mission-ary friars who accompanied the *conquistadores* were catechizing in an indigenous village. They preached about baptism and were frustrated by the many indigenous questions. "But why should we be baptized," an elder asked? A friar coldly responded, "So you will not go to hell." "Well then," replied the man, "where are all my ancestors and family members who have died without the Christian baptism?" "They are in hell," re-sponded the frustrated friar. "Then," said the indigenous, "you'd best not baptize me, *Padrecito*, because when I die, I want to go to hell so that I can be with them."[5]

The mystical-indigenous imagination of the poor is unique. It is highly communal and has a singular sense of time, space, and nature. It is nepantlic. Its center is God, the Giver of life, the Giver of breath, the Creator of light, the One for whom all things live, the One who is close and near, the Mother and Father, the Heart of the heavens, the earth, and the *pueblo*.[6] It has a profound respect for the harmony between woman and man, between humanity and nature, and is deeply religious and ori-ented toward service.[7]

The operative theology of the preacher who accompanies the indig-enous poor begins in *this* imagination. Its integration is an exciting, if perilous, journey of discovery in creative compassion and sacrifice that is aptly described by Margaret Craven in her moving novel, *I Heard the Owl Call My Name*. Mark Brian, an Anglican priest assigned to an indigenous

4. I am indebted to Arias Montes for these stories. See *Y la Palabra de Dios*, 134–38.

5. Story told by Arias Montes to the author in a conversation in June of 2005, Oaxaca, Mexico.

6. Arias Montes, *Y la Palabra de Dios*, 133–39. These are popular Mexican indig-enous names for God.

7. Ibid., 129.

culture in British Columbia, slowly comes to an awareness of the imagination of the poor. He moves, as all preachers from dominant cultures must,
from suspicion and rejection to acceptance. His skin is white, his customs
are different, but his heart is transformed by the *Kwakiutl*. This biblical
metanoia, a literal "change of heart," is likewise seen in the Dominican
friars of La Española (Part One). Recent Church documents call the journey "inculturation." True inculturation means that the evangelical tables
are turned; the preacher, in the process of sensitive proclamation that
touches the very roots of indigenous culture and reality, is the one who
is truly evangelized. He or she ultimately realizes that the gospel of the
God of Jesus, in an indigenous *pueblo* moved by the Spirit (John 3:8), has
already been proclaimed and lived for centuries:

> The fundamental idea that animates the inculturation of the
> Gospel is that the presence of God and of [God's] Son Jesus
> Christ and salvation do not arrive from the word of the evan-
> gelizer, but that they are antecedent realities to any evangelizing
> action, because they are the work of the Spirit who blows where
> [God] wills. The Spirit of God has been and is present and op-
> erative in all creatures, in all times and places, independently of
> evangelization and even independently of whether or not one is
> aware of that [divine] presence.[8]

The beginning of meaningful preaching in this context, then, is to
develop an "operative theology of preaching," to use a phrase coined by
preacher Gregory Heille, OP. From what imaginative sources does it pro-
ceed? The principal question for the preacher, in such a context, is: where
do I discern the *semillas del Verbo*, the seeds of the Word, in this particular
culture and *pueblo*? Or even better, what is the *presence* of the Word in this
culture, as José Marins asks? Traditional North Atlantic Christian theory
of evangelization limits the Incarnation of the *Logos*. There was already a
presence of the Word in the indigenous culture long before the Europeans
arrived in the Americas. The mysticism of the imagination of the indigenous poor expresses the cultural presence of the Sacramental Word.

Catherine of Siena, the great Dominican contemplative, speaks from the
depths of the mystical imagination: "Eternal Trinity, in your light I have
come to taste and see your own unfathomable depths and the beauty

8. Ibid., 114.

of what you have created. You are the light-giver. By your light, I have come to know your truth." This mystical tradition relies on what Gustavo Gutiérrez calls "complex unities"—pluralities maintained in unity through creative tension. Indigenous culture and imagination redefine Christian mysticism. It is nepantlic, a root manifestation of "mystical" unity within the very real diversity of the world.

Mysticism has always reserved, even without knowing it, a special place for *nepantla* and "complex unities." God, through whom we experience the all through the *"nada"* (John of the Cross), the "unfathomable depths of God" and the "beauty" of created things (Catherine of Siena), the "breakthrough" wherein the diversity of the universe becomes part of the oneness of God (Meister Eckhart), the joyful ecstasy through the "love letters" of sorrow (Teresa of Avila), the "all is straw" with the consequent inability to articulate (Thomas Aquinas), the mystical experience of the crucified Jesus in the tranquil river cave (Dominic of Guzmán), the experience of Jesus through the sufferings of the indigenous poor (Bartolomé de Las Casas)—all express the tension beyond comprehension in the mystical *nepantla* of diverse unity.

But indigenous imagination is not expressive of the traditional or "stereo-typed" mysticism prevalent in Western thought, for its central characteristic is the option for the poor. The "mystical," for the indigenous poor, is God's gratuitous and unmerited love, which is pure gift. The presence of Jesus, the "presence of the Word," is especially discerned in the suffering poor. The face of Jesus is seen in the innumerable faces of the *pueblo.*[9] This makes the mysticism of the poor, and their imagination, strongly Christocentric. Jesus the Sacramental Word, assuming human flesh, is both cultural and historical—an indigenous mysticism of the Incarnation:

> In the logic of God, Christ in the incarnation became Jewish and thus, assuming a very concrete culture and religion, enters into all human reality of that time, of the past and of the future. For having entered into the concrete totality of human reality, one can appropriately say that the son of God became man, became woman, Jew, Greek and Roman; became *Otomí, Tarahumara, Náhuatl, Aymara, Quechua, Mapuche;* became *Mixteca, Zapoteca, Mixe, Chatino, Amuzgo* . . . And from the incarnation in the culture and people oppressed by the Romans, he becomes one with

9. *Puebla* 31–39.

all people and every human being and saves all humanity. By his death and resurrection he purifies and saves all culture and all religion, he transfigures creation and history, opening them up to the definitive and eternal Reign.[10]

Chilean theologian Segundo Galilea says that to be mystical is to see all things—the self, others, history, and creation—with the eyes of Jesus.[11] But how can we possibly "see" with the eyes of Jesus? Only through the grace of Jesus, he says. The poor, through grace, "see" Christologically, with the eyes of hope, justice, and compassion—special "eyes" for the reign of God. Mexican theologian Camilo Maccise, OCD, former Master General of the Carmelites, likewise locates the mysticism of the poor in Jesus. In a particularly thought-provoking work on John of the Cross and the indigenous poor, Maccise says that the mysticism of John of the Cross is centered in two things: union with God and following Jesus the Word of history.[12] John of the Cross, he maintains, focuses on Jesus, the Word of God for the *pueblo*.[13] Jesus is a liberating Word for the poor, and it is the mysticism of the poor that hears this incarnate Word and follows his voice inviting justice and dignity for all God's children. As in most Latin American theology, Maccise reserves a special place for the cross of Jesus. John of the Cross helps the indigenous poor articulate a unique mysticism centered in "suffering love" as a sacrament of life.

Manuel Arias Montes gives special emphasis to the "Word made flesh" in indigenous culture, speaking of the mystical relationship of Jesus to the poor. There are two principal poverties. The first, says Arias Montes, is systemic poverty, an evil opposed to God's reign as proclaimed by Jesus and his followers. This poverty is denounced by the ecclesial community as an injustice "that cries out to the heavens." The follower of the poor Jesus, in mystical negation, strives for its elimination. The second is poverty assumed in solidarity, like the *kenosis* assumed and lived out by Jesus mystically in the heart of the Church community. This is a poverty that is taken on, like Jesus and his *kenosis*, voluntarily. The marginalized reality of the poor is mystically lived by the ecclesial hearer in a Christocentric following of the kenotic Jesus.[14] The mystical is complimented by the prophetic

10. Arias Montes, *Y la Palabra de Dios*, 106.

11. Galilea, *Ascenso a la Libertad*, 83–84.

12. Maccise, *Perspectivas Latinoamericanas*, 18.

13. Ibid., 23–24.

14. Arias Montes, *Y la Palabra de Dios*, 116–24.

in the search for justice, and the two are united as the follower of Jesus mystically experiences, in prophetic solidarity, the option for the poor.

Gustavo Gutiérrez reminds us that it is perhaps biblical Job that best bespeaks this combination of mysticism and prophecy.[15] For the poor, mysticism is mysteriously—and gratuitously—connected to the extreme poverty of the concrete poor. But God's justice and mercy are not opposed. Rather, they are mysteriously one and the same. Contemplation means this—that despite the suffering of the innocent, God is love, compassion, justice, and grace.[16] Justice and mercy express the very being of God. God accompanies the poor not because of *our idea* of God but because of *who God is* in God's essence—the God of justice and grace who accompanies the poor in their suffering.[17] The human being, Job learns with difficulty, cannot understand divine mercy and justice. Either God is responsible for human suffering, in classic theology of retribution, or God is blamed for the suffering of the innocent. What is required—and what Job eventually comes to see—is a contemplative leap into the infinite sea of God's grace and justice.[18]

How is this mysticism, centered in the incarnate and Sacramental Word, lived and expressed in indigenous Mexican culture? Arias Montes says:

> [T]he use of various names for God, the continual relating of the divine masculine with the divine feminine, the explaining of the profoundly religious [through an attitude of] profoundly social service, the considering of the earth as mother [and] generator of life, the naming of God in the harvest or whatever task, the maintaining of community life, the sharing of solidarity as the will of God, [these are all things] that do not pass unperceived, if we let ourselves be touched by the indigenous spirit; with open hearts and attentive ears, we hear this in [indigenous] narratives, [and] at the same time we confirm that [this] message is a permanent and evident actuality.[19]

Indigenous imagination is "God as integral part of everyday life"; it is deeply communal, thoroughly nepantlic, inseparably connected with

15. Gutiérrez, *Hablar de Dios*, 125–26, 220–26.
16. Ibid., 179–202.
17. Ibid., 205–6.
18. Ibid., 203–26.
19. Arias Montes, *Y la Palabra de Dios*, 74.

creation and the cosmos, and directed toward loving and sacrificial service. These five "categories" of the imagination of the poor can be spoken of, in traditional Christian theology, as Christology, ecclesiology, word and sacrament, grace, and eschatology.

In the indigenous imagination, God is everything. God is creator and giver of life; we are creature. A basic stance toward God permeates all reality in the indigenous context. God is found in all things and is inextricably present in nature. This is *not* what Western imagination categorizes as "pantheism" or even "panentheism." God is present in all things but *above* all things. God is nepantlic—*within* creation but *above* it.

Latin American indigenous cultures have been stereotyped in the North Atlantic as "polytheistic." This comes from prejudicial thinking and the dominant triumphal theology, what Ivone Gebara calls "monotheistic dominance" and what Martin Luther calls *theologia gloriae*. The stereotype falls far short of the mark. Rather, in *Mexica* culture the one and only God is Ometéotl, the Giver of life at once feminine and masculine, the God of the near and the close, the God for whom all things live, the Creator of persons, the Owner of heaven and earth.[20] In *Mixteca* culture, the true God is the Creator who is the Heart of the heavens, the Heart of the earth, and the Heart of the people.[21] All indigenous Latin American cultures share this faith in God. Arias Montes, when he was a newly ordained priest assigned to a small indigenous village in the state of Oaxaca, tells an amusing story of his time there. As he became better acquainted and more comfortable with an older indigenous woman, he said to her, "Do you really believe that the moon, the sun, the rain, even the stones, are gods?" She abruptly responded, *"¿Estás pendejo, Padrecito? ¡El único Dios creaba todo lo que hay!"* Spanish-speaking readers will immediately perceive the humor. A watered-down translation would be, "Are you crazy, Father? The one God created everything!"[22] Indigenous cultures believe in the one creator God of life.

The indigenous poor express their faith through what has been called *la religiosidad popular*—"popular religiosity." *Religiosidad popular* is not "religion," as such, at all. Rather, it is the *faith lived* through the symbols,

20. Guerrero, *El Nican Mopohua*, 173–74.

21. Arias Montes, *Y la Palabra de Dios*, 134.

22. Conversation with Arias Montes, June of 2005, Oaxaca, Mexico.

metaphors, and culture of the *pueblo*.[23] This faith is centered in the God who is *Padre-Madre* (Father-Mother), *Dador de vida* (Giver of life), *Dios por quien todo se vive* (the God for whom all live), *Corazón de la Tierra, del Cielo, y del Pueblo* (the Heart of the Earth, the Heavens, and the People), Ometéotl (the one God with the masculine and feminine face)—in short, the God of life. *Religiosidad popular* is the faith expression of deeply held indigenous values.[24] It connects the *pueblo* with their indigenous roots and is manifested in practices like pilgrimages, popular devotions to the Trinity, Jesus, Mary and the saints, blessings, service groups dedicated to the village or neighborhood *patrón* (*hermandades, cofradías, cargueros,* etc.), and other customs often dating back to pre-Columbian times.

Religiosidad popular is often not connected to the official rituals of the Church institution. Rather, it is the deep-rooted faith of the *pueblo* in the God of Jesus as expressed through their culture. José Luis Guerrero, a priest and theologian from Mexico City, calls the *religiosidad popular* an expression of the "underground Church."[25] He maintains that this "underground Church" began early in the history of Mexican Christianity. The precipitating event was the famous meeting, in 1524, between the *Doce Apóstoles* (the first twelve Franciscan friars in Mexico are referred to as the "Twelve Apostles") and the indigenous priests, the *papahuaque,* of the *Mexica* culture.[26] The meeting went for several days at great risk to the indigenous priests. It was, at first, marked by a certain courtesy on the part of the Franciscans, surely because of the absolute respect shown to them by the *papahuaque.* After a few days the "dialog," never really a dialog with its purpose of forced conversion, deteriorated. The indigenous priests knew that they were being coerced—ultimately by Spanish weapons that supported the *Doce Apóstoles*— into accepting this new religion. The crisis came when the *Doce* referred to the indigenous as "immoral devil worshippers" and "idolaters."[27] The *papahuaque* knew that they would be forced to accept this new *teotl* Jesus.[28] They finally

---

23. Arias Montes refers to *religiosidad popular* as a perception of "the divine dimension within ordinary life." See *Y La Palabra de Dios,* 72–73. See also 258–59 n147.

24. Ibid., 110.

25. Guerrero, *El Nican Mopohua,* 66–67.

26. Ibid., 61.

27. Ibid., 63.

28. Dominant culture translation of this *Náhuatl* word is "god" or "goddess." It is incorrect. The *teotl* is an expression of the one God Ometéotl. All that proceeds from

acquiesced to the obligatory evangelism of the Franciscan friars. In a poignant speech, they told the Franciscans to "do with us what you will."

The *pueblo*, though accepting the forced baptism of the Europeans, continued the "underground Church" in which they practiced the "old ways." The old ways were simply adapted to this new faith. But after several years—in 1531—an event occurred that would bring this "underground Church" into the open. That event was the apparition, on the hill of Tepeyac, of Santa María Tonantzin, as Our Lady of Guadalupe is often called by the indigenous poor. The *Guadalupana*, for Guerrero and other indigenous theologians, was the divine intervention, the miracle of God, which returned dignity and respect to an oppressed indigenous culture.

Indigenous Mexican theologians maintain that the first evangelization was tainted by the culture and the socio-religious beliefs of the Spaniards. The ancient indigenous culture led people to a faith that gave meaning to their life experience. What the *Doce* and the other European evangelizers taught, with very few exceptions, was contrary to this lived faith. The God preached by the Spaniards was a confusing God, a punishing God, a cold God, not the Ometéotl of compassion and sacrifice from their own culture, or the authentic God of the Hebrew and Christian Scriptures.

As a result of the meeting between the *Doce* and the *papahuaque*, a course of "resigned resistance" occurred. The people continued believing in the true God of their ancestors. They already had *teotles*, but they accepted the Christian God, Jesus, Mary, and the saints. In 1531, Santa María Tonantzin represented the miracle of God on behalf of the *pueblo*—nothing less than revolutionary—that would be the real proclamation of the good news of the God of Jesus.

Flor y canto—flower and song—are essential expressions of Mexican culture and *religiosidad popular*.[29] They refer to the divine gift of life and are expressed through indigenous poetry and art. Where there is *flor y canto*, there is God. *Flor y canto* speak of joy and sorrow, hopes and dreams. The

---

this God is *flor* (flower)—that is, life, which has its roots in the heavens with Ometéotl. See Guerrero, *El Nican Mopohua*, 41. The various *teotles* are manifestations of the unity, oneness, and life of God. These manifestations are most often expressed through personified nature, for instance Tláloc is the *teotl* of rain, Quetzalcóatl is the *teotl* human feathered serpent, and Tonantzin is the *teotl* Mother. See Arias Montes, *Y la Palabra de Dios*, 136. See also López Hernández, "Teologías Indias de Hoy," and "Los Indios ante del Tercer Milenio." In my opinion, it is best to leave the word untranslated.

29. Guerrero, *El Nican Mopohua*, 35–37.

paradise of Tláloc, in indigenous eschatology, was permeated with flower and song. In the *Nican Mopohua*, the *Mexica* account of the Guadalupe apparitions written in *Náhautl*, Juan Diego Cuauhtlatoatzin ("the eagle who speaks") wonders, as he observes the transformation of Tepeyac, if he is in the ancient paradise of Tláloc, the Xochitlalpán of his ancestors.[30] Tepeyac, desecrated by the Spaniards in the destruction of the indigenous sanctuary to the *teotl* Mother Tonantzin, is now covered with flowers— in December!—and bathed in divine music. *Flor y canto* tell a people who have been decimated that the Giver of life has not abandoned them. *Flor y canto* speak of the divine presence in nature and life. We preachers who work with indigenous Mexican people—or any exiled community— should take note. A Dominican friar in colonial Oaxaca, Luis de Cáncer, preached by *singing* the old indigenous *cantares* of the *pueblo*.[31]

José Marins rightly observes that Latin American devotional centers are found in the crucified Jesus and his mother Mary. This poor indigenous Christology—the Paschal Mystery vividly depicted through images of the crucified Jesus and the Virgin Mary—is central to the theology and the imagination of the poor. Phillip Berryman says, "Latin American theology tends to be very Christological, very Christ-centered . . ."[32] But the center from which this arises is an indigenous Christological ecclesiology, reminiscent of the theology of Dietrich Bonhoeffer. Christ *is* the Church of the poor in his body, in the faith of the *pueblo*. Devotional images of the crucified Jesus, and Mary, are popular representations of the Paschal Mystery. The image of the crucified Jesus represents the death of Jesus and the image of Mary the resurrection, according to Marins. Perhaps this approaches what the Eastern Church means when it speaks of Mary and the Holy Spirit as the "hypostatic maternity" of Jesus the Word, and consequently, of the Church.[33] The crucified Jesus is seen in every town church and in every home. Likewise, Mary, who in the *religiosidad popular* is life-giving symbol of the resurrection, is commonly seen throughout Latin America. The *Aparecida* of Brazil is African-American and personifies life through the struggle of the poor for human dignity, equality, and justice. The *Guadalupana* is an indigenous woman of the

30. Arias Montes, *Y la Palabra de Dios*, 59. See also Guerrero, *El Nican Mopohua*, 251 n80. Xochitlalpán is associated with the Paradise of Tláloc, the rain *teotl*.

31. Arias Montes, *Y la Palabra de Dios*, 86.

32. Berryman, *Liberation Theology*, 157.

33. Evdokimov, *In the World*, 159–61.

Mexica culture. The Paschal Mystery is nepantlic—the death and the resurrection of Jesus lived in the *pueblo* and also observed in many contemporary Latin American images of the crucified Jesus and the Virgin Mary. The crucified Christ is depicted as a *campesino* hanging on a shovel and pitchfork; as an indigenous suffering on a rough-hewn cross; as a *Mexica* crowned with a *penacho* (a royal indigenous head covering); and as the crucified Jesus emerging from an ear of *maíz*. There are touching images of the *Pietá*, as well, that represent Jesus and Mary as indigenous poor. Many are already familiar with the image of Mary as *La Madre de los Desaparecidos* (the mother of those "disappeared" by military *juntas*).

Images of the crucified Jesus and Mary show the nepantlic unity of death and life. The preacher in a Latin American context should give them special attention. Perhaps the crucified Christ and the *Dolorosa*, Our Lady of Sorrows, are so popular because the poor instinctively see their own suffering in these icons. They occupy central places in the town churches and in the homes of the people. They are seen in the *campo* and the central marketplaces of large cities. Many hills in Latin America have crosses at their summits, since the mountain has been a special manifestation of God's creative mercy since ancient times. Most significant hills and mountains throughout Latin America were cultic centers for the indigenous in pre-Columbian times. Many had temples that were destroyed by the Europeans during the Conquest, such as the temple to Tonantzin on Tepeyac. Devotions and popular faith rooted in the ancient indigenous customs express a communal outlook that transcends individualism. Jesus is not "*my* savior," but "*our* savior," in the ecclesial imagination of the poor. The crucified Jesus and the Mary of life, for whom "the Mighty One has done great things" (Luke 1:49), typify this ecclesiology.[34]

Gregory Heille says: "All good Christian preaching leads to the foot of the cross." The Latin American poor stand at the foot of the cross with Mary, the women disciples, and John. The preacher must respect the attachment of the *pueblo* to the cross. This was Martin Luther's sense as well, for he would never allow the crucifix to be removed from any church building in which he preached. Leonardo Boff maintains that the real art of theology is to know how to preach the cross and death of Jesus.

While the crucifixion of Jesus is easier to portray, how does one rightly depict the resurrection? The imagination of the poor is concrete. It looks to signs, symbols, and images. In Mexican indigenous imagina-

---

34. See Arias Montes, *Y la Palabra de Dios*, 178.

tion, Our Lady of Guadalupe is a concrete sign of the resurrection. Arias Montes says that the Church the *Guadalupana* wants built on Tepeyac is not so much a *building* but a Holy Temple, a *people* who embody justice and peace.[35] Santa María Tonantzin is the presence of the risen Christ, a symbol of the body of Christ, the Church. She is the transverbation of the Word in efficacious sign for the ecclesial community of hearers. She carries the indigenous Word, for the black ribbon the *Guadalupana* wears on her hands is the *Mexica* sign of pregnancy. She proclaims the Word of life to Juan Diego Cuauhtlatoatzin, and it is *he* who converts the bishop in a reverse evangelization that surges from deep within indigenous culture.

Santa María Tonantzin invites the male-dominated Church institution to respect women, and their preaching, in the Church community. She returns to the indigenous the dignified image of women that was a casualty of the Conquest.[36] The *Guadalupana* is not so much the "Mother of God" as the "God-mother."[37] That is why the European friars were so afraid of her, for there is no early written record of the apparitions in Spanish documents. She was too revolutionary, and counter (North Atlantic!) cultural. Santa María Tonantzin appears on the lifeless hill of Tepeyac because the *conquistadores* had practiced a "scorched earth" policy. The sanctuary to Tonantzin, the *teotl* Mother, had been destroyed, not a stone left upon another, and Tepeyac itself was devastated—the trees, the flowers, the songs, an indigenous culture. Especially dangerous was the ancient faith. The friars tried to eradicate all traces of "idolatry." It is indeed a tragedy of history that the friars were closed to the presence of the Sacramental Word in the ancient indigenous faith of the people. They blasphemed against the Holy Spirit, committing the unforgivable sin (Mark 3:28–30).

While Christian Europe was arguing over Reformations, Counter Reformations, and the indigenous capacity for faith, God brought about a veritable revolution. For the appearance of Our Lady of Guadalupe to Juan Diego Cuauhtlatoatzin on that December day in 1531—only ten years after the fall of Tenochtitlán, the indigenous capital that is present day Mexico City—was not a reformation of Christianity. It was a *revolution*, a transformation by the power of the Spirit, which touched the very core of faith in the God of Jesus. Santa María Tonantzin shared the risen

35. Ibid., 74.

36. Arias Montes, *Y la Palabra de Dios*, 61. The *machismo* often spoken of in Mexican culture is entirely European.

37. Ibid., 60. Arias Montes refers to her as the "feminine face of God." See also Elizondo, *La Morenita*.

life of the Christ with an indigenous people the powerful had tried to destroy. The crucified and life-giving Sacramental Word, in a *pueblo* dead and risen, proclaimed that the poor were just the ones whom the God of Jesus inevitably chooses.

∼

The indigenous imagination is communal and has an innate appreciation for the Church as the people of God and the body of Christ. The individual is important, but only finds personal identity within the community. The individual belongs to a family, the family belongs to a community, and the community belongs to a *pueblo*. This is distinct from North Atlantic thinking, preoccupied as it has been with the ego as subject since Descartes and the *cogito*. José Marins observes that in Africa, the *cogito* is rendered, "I dance, therefore I live," and in Latin America and the Caribbean, "I celebrate *fiesta*, therefore I am *pueblo*." In the West, the individual is often prior to the community. This is in contrast to the imagination of the poor, which places the needs of the community above those of the individual. Individual rights are not disregarded by indigenous communities. Rather, the individual finds dignity and justice *only* in the context of community. If one member of the community suffers, the entire *pueblo* suffers, and if one member of the community is joyful, the entire community is joyful. Perhaps this is best seen in the word *acompañar*—"to accompany." As Gutiérrez and others have pointed out, etymologically the word means "to share bread."[38] Everything is shared by the community. If someone is hungry, the community shares the little they have (Matt 14:14–21; Mark 6:35–44; Luke 9:12–17; John 6:1–13), for all feel the hunger. A common saying in poor Latin American homes, when an unexpected visitor arrives, is *Ponemos un poquito más de agua a la sopa*—"We'll just add some more water to the soup."

The Latin American *fiesta* is an example of the imagination of the poor and its emphasis on community. The entire *pueblo* gathers to celebrate key events in the life of the community. Food is shared, stories are told, songs are sung, and embraces are exchanged. In the *fiesta*, the *pueblo* comes together simply for the joy of *being together*, of celebrating life. The Eucharist, in poor Christian communities, is a *fiesta* of the *pueblo* where manna from heaven is shared with the poor and the story of the community is proclaimed. It is a celebration of life in the midst of death. In

38. Nickoloff, ed., *Gustavo Gutiérrez*, 131.

the *fiesta* of the Eucharist, the community gathers in *acompañar*, breaks word and bread, and praises the God of life.

The God of Jesus is relational. Human experiences of love and community point to the love of the Triune God, and the love of the Triune God is the gratuitous source of community. "The Christian God is not a lonely God," according to Karl Barth.[39] Arias Montes says that community is a reflection of the love expressed within the Trinity.[40] The Holy Trinity is the foundation of indigenous ecclesiology, where the communal life of the Church is often lived locally through the *comunidades eclesiales de base*. The *comunidades*, in turn, are local expressions of the indigenous and communal roots of the people.[41] The base communities remind us that the Church is community and sacrament, invited to faithful praxis by the Spirit of love.

The indigenous imagination is nepantlic, "situated in the midst of" diverse creative tensions that always move in a circle of unity. God is the "Father-Mother" God, the "creative tension" of the three divine persons in the One who transcends all history, yet is integral part of history in life-giving Spirit through the Sacramental Word. The divine creative tension lives community in unity. The Church community reflects the divine diversity in unity, the God three in One, for God in Jesus becomes incarnate in human community and, in the Spirit, "raises" the *pueblo* to divinity, as the Fathers and Mothers say so often.

I have referred to the Christology of Javier Garibay and *nepantla*. But Garibay likewise insists that *nepantla* is central to *all* theological reflection in a poor indigenous context. He describes the situation of the *Mexica* after the Conquest, when they found themselves adjusting to a radically different reality. Garibay uses the historical accounts of Franciscan friar Gerónimo de Mendieta (1525–1609) to examine and analyze theologically the result of this new context on a formerly autonomous people. The faith of the *pueblo* was deeply affected by this new and oppressive reality.

Garibay maintains that the primary *nepantla* ironically found in the theology of Mendieta is between the "moment of grace" (a sincere attempt to live the gospel of Jesus and the Franciscan lifestyle as it was interpreted

---

39. Quoted from Kallistos Ware, "Seek First the Kingdom," 14.

40. Arias Montes, *Y la Palabra de Dios*, 178–85.

41. Ibid., 183–85.

by the sixteenth century Spanish friars) and the "moment of sin" (the root injustice of imposing one culture and faith upon another). This "moment of grace" and "moment of sin," two contraries, were brought together forcefully in the *nepantla* of the new context.[42] Garibay cites a story by nineteenth century friar Diego de Durán, who had been invited by the indigenous to a village for a religious festival. They warned him ahead of time: "*Padre*, you may not like some of the things you see in our rites celebrating the *fiesta*, but we are just being *nepantla*" (*estando nepantla*). The priest wondered what was meant by the term normally rendered "situated in the midst of." When he saw the festival, he knew they were speaking of a unity of indigenous and European customs, integrated by the *pueblo* in *nepantla*, during the years since the Conquest. The people retained their own indigenous faith values and nepantically combined them with the customs imposed by the Spanish friars.[43]

Nepantla reveals the unity that respects indigenous life, proclaiming the good news of Jesus even in the midst of the "moment of sin." The primary question then becomes: where is grace in the midst of sin? Or, as Gutiérrez prefers, how are the poor told that they are *loved* by a gracious God? Paul summarizes the *nepantla* of sin and grace: "The law entered in so that transgression might increase but, where sin increased, grace overflowed all the more" (Rom 5:20). Indigenous unity incorporates a structurally sinful situation into the grace of traditional faith expression. *Nepantla* is the grace of the gospel palpable in the faith of the *pueblo*, lived in indigenous *comunidades eclesiales de base*, and expressed in the *religiosidad popular*.

The Sacramental Word, then, becomes an expression of *nepantla* for the *pueblo* in the *huetlatolli*—the "ancient word." The *huetlatolli* were ethical customs, along with the earliest theologies and philosophies, recorded by indigenous scholars in Spanish. This ancient word was by and large "accepted" by the Spaniards because it proposed a way of living that was in keeping with the gospel. The indigenous retained their sacred customs, which were then nepantically "adjusted" to the "new ways" of the Spaniards. *Huetlatolli* became, in *nepantla*, the word of Scripture, now deeply expressive of indigenous values. *Huetlatolli*, the ancient indigenous word, is proclaimed as the good news, denouncing the injustice suffered by the indigenous poor and announcing Jesus Christ Sacramental Word

42. Ibid., 9.
43. Ibid., 227.

of the God of the poor. The gospel, proclaimed by the preacher in solidarity with the *pueblo* from the perspective of the imagination of the poor, is the "presence of the Word" in the *huetlatolli*.[44]

Nepantlic word is expressed in the *vírgula* of the ancient Mexican indigenous codices. The *vírgula*, a circular glyph coming from the mouth of a speaker, symbolizes the indigenous word spoken in prudence, humility, sacrifice, and service. It is heard, and received, in community, in the *pueblo*.[45] The *vírgula* is used only for those in authority entrusted with the spoken word, and the *pueblo* is edified by the speaker's sacrificial service. A contemporary example of the *vírgula* can be seen in a creative Jesuit indigenous catechism that uses this ancient art form in the portrayal of Jesus and the disciple-proclaimer.[46] The catechism is done in the style of the historic Mexican indigenous codices and consists strictly of New Testament stories. The *vírgulas* express through their graphics whether the words proceeding from the mouth of the speaker are good news or bad news.

The spirit of the *huetlatolli* is also manifested in what has been called a "parabolic imagination" that proclaims that the powerful will be humbled and the poor exalted. Parabolic imagination turns things upside down. This is precisely what the parables of Jesus do. In the words of Robert Farrar Capon, "the least, the last, the lost, the little," who experience life from the underside of history—in our context the indigenous poor—are the ones who are lifted up and exalted by God.[47] Paul Janowiak suggests that this imagination is central to the understanding of the imagination of the poor.[48] The ninety-nine are left in the desert so that the shepherd can seek the lost sheep (Luke 15:4–6). A house is scoured by a desperate woman until one lost coin is found (Luke 15:8–9). A lost son is sought by a distraught and compassionate father (Luke 15:11–32). A poor beggar is comforted, while a rich man is tormented (Luke 16:19–31). The invited wealthy are cast aside in favor of the poor who come in from the byways to feast at the sumptuous table of the king (Matt 22:1–14). The son who says "no" is chosen over the son who says "yes" (Matt 21:28–32). The last

44. Ibid. Garibay's discussion of the *huetlapolli* is found on 230–43.

45. I am indebted to Marco Antonio Tovar, an anthropologist who works in the library of the *Museo Nacional de Antropología* in Mexico City, for his cogent explanation of the *vírgula* and its relationship to Mexican indigenous reality.

46. Basilas, ed., *Jesús Nuestro Amigo*, 1999.

47. See Capon, *The Parables of the Kingdom*.

48. Conversation on 19 July 2005 in Portland, Oregon.

receive the same as the first (Matt 20:1–16). The insignificant mustard seed grows into a large shrub and is likened to the reign of God (Mark 4:30–32). The merchant looking for the finest pearls finds the one of great price and sells everything to buy it (Matt 13:45–46). The prayer of the sinner is heard over the prayer of the just (Luke 18:10–14). Through these and other parables, Jesus reverses the expected order. The poor become beneficiaries, while the powerful are humbled.

The parable is not limited to the experience of the people of first century Palestine. Wilfred Harrington, OP, says, "[The parables] must speak in such a way that we strive to hear not so much the exact words in which Jesus first spoke the parables, than to hear them as his living voice today."[49] The imagination of the poor is parabolic because of the way the poor *hear*. The parables of Jesus are "reversals" in action. They cause more confusion and misunderstanding than clarification. "With Jesus, however, the device of parabolic utterance is used not to explain things to people's satisfaction but to call attention to the unsatisfactoriness of all their previous explanations and understandings," says Capon.[50] However, in parabolic imagination the poor and the exiled—"the least, the last, the lost, the little"—actually *understand* the parable as it is told by Jesus. The creative power of the indigenous imagination instinctively "knows" who the exalted are in the story. The poor are Lazarus. The poor arrive last but are given the same. The poor are the mustard seed, the lost sheep, and the lost coin. When the *pueblo* hears a parable, there is rejoicing because "[God] has brought down the powerful from their thrones, and lifted up the lowly . . . filled the hungry with good things, and sent the rich away empty" (Luke 1:52–53). When the powerful hear a parable, there is "weeping and gnashing of teeth" (Matt 8:12; 13:42, 50; 22:13; 24:51; 25:30; Luke 13:28), for the parable denounces injustice and becomes a condemnation. The wealthy and the powerful, the "privileged" of society, do not understand, or refuse to understand, for they know the parable is a denunciation of their privileges. But the poor "hear the word and accept it and bear fruit thirty and sixty and a hundredfold" (Mark 4:20). The parables are the "theological reflection" of the poor on the reign of God—not as proposed by the powerful, but as transformed by Jesus in the Spirit.[51]

---

49. Harrington, *Parables Told by Jesus*, 4.

50. Capon, *The Parables of the Kingdom*, 4.

51. Mesters, *Las Parábolas de Jesús*, 55–61.

~

The imagination of the poor is deeply intertwined with nature and creation. There is a harmony in nature that is integral to its being. Women and men, created to be in accord with themselves and creation, are to respect nature. In indigenous Mexican culture, a person at birth is given a name—a *náhual*. This name is known only to the parents and the child and can never be revealed to anyone else. The name is most often an animal. There is a natural respect, in the indigenous imagination, for creation, for animals, and for all things. Even "inanimate objects" are full of life—rivers, rocks, water, and song. Peruvian poet and novelist José María Arguedas is one of the best at capturing the indigenous sense of grace in nature. Much of his poetry is written in *Quechua*. Songs and sounds are important conveyors of imaginal meaning—the tolling of bells, the sounds of birds, insects, and simple toys, the indigenous *huaynos* (ballads)—all bring the reader to appreciate the creative imagination expressed through indigenous reality. Arguedas, a favorite of Gutiérrez, is unfortunately not well known in Western circles, as John Murra says, because of the challenge of translating his novels, which use *Quechua* words, culture, and grammatical constructs interspersed with Spanish. However, an excellent translation of an Arguedas novel—*Los Ríos Profundos*—is available in English with the nuances intact and a fine introduction. The "inanimate" is anything but! Full of life and wonder, rivers, mountains, seas, stones, earth—everything manifests life as gift of the Creator.[52]

The imagination of the poor is rooted in the earth. *Pachamama, madre-tierra*, mother earth, is sacred to the *Quechua* and *Aymara* indigenous cultures of the Andean highlands as well as to Mexican indigenous cultures.[53] But mother earth is sacred to all indigenous. Chief Seattle, leader of the Duwamish people in the 1850s during the United States incursion into the Puget Sound area, shows the profound connection between indigenous culture and the earth:

> How can you buy or sell the sky, the warmth of the land? The idea is strange to us. If we do not own the freshness of the air and sparkle of the water, how can you buy them? Every part of this earth is sacred to my people. Every shining pine needle, every sandy shore, every mist in the dark woods, every clearing

52. Arguedas, *Deep Rivers*.
53. Arias Montes, *Y la Palabra de Dios*, 139.

and humming insect is holy in the memory and experience of my people. The sap which courses through the trees carries the memories . . . We are part of the earth and it is part of us . . . The perfumed flowers are our sisters; the deer, the horse, the great eagle, these are our brothers. The rocky crests, the juices in the meadows, the body heat of the pony . . . all belong to the same family . . . This earth is precious to [God], and to harm the earth is to heap contempt on its Creator.[54]

The earth is sacred. To hate the earth is to hate God. The earth is gift to the *pueblo*. If the earth suffers, everything suffers. Humanity cannot exist without the natural reciprocity of all creation. If nature's harmony is disturbed, everything is dissonant. Many from indigenous Mexican cultures sadly remember what was done to the hills and landscape of *madre-tierra* during colonial times. Trees were cut for lumber and industries, leaving the hills bear. The results are still seen and are deeply lamented by the indigenous cultures.

The "fundamental trait of indigenous spirituality," according to Arias Montes, is the ability to see the presence of God in all created things.[55] Nature brims with the presence of the divine. All creation—the heavens, the world, humanity, the cosmos—palpitates with the divine presence. Nature overflows with the presence of God. A "privileged place" of the presence of God—a *locus theologicus*—is the *community*. The life of the *pueblo* is deeply important. At the same time it is precisely *all life*, in the context of the human community, which is "embraced" by the God of compassion. Community and creation are one in *nepantla*. The human, the natural, and all creation overflow with the life and mercy of God in divine creative love. The human community reflects the marvelous creation of God. This is called "grace" in theology, where creation is "salvific act" of God.[56] God's deepest desire is self-communication in grace (Rahner). God *wants* to be in relationship. Through the Incarnation of Jesus and the outpouring of the Spirit, humanity is glorified and becomes *imago Dei*. God's gratuitous and unmerited love—a constant theme for Gutiérrez—is always present in created reality and is gracious gift for humanity.

54. Excerpts from 1854 speech to Franklin Pierce on the desire of the United States to "purchase" the Puget Sound area. The speech was originally delivered in the Duwamish language. This rendering is by Texas professor Ted Perry.

55. Arias Montes, *Y la Palabra de Dios*, 148.

56. Gutiérrez, *Hablar de Dios*, 166.

Indigenous theology and imagination are fundamental expressions of what Rahner calls "uncreated grace" or Orthodox theologians "divine uncreated energy." Grace is everywhere in the imagination of the poor, in everyone and everything. Grace permeates created historical reality. God is not just the North Atlantic "transcendent Other," the *totaliter aliter*. Rather, God is infinitely close to creation and humanity. Western theology has by and large lost this subtle and important theological paradox— how is God the totally other "Absolute Mystery" and at the same time infinitely present *within* created nature? Scripture, the Christology and ecclesiology of the Fathers and Mothers, and theology throughout the first millennium were much more open to *symbol* as manifestation of the "real." Theology, during those early centuries, was most rightly expressed through the power of symbol as liturgical prayer and as contemplation of the divine mystery. Later, in the second millennium, theology lost its integral connection with symbol and became dialectical and rational.[57] This effectively distanced much North Atlantic thinking, both Catholic and Protestant, from one of its most important themes—grace.

Indigenous imagination respects the symbolic. North Atlantic theological imagination will never appreciate the indispensible contribution of the imagination of the poor until it becomes, once again, a theology of *symbol*. This is so integral to a proper understanding of grace and one of the reasons why the institutional Church, and even the academy, has such a difficult time with newer indigenous and feminist theologies from Latin American. If Jon Sobrino and Roger Haight, accepted Jesuit scholars who have pushed against the fringes of symbolic theology, have been censured by ecclesiastical authorities, one can only imagine what theologians like Ivone Gebara, a Brazilian woman, and Manuel Arias Montes, an indigenous Mexican, have endured at the hands of the local and universal Church institution in their quest for a contemporary indigenous and holistic theology of symbol. The institutional Church and the male-dominated North Atlantic theological academy are still far from the symbolic imagination of the Fathers and Mothers. Theology, with all due respect to Barth and Rahner, can no longer look solely to dialectical and sacramental methodologies and imaginations revolving around scholasticism and the Western tradition. Contemporary theology and preaching must express symbol and *nepantla* in the imagination of the poor. God's grace and the Incarnation of Jesus, by the creative breath of

57. Codina, *Creo en el Espíritu Santo*, 35–36.

the Spirit, are, after all, totally unlimited and entirely unpredictable: "The wind blows where it chooses, and you hear the sound of it, but you do not know where it comes from or where it goes. So it is with everyone who is born of the Spirit" (John 3:8). God's gracious presence, mysterious and transcendent, is at "the heart of human history" (Gutiérrez). "All is grace," says Bernanos' country priest—and the imagination of the poor.

> I am the LORD your God, who brought you out of the land of Egypt, out of the house of slavery; you shall have no other gods before me. You shall not make for yourself an idol, whether in the form of anything that is in heaven above, or that is on the earth beneath, or that is in the water under the earth. You shall not bow down to them or worship them; for I the LORD your God am a jealous God, punishing children for the iniquity of parents, to the third and the fourth generation of those who reject me, but showing steadfast love to the thousandth generation of those who love me and keep my commandments. (Exod 20:2–6)

Every preacher has an operative theology, says Gregory Heille. The operative theology of the Conquest was idolatrous. The idol was a god of the crown, punishing and hateful—a god of gold-lust and wealth who wielded the sword of the *conquistador* and demanded blood sacrifice as an offering to the golden calf of power. The golden calf is still adored in international banking systems, consumerisms at any cost, neo-liberal and unregulated capitalisms that have thrown the world into global economic crisis, and the military-industrial complexes of the powerful. If we render *any* homage to these "principalities and powers" (Eph 6:12), our preaching and our theology will be idolatrous. We dare not return to the land of Egypt and the slavery of dominant homiletics.

But we preachers can choose, by the wholly unmerited grace which calls us to proclaim the good news of the God of Jesus in the Spirit, to place ourselves within the embrace of an operative theology that *reverences* the imagination of the poor. This operative theology, taken on by the preacher in an imagination that is mystical, ecclesial, nepantlic, and graced, is grounded in solidarity with the indigenous poor. It is not something that we preachers just "do." It is free and gracious gift of the God who is Mother and Father, Giver of life, and Heart of the earth, the heavens, and the *pueblo*. The grace is *God's* indigenous imagination: "If the poor are God's privileged, then . . . the God imagery of the poor is the privileged imagery of God."[58] The indigenous poor have a living and unique imagination centered in the God of life. Preachers remove their sandals here, for it is sacred ground (Exod 3:5). The poor, through no quality of their own but simply because they are the chosen of God, are embraced by the mystery. The preacher who humbly accompanies in solidarity will be caressed by the grace of the mysterious God of Jesus, who in the Spirit blesses graciously, through the imagination of the *pueblo*, the now unclad "feet of the messenger who announces peace, who brings good news, who announces salvation, who says to Zion, 'Your God reigns'" (Isa 52:7).

58. Virgilio Elizondo in Preface, González, *Mañana*, 17.

9

Flor y Canto, Return to the Source

Thomas Aquinas said that it is easier to say what God is *not* than what God is.[1] This theological methodology is known as the *via negativa*. Although meant by Aquinas to refer to the theology of God, it readily can be applied to the theology of preaching. It is easier to take the *via negativa*, by saying what preaching should not be, than to say how preaching should be done. *Caminante, no hay camino*—as Antonio Machado has said: "Journeyer, there is no road, no path . . ."[2] The path is made in the journey. The only thing the *caminante* can rely on is the *estelas en la mar*—wakes, or signposts, upon the sea.[3]

The preacher follows a path that is no path—the *nada* of John of the Cross. But there are wakes and signposts on the uncertain waters. It is in the discerning of the wakes, the *estelas en la mar*, where many preachers stand or fall. An operative theology, prayerful reflection, hermeneutics of

1. *Summa Theologiae* I, q. 3.

2. Machado, *Poesías Completas*, 158. Part of a larger poem (*Proverbios y Cantares*, CXXXVI), the words in question form some of Machado's best known verses. The second section of the poem refers to the human journey as likened to Jesus walking on the water and is connected with the twenty-ninth section, the verses to which I refer. Machado wrote the poem during his journey to France after his exile by Franco.

3. My hermeneutic of Machado revolves around two translations of the word *estela*. It most commonly means "wake," as the wake left on the sea by a ship. But *estela* is also used in reference to the great stone "totems" of the ancient Mexican indigenous cultures. Examples can be seen at the *Museo Nacional de Antropología* in Mexico City. These large stones were "signposts" for the ancient cultures. They tell stories, for engraved upon them are the glyphs of the ancients. The one solid *Estela* for the preacher, like these stone signposts, is Jesus Christ Sacramental Word of the God of the poor. The other *estelas* are like the original meaning of *estela* in Machado's poem—wakes upon the sea.

the readings and of the community, study and thoughtful preparation, all of these are "wakes upon the sea." But there is no "tried and true" path, no sure methodology that will result in the impeccable homily. Nothing can be said about what goes into the "perfect" homily—there is no such recipe! Jesus was almost stoned to death after his first preaching—"perfect" since it proceeded from the voice of the Master.[4] Our own preaching always falls far short of the Sacramental Word, the *Estela par excellence*.

There are many examples of what should *not* be done when preaching from the imagination of the indigenous poor. Consider the following account from Arguedas' *Los Ríos Profundos* of the "saintly" Padre Linares, rector of the boy's school in the Andean town of the novel's setting, who regularly accepted the invitation of the wealthy landowners to celebrate the Eucharist and preach in the chapels of their *haciendas*:

> The Rector began his sermons softly. He praised the Virgin Mary in moving tones; his voice was high and pleasant, but he easily became excited. He hated Chile and always found ways to pass from religious themes to the praise of his country and its heroes. He preached a future war against the Chileans. He called on the young men and boys to be prepared and to never forget that to obtain revenge was their greatest duty; and thus, exalted and speaking in violent terms, he would remind the men of their other duties. He would praise the landowners—they were the foundation of the republic, the pillars of its wealth. He referred to the piety of the gentry, to the care they took of the hacienda chapels and the way they made the Indians go to confession, take communion, get married, and be content with their humble lot. Then he would once more lower his voice to recite some passage on Calvary.[5]

Although the landowners consider Padre Linares the best preacher the town has seen, his sermons oppress the indigenous *Quechua* who are virtually enslaved on the *haciendas*.

But a preacher who accompanies the poor and respects their imagination needs more than simple awareness of the homiletic *via negativa*. Are there really any *estelas en la mar* on which the preacher can lean? There is one *Estela* that is sure: Jesus Christ Sacramental Word of the God of the poor. The Renaissance painter Fra Angelico often depicted

---

4. Peñalosa, *Manual de la Imperfecta Homilía*, 5–6.

5. Arguedas, *Deep Rivers*, 43.

Domingo de Guzmán, the founder of the Order of Preachers, clinging to the cross of Jesus. Johannes von Staupitz tells a frightened young Luther, "Bind yourself to Christ, and you will know God's love." Jesus the Sacramental Word is the *Estela—the* Signpost—to which the Christian preacher, like Dominic, clings without fail. Or perhaps better, it is *that* Word that clings to us, that "binds" himself to us—"No one can come to me unless drawn by the Father who sent me; and I will raise that person up on the last day" (John 6:44), and, "I am the way, and the truth, and the life. No one comes to the Father except through me" (John 14:6).

But there are other *estelas* that sprout from the Word, like the shoots from the vine (John 15:1–5), by the power of the Spirit. In the last chapter, I presented four characteristics of the imagination of the poor. There is a fifth of great importance for the preacher: sacrificial service of the community centered in the option for the poor. A center piece of Latin American theology is proclaiming to the poor God's gracious love.[6] How does the Church preach God's passionate, merciful, gratuitous love in Jesus and in the Spirit—*the* Christian faith—to the poor (Gutiérrez)? How are the poor told of the option that God has taken on their behalf? This is *the* hermeneutical problem that confronts theology as addressed to followers of Jesus. In the style of Dietrich Bonhoeffer, faith and obedience are united. God's option becomes *my* option. Believers place themselves in radical solidarity with the poor. The questions of the poor become the questions of the Church. The pastoral agent, in solidarity with the poor and their imagination, proclaims God's option for the poor again and yet again. The poor, in turn, experience the love of God through the solidarity expressed among the *pueblo*. If the presence of the God of Jesus in the Spirit is discerned in the faces of the poor (*Puebla* 31–39), there is a mystical communion—the presence of God is manifested in the *pueblo*, and Jesus identifies himself with the poor and the least (Matt 25:31–46). The cry of the Spirit, as Víctor Codina says, becomes the cry of the poor. The poor suffer premature death in all its forms—injustice, hunger, unemployment, oppression, repression, exile. But their imagination is rooted in the Spirit of life, experienced by the poor in God's option for life through the cross and resurrection of Jesus.

Praxis and mission are the litmus test of discipleship, faith in *nepantla* with obedience, and the goal of the ecclesial community. Praxis is the starting point. It is centered in the grace of God and directed toward the

6. Nickoloff, ed., *Gustavo Gutiérrez*, 272.

mission of Jesus, the reign of God. God opts for the poor in the praxis of the ecclesial community:

> [T]he church [is the] creation of the grace of God and [the] fruit of the cross of Christ. Its contrast to pagan society does not stem from "efficiency and moralism," but from the miracle of the in-breaking reign of God. It is for this reason that the guilty and the unsuccessful have a place in the church, for grace comes to perfection in human impotence. And it is for this reason that the miracle of new creation shines most beautifully in the church when it emerges as love and reconciliation in situations which— seen from a human perspective—seem lost and hopeless.[7]

The mission of the Triune God is ecclesial praxis. Víctor Codina and José Comblin remind us of the image of St. Irenaeus of Lyons often forgotten in the North Atlantic imagination: the two "hands" of God are Jesus and the Spirit. They are the "mission" of God which, as Allan Figueroa Deck says, "has a Church."

Praxis discipleship is grace. Praxis is, at core, the work of the God of Jesus in the Spirit whose option is for the poor and the exiled. The center is grace—a grace that is not "cheap." The faithful disciple, in praxis, is invited into God's mission with all its costly consequences:

> Discipleship of Jesus in no way begins by being asked to live more heroically than others do or have done in the past. It rather begins with a super-abundant gift. Jesus points with his entire existence to the miracle occurring in history, to the arrival of the reign of God. This miracle could not be brought about by human strength; it was uncontrollable and completely gratuitous. Discipleship means to sense the miracle of the reign of God and to pursue radically the path of Jesus, fascinated by the gift of a new possibility of human community.[8]

For the preacher, the event of proclamation holds a place of honor in Christian praxis. When Bartolomé de Las Casas, after trying many other options, approached Domingo de Betanzos to discern his true calling of accompanying the indigenous poor, Domingo told him that *now* was the time for *preaching*.[9] The same advice applies to the twenty-first century

---

7. Lohfink, *Jesus and Community*, 180.

8. Ibid., 179.

9. Pérez Fernández, *El Itinerario Espiritual*, 16.

disciple of Jesus. The preacher, as ecclesial disciple, is invited to take on the imagination of the poor in solidarity. This involves three tasks. The first is to nurture a strong operative theology; the second is to develop methods of textual and congregational hermeneutics; and the third is to cultivate the rhetorical skills necessary for touching the imagination of the people.[10]

First, the preaching task involves nurturing a strong operative theology. Theologically, preaching is *epiclesis*, a "calling down" of the Holy Spirit that makes *this gathering Church*, in the words of Dietrich Bonhoeffer; and *anamnesis*, a "doing in memory" of Jesus—Metz's "dangerous memory"— by the power of the Spirit. It is liturgical *prayer*. Its language is not didactic but *symbolic*—the root meaning of inductive preaching and the "new homiletic." Preaching does not *lead* to the Eucharist, as some liturgists suggest. It *is* the Eucharist, a part of the entire sacramental action where no one moment is "magic," but all is *epiclesis* and *anamnesis*. Luther and many others have referred to preaching by using *sacramental* language. Preaching is, in the most profound sense, a *sacrament*.

The preacher must spend time in study and prayer to discern his or her operative theology. Preachers are theologians. We may not be professional academic theologians. But we are "resident" theologians in the communities in which we preach, where what we do is much closer to the Eastern Orthodox notion of theology as contemplation of the Holy Trinity than it is to the North Atlantic academy. Study, for the preacher, is a way of life, a discipline of contemplating the Trinity in the events of everyday life. This contemplation—Thomas Aquinas gives priority to study and prayer as contemplating and "sharing the fruits"—means struggling with challenging texts and taking the time in our busy schedules to be attentive, in contemplation, to the urgings of grace. We do not preach academic theology, nor do we preach a particular method of prayer. But we do take theology and the gleanings from contemplation and apply them pastorally to the people with whom we minister. A privileged locus for this is the world of theological study and contemplative prayer. It is often said that academic theology is "second theology," and preaching occupies the privileged place of "first theology."[11] While every theologian may not be a gifted preacher, every preacher must be a gifted theologian. And every preacher must be a person of prayer.

10. Heille, ed., *Theology of Preaching*, 11.

11. Ibid., 12.

Second, the preacher must develop a methodology for textual and congregational hermeneutics—the "science" of the *interpretation* of Scripture and the community. This means the tedious but rewarding task of biblical exegesis and hermeneutics of the texts to be preached. Sandra Schneiders suggests a methodology for approaching the scriptural text—to consider "the world behind the text, the world of the text, and the world before (in front of) the text."[12] Carlos Mesters calls this *pretexto, texto,* and *contexto*—"pre-text," text, and context. The world behind the text, the *pretexto,* is the familiar exegetical methodology which every seminary student learns—historical-critical exegesis. The subject of the world behind the text is the text in its historical milieu. What is the meaning of a particular word? Why does the author insist on a particular phrasing? What is the world of the author? When was this text written? To whom was it originally addressed? What clues for interpretation are gleaned from the original languages? This is important preliminary work that seems trivial but is necessary to an integral textual hermeneutic.

Then the world of the text (*texto*) is visited. The world of the text moves beyond traditional historical analysis to literary criticism. Its subject is the text as literature. What does the text itself—independent of the author—say to the reader? How is this text evaluated as literature? Who is the "actual reader," and who is the "implied reader"? What is the historical and cultural context of the reader? Here the preacher begins to move into postmodern literary methodologies.[13] This work is necessary to the act of preaching.

Finally the world before, or in front of, the text (*contexto*) is visited. The subject of this methodology is the reader or, in the context of the poor, the *community* of readers. This is the contextual world of the reader as the "hearer of the word." In the imagination of the poor, the indigenous poor are the *subjects.* What does the preacher proclaim when the poor are subjects, not "objects," of preaching? This is an important question, for in this third step the preacher moves from textual to congregational hermeneutics. A significant way in which the preacher can engage this interpretation is what Reuel Howe calls "Partners in Preaching."[14] He maintains that it is necessary for the preacher *to listen* to the people. This is an important—and often neglected—task in homily preparation. What

12. See Sandra M. Schneiders, *The Revelatory Text.*

13. For a cogent discussion of these methodologies, see Adam, ed., *Handbook.*

14. See Howe, *Partners in Preaching.*

are the *people* saying about the text? What is the context of this historical community? Will the God of mercy touch their lives through this preaching? Howe proposes the formation of small groups of parishioners who meet with the preacher weekly to share the Sunday readings. "Partners in Preaching" has various manifestations; but all are based on significant input from the community. In the context of the imagination of the poor, this means careful *listening* to the voice of the *pueblo*.

Third, the preacher cultivates the rhetorical skills necessary for the preaching to touch the lives and the experience of the people. We have already seen Pedro de Córdoba's methodology for preaching. The *religiosidad popular*, and its manifestation in *flor y canto*, proposes other creative approaches. Perhaps the best thing that a preacher who accompanies the indigenous poor can do is to develop an aesthetical theology, for *flor y canto* so deeply touch the beauty of nature. Recall the discussion of grace in the previous chapter. Where does the preacher perceive beauty? What is the preacher's theology and imagination? A simple "jump start" could be a walk in the woods. Or perhaps the preacher has an ear for music, a heart for poetry, or an eye for art. What do these say to the experience of the people? What do *flor y canto* mean for the indigenous poor?

A good methodology for preaching in any context is the traditional Dominican *contempló*, *studēo*, and *praedico*—prayerful reflection on the readings, study involving exegesis and hermeneutics, and the actual preaching event itself.[15] These three essential branches that sprout from the Sacramental Word (John 15:1–6) are described as follows: first, *contempló*: Early in the week, the preacher sits quietly and passes time with the Sunday readings in *lectio divina* or another scriptural method for prayer, such as Jesuit *collatio*. Scriptures, whether chosen by the preacher or followed from the lectionary, are read slowly and prayerfully. The preacher asks: What do these readings say? Are there any phrases that stand out? What are the people doing? Who are the principal characters? What is the setting? Can I see myself in the readings? And, most importantly in the context of the indigenous poor, what might these readings say to the *pueblo*? Do they address what has happened in the community

15. The words *contempló*, *studēo*, and *praedico* were first applied in reference to Dominican methodology for preaching by Mary Margaret Pazdan, OP, Professor of New Testament at Aquinas Institute of Theology, St. Louis.

during the past week? It is helpful during this stage to reflect with a community. But it is also imperative that I take my own time in *lectio divina*. This perhaps most important step in Dominican methodology respects the scriptural word and what it says in *this* context. No commentaries are consulted yet. Rather, I open my heart to the Sacramental Word of the God of the poor in the Spirit. What does that Word proclaim through *this* scriptural word in *this* context? The Word is "transverbized" in the heart of the preacher, for as it is often said, if this word does not say something to *me*, it certainly will say nothing to the people.

Second is the *studēo*. Joaquin Antonio Peñalosa writes about "remote" and "proximate" preparation for the weekly preaching. Study, he says, is a habit developed over the preacher's lifetime—the "remote" preparation. "Proximate" preparation means bringing this lifetime habit to bear intensely on *these particular readings*.[16] Study involves several steps; but there is no solid *camino* nor sure-fire method—just *estelas* on the sea. Study should include consultation with the best commentaries and in-depth word study and exegesis—i.e., the tedious work of concordances, lexicons, and biblical languages. Karl Barth says the first step in homily preparation is *to go to the text*. The text, he says, *means* the text— the original scriptural languages.[17] Brush off those Greek grammars and lexicons! There are resources available on the Internet as well as specific Scripture computer programs, but be highly selective—don't rely on simple Internet searches or use programs from the clearance tables at your local software store! Invest in a good exegetical program like the *Logos- Libronix* software or *Bible Works*. Join the Society for Biblical Literature. Don't be afraid to use the local university library, if one is available.

The preacher must remember, as well, "remote" preparation. Read, or reread, the books you did not get a chance to study in the seminary— the classics, like Schillebeeckx's *Christ the Sacrament of the Encounter with God*, Rahner's *Hearer of the Word*, Barth's *Epistle to the Romans*, Semmelroth's *The Preaching Word*, or Bonhoeffer's *Discipleship*. Consult the Fathers and the Mothers. What does Irenaeus or Hippolytus say? What does Gregory of Nazianzus suggest? Why did Macrina the Younger tell her brother Basil, after he returned from studies in Athens, that she had to teach him "real theology"? What did Chrysostom or Augustine say regarding classic Christian rhetoric? But also read the new theolo-

---

16. Peñalosa, *Manual de la Imperfecta Homilía*, 15–31.

17. Barth, *Homiletics*, 96–98.

gies, particularly those presenting different or challenging ecclesiologies. Subscribe to *Journal for Preachers* or *The Living Pulpit*. Don't forget the "new homiletic." Thomas Troeger, Barbara Brown Taylor, Fred Craddock, Eugene Lowry, David Buttrick, Anna Carter Florence, and Walter Bruegge-mann all remind us what "inductive preaching" is all about, and why it is so important. During these first two stages, it is important not to neglect newer methods of biblical interpretation, like social scientific studies, ancient Mediterranean cultural contextual studies, contemporary liter-ary approaches to Scripture, or reader contextual methods. I have already spoken of ways to approach these postmodern methodologies.

Third, there is *praedico*—the actual preaching and the organization of the material. How shall I preach? Will I write the text out? Will I use the text during the preaching? How will I familiarize myself with it before hand? Will it be "proclaimed" or "read"? If I do not use the text, how will I consign it to memory? These are all important questions for *praedico*, remembering the counsel of Robert Farrar Capon: do everything to pre-pare the preaching responsibly, but on Sunday morning turn things over tp the Spirit of the Sacramental Word.

Many preachers now use a system of "moves," though they have also been called "points" (James Henry Harris, Joaquin Antonio Peñalosa) or "sequences" (Joseph Webb). These have been the basic building blocks for preachers the last twenty-five years or so. They generally follow the in-ductive method. Unlike the deductive method, which "deduces" from the general to the particular, inductive thinking "moves" from the particular to the general. In the 1970s, preachers such as Fred Craddock (also a New Testament scholar) and David Buttrick pioneered what became known as the "new homiletic," which was marked by homiletic moves and the inductive approach to preaching. The new homiletic departs from the use of a deductive outline or text and thinks in "moves"—how does my preaching "flow," inductively, from one move to the next?

At the beginning of the chapter, I promised some *estelas en la mar* for preaching the Sacramental Word of the God of the poor, in the Spirit, from the imagination of the poor. There are, of course, an infinite number of *estelas* available to every preacher. I find it helpful, though, to begin from the standpoint of five theological categories: The Church, the poor, grace, Scriptures, and Christian hope.

∿

As I have stressed throughout this book, Trinitarian theology, Christology, pneumatology, and ecclesiology are all integrally connected, inextricably intertwined in *nepantla*. All of these can be combined into one *estela*—the Church. A strong, living ecclesiology is indispensable to any theology of preaching. But living ecclesiology means a *Church* that is vibrant with the Holy Trinity and the Spirit in its Christological proclamation of the Sacramental Word. The Second Vatican Council tried to recover the Trinitarian ecclesiology of Scripture and the Fathers and Mothers of the first centuries in *Lumen Gentium*, when it placed the Church in analogous and mysterious relationship with the Holy Trinity. As God in Godself is communitarian and relational, so is the Church. This is what, I think, Dietrich Bonhoeffer means when he insists that the proper analogy for God is neither *being* (neo-Scholasticism) nor *faith* (Barth), but *relation*. The Church is the people of God, corresponding to its relationship with the first Person of the Holy Trinity. The Hebrew Scriptures develop the image of the people of God. God directly identifies who God is *in relationship* with the people (Exod 3:14). God promises to dwell among the people—to "tent" among them—and to be their God (Exod 29:45). They are to be holy because God is holy (Lev 19:2). The Church, the council says, is also the body of Christ, corresponding and correlating to the Son in the Incarnation. The council reminds us of our rich heritage in the Pauline imagery of the body of Christ (Rom 12:5, 1 Cor 10:16, 1 Cor 12:12–27).

But although the Church is Trinitarian, the Spirit was not sufficiently treated at the Second Vatican Council. There was need for further development of the mystery of the Spirit in analogous relationship with the Church. This was pointed out by many Orthodox and Protestant observers, as well as official Catholic *periti* to the council like Hans Küng, who suggested further exploration of the Church as the "creation of the Spirit" so that the Trinitarian imagery could be enriched. Paul, connecting the Spirit with the members of Christ's body, calls individual members of the Church the "temple of the Holy Spirit" (1 Cor 6:19) and integrally connects humanity, creation, and the Church with the Spirit (Romans 8).

The Second Vatican Council and contemporary theology remind us that the Church cannot be divorced from the Holy Trinity without damaging its very essence. Jesus Christ *is* the Sacramental Word of the God of the poor and, ultimately, the one necessary *Estela* (Luke 10:42) for preaching. But St. Irenaeus of Lyons said many centuries ago that the Holy Trinity means that God has "two hands": Jesus and the Spirit. These are the "missions" of the Trinity and the missions of the community "full of the Trinity": the Church. The life of the preacher revolves wholly around Jesus, the Sacramental Word of the poor—prayer, play, pondering, preaching, and pastoral endeavors. Preaching is *epiclesis*, the presence of the Spirit invoked by Jesus in the resurrection upon the Church community, as Paul Evdokimov says; and *anamneses*, the dangerous memory of the living Sacramental Word in the Spirit. Preaching is, as Bonhoeffer says, the living Christ walking among the people. The imagination of the poor in preaching is prophetic, and its prophetic dimension depends wholly on the centrality of Word and Spirit, the "missions" of God. The Barmen Declaration affirmed over seventy years ago: "Jesus Christ, as he is attested to us in Holy Scripture, is the one Word of God whom we have to hear, and whom we have to trust and obey in life and in death." That one Sacramental Word speaks with God's voice in the Spirit, which hovers over the waters—the Church community—and creates new life (Gen 1:2) through our inadequacies and shadows in the pulpit.

North Atlantic preachers are, by and large, individualistic in their approach to preaching. This comes, perhaps, from generations of the Western focus on the interior self and the individual as locus of the imagination. But the imagination of the poor, before anything else, is communal. The poor, like the Trinity, live community in relationship. Despite many years in a post-Vatican II Church, Catholics in the North Atlantic have yet to appreciate fully the biblical images of the people of God and the body of Christ developed by the council—let alone any kind of theology of *epiclesis*. Nor have North American Protestants fared better—particularly the more fundamentalist communities. Do we preach only "Jesus and me"? Or is it Jesus the Sacramental Word of the God of the poor by the power of the Spirit, and the community of his followers, that we preach?

There are various ways of getting at a more communal approach to preaching. Is preaching expositional sermon—"monologue"—or is it homily, a "dialog," with the people? Do we engage the community as preachers? Are they actively "participating"? This mean much more than mere "listening"—although there is an *active* listening in true ecclesial preaching that the preacher can discern through the people's attention span! The preacher, in the style of Latin American indigenous communities and the *comunidades eclesiales de base*, can engage the community in a Marins-style "chit-chat"—an invitation to the people to converse briefly with one another about something said in the homily or a particular question.

The preacher should be deeply conscious, at every moment of preaching, of the imagination of the poor. Preaching is primarily a liturgical act. Like the liturgy itself, it is not the precise language of the theological classroom. Rather it lives, as does the imagination of the poor, within the realm of theological metaphor and symbol. There should be an innate confidence on the part of the preacher in the imagination of the poor to make the necessary connection between liturgy and life, between symbol and meaning. Indigenous theologians are right when they say that contemporary theology has not sufficiently accounted for the *religiosidad popular*. A respect for the faith of the people and the imagination of the *pueblo* means an assurance in their capacity to make meaningful and symbolic connections that come out of the experience of *nepantla*. The preacher accompanies the poor through vivid use of theology, metaphor, and symbol so that the Sacramental Word of the God of the poor is transverbized into the *pueblo* by the power of the Spirit. The preacher remembers that preaching is part of the entire liturgical act. It calls down the Spirit on the poor and makes them *pueblo*, accompanying the people in an *anamnesis* that powerfully recalls the Sacramental Word and the "dangerous memory" evoked from it.

I am often asked by sincere North Atlantic preachers who do not directly minister in poor communities what they can do to foster solidarity with the *pueblo*. The asking of the question itself shows solidarity with the poor. But more is required (Mic 6:8, Luke 12:48)—perhaps even *much* more of the preacher who works in a wealthy community, for the comfortable do not like to be made uncomfortable—and that is what preaching the Sacramental Word from the imagination of the poor often does. Where did preachers ever get the idea that people always had to *like* their preaching? That is, unfortunately, still drilled into homiletic students in the United States. Critically negative comments on a student homily are often given priority for the wrong reasons in too many schools of theology and ministry. Positive comments are associated with "good" homilies, negative with "bad." I remember an older friend, a mentor preacher now retired, who passed the majority of his pastorates in wealthy communities. He was one of the kindest priests I have ever met. He also had a deep love for the poor and a thirst for justice that he constantly referenced in his preaching. This made him unpopular in most of the communities in which he ministered. A pastor in a wealthy community is called to be a prophetic witness, and that is *not* a place any of us like to be.

But prophetic preaching from First World "comfortable" pulpits does not exclusively mean denunciation of structural sin. What if the preacher looked for the *anawim* in his or her own community and made special attempts to engage them in the preaching? The poor *are* the exiled and the excluded, Víctor Codina and Pablo Richard remind us—in *every* context. If you are a male preacher, how do you invite women into the preaching? How does the preacher accept and include the immigrant and the stranger? Is there a large African-American community in the parish in which you minister? Are we preachers sufficiently sensitive to the physically disabled, older people, homosexuals, the young, in our preaching? This kind of preaching is challenging—but what truly ecclesial preaching is not?!

All preaching is flawed. The preacher, no matter how "good," no matter how "easy" preaching becomes, no matter how competent in the use of inductive methodology, the "new homiletic," or even traditional deductive preaching, is simply not up to the task, for preaching is really the work of the Spirit. The problem is that most preachers don't *really* believe preaching is the work of the *Spirit*. Barbara Brown Taylor speaks powerfully about the carelessness with which we preachers approach the Sunday homily:

> Any way you look at it, the act (preaching) is a foolhardy thing to do. Who will volunteer to conduct lightening from heaven to earth? Who will offer a guided tour through the beating heart of God? People more faithful than we have gotten killed doing things like that, and yet plenty of us climb into pulpits Sunday after Sunday with no more sense of danger than if we were climbing into our cars to go fetch a quart of milk. We don't even put our seatbelts on. Why? Because we do not expect anything serious to happen, any more than our congregations do.[18]

18. Taylor, *When God Is Silent*, 86.

Preaching, in a nutshell, is wholly the work of the God of the poor, through the Sacramental Word and by the power of the Holy Spirit. There is no amount of human effort that is going to make this homily "perfect." Preaching is, very simply, not about *us* as preachers. It is about *God*. Paul is blunt: "For we do not proclaim ourselves; we proclaim Jesus Christ as Lord and ourselves as your slaves for Jesus' sake . . . But we have this treasure in clay jars, so that it may be made clear that this extraordinary power belongs to God and does not come from us" (2 Cor 4:5, 7). This is a tough pill to swallow for many preachers. We have become too accustomed to Pelagius and his disciples. Isn't preaching, after all, about the *effort* with which the preacher prepares? We *must* emphatically answer "no." Preaching is *grace*, not effort. Bonhoeffer insightfully says that if the preacher is exhausted after the homily, then something is wrong. Christian belief, from the very first centuries, is that the reign of God is not brought about by our efforts but wholly by the free, gratuitous, undeserved, mysterious grace of God.

The imagination of the poor is not Pelagian. It moves in the Trinitarian circle of grace. But it is unlike the "cheap" grace of classic North Atlantic "Pauline justification." It is, perhaps, much closer to the Eastern Church's "synergy" of the Spirit and the Church. Víctor Codina points to what Chrysostom said centuries ago: "God does the work, and we do the sweating." José Marins often says in workshops with base ecclesial communities, "God will *never* do for you what *you* can do for yourself." God works *through* our humanity. "Oh necessary sin of Adam and Eve," we sing in the Easter proclamation. St. Athanasius said that the reason God in Jesus takes on our humanity is precisely to *divinize* it in the Spirit. Our inadequacies have been seen by North Atlantic justification theology as something that God "uses" *in spite of* the flaws—not *because of* them. This is the flip side of Pelagianism, and it, too, is heresy because it denies both Pauline theology *and* the doctrine of grace that St. Thomas Aquinas worked so diligently to define. Aquinas, says Anton Pegis, directed his efforts toward the basic problem of Platonism, an "error regarding existence."[19] Platonism, which so affected (and still affects!) Christian theology, separates the material from the "spiritual." The error is unmasked by Aquinas, according to Pegis, in three primary areas: being, humanity, and knowledge.[20] Platonic thinking tears soul from body in the human

19. Pegis, *An Introduction to St. Thomas*, xv.
20. Ibid., xvi.

being. The body, the material, is insignificant; the soul, the spiritual, is "real." Aquinas' thought provides a radical break from this thinking, which is why he was, and is, so controversial in the history of theology. In theological terms, though, Aquinas is thoroughly Pauline. Grace is not shared by God *in spite of* this human body, which is "nothing" in Platonic and Neo-Platonic thought, but *because of* this humanity—body *and* soul—created in God's image and likeness (Gen 1:26). For Paul *and* Aquinas, God's gracious love is lavishly outpoured—even in the midst of personal and structural sin—in a superabundance (Rom 5:20) upon humankind: "God *so loved the world* that (God) gave (God's) only Son, so that everyone who believes in him may not perish but may have *eternal life*" (John 3:16).

God does not despise the world. God loves the world. Grace means this and only this: that our human failures, flaws, errors, and sinfulness are not the badges of shame that classic justification theology has led us to believe. They are something God *takes on* in Jesus and *recreates* in the Spirit, in God's mysterious plan, wholly for God's purposes. God acts not in spite of our flaws but *through* them, *because of* them. This is a mantra every preacher should repeat. Preaching is flawed—sometimes seriously. But that does not matter. The Sacramental Word of the God of the poor is transverbized by the Spirit in preachers (*epiclesis*) so that it can be transverbized into the Word in the womb of the *pueblo* (*anamnesis*).

Preaching should arise from the classic themes presented in Scripture. The Bible has been called "the book of the Church." God's word, though written during a specific historical time, is normative for followers of Jesus, the Church community, in every age. This is particularly important for the preacher. The Church's book speaks the language of the Spirit, the language of the Sacramental Word. This language is *contextual*. That is why Dietrich Bonhoeffer could rightly say that the call of Jesus is as clear for us today as it was for the first disciples. Scripture, the book of the Church, transcends time and culture, which is why it can be of *every* time and culture and should never be interpreted in isolation, but always in *community*. Preaching is the privileged *locus theologicus* for this hermeneutic.

There are some who advocate going outside Scripture for the material of the Sunday preaching. For instance, there is a movement in some

Catholic dioceses to return to the "doctrinal preaching" of the past (I'm sure Protestant and Orthodox Churches have their own equivalent!). These dioceses might have doctrinal outlines for preaching the liturgical year that come from the bishop or the chancery. The connection of these outlines to Scripture is, many times, tentative at best. On the other hand, some liturgists advocate periodic preaching from the classic texts and prayers of the liturgy itself. Both approaches are incomplete, and, in my opinion, they should be avoided. Many years ago, Karl Barth rightly observed: "The first step in preparing a sermon is thus to realize that we must seek the material for it exclusively in the Old Testament and the New. This alone is the material that we must proclaim to the congregation, for as the community of Jesus Christ it is waiting for the food of holy scripture, and nothing else."[21]

This holds especially true, I think, for the preacher who works in a poor community. African-American preaching, so strongly based in Scripture, provides us with a model of preaching that is founded upon the word of God and at the same time speaks strongly to the situation of the poor. Archbishop Oscar Romero has shown us the same path. While avoiding the trap of reactionary Church polity that would regime our every move as preachers into a new biblical fundamentalism, it is, nevertheless, important to advocate for strong scriptural preaching. The powerful biblical themes of creation and covenant, exodus and exile, justice, faith, righteousness, grace, prophecy, compassion, "loving-kindness" and "steadfast-love" (*hesed*), God, Jesus, Spirit, humanity, nature, and the community—all provide ample opportunity to accompany the poor in solidly scriptural preaching.

Perhaps the *estela* of the theological locus of the scriptural word is more *via negativa* than anything else. This *estela* is not license for the preacher to develop a new biblical fundamentalism. Fundamentalism of any kind is an abuse of Scripture as the book of the Church. The fundamentalist preacher himself or herself becomes the scriptural interpreter, outside any kind of ecclesial context. The worst abuses are by those who are convinced that "my way" is "*the* way." The words of Scripture must be the primary material for the preacher, but if they are disconnected from Augustine's "First Book" of creation and life; if they are unrelated to the everyday experiences of the *pueblo* and the poor; or if, in the preacher's zeal to preach only the scriptural word, Church, liturgy,

21. Barth, *Homiletics*, 92–93.

and life are forgotten; then preaching becomes just another form—and a particularly diabolic form at that—of biblical fundamentalism.

Preaching fosters Christian hope. Hope, as we have said, has to do with eschatology. But the eschatology of a healthy theology of preaching is different from that of traditional North Atlantic theology. The eschatology of the theology of preaching has much more to do with the *first days* than the "last." Preaching is deeply connected with the first days of creation leading to the "Eighth Day" (Codina, Evdokimov). It is the sacrament of the *dabar YHWH*. Dietrich Bonhoeffer, in lectures to his students on the first three chapters of Genesis, says that the word of God is inseparably related to creation.[22] Preaching always looks "backward," in hopeful anticipation of the Eighth Day, to those first days, the "and God said" (Gen 1:3–31). Preaching proclaims the "new creation" of the Spirit through the Sacramental Word present in God's holy people:

> Martha said to Jesus, "Lord, if you had been here, my brother would not have died. But even now I know that God will give you whatever you ask of him." Jesus said to her, "Your brother will rise again." Martha said to him, "I know that he will rise again in the resurrection on the last day." Jesus said to her, "I am the resurrection and the life. Those who believe in me, even though they die, will live, and everyone who lives and believes in me will never die." (John 11:21–26)

Martha's immediate concern is that of the traditionally "hopeful" Church —"the resurrection on the *last day*." Jesus tells her that *he is the new creation*, the resurrection and the life. Those who believe in him will live *now*. They become, with Martha, Mary, and Lazarus, a new creation *now*. The concern of the preaching Church is not what God, in God's mysterious plan, will bring about during the "last days." Rather, the new creation is brought about *now*, through the Sacramental Word, in the wind of the Spirit that blows over dried up, old dead bones and makes them live (Ezek 37:1–14). "Lazarus, come out" (John 11:43)—at the Sacramental Word who is Jesus, the Church becomes a new creation. In turn, this newly born Church community proclaims the "preaching Word" that places us, not in the "last times," but in the first days of creation with eyes set on the Eighth Day that will never end.

22. Bonhoeffer, *Creation and Fall*.

Preaching is not primarily directed to the Church *qua* Church. It ultimately has only one purpose—the proclamation of the reign of God, the mission and the praxis of the ecclesial community not really the Church's at all but belonging to the Holy Trinity. The purpose of preaching is solely to animate the community towards *praxis*, to "make this gathering Church" (Bonhoeffer). This is the mission entrusted to the Church by Jesus and the Spirit. It can even be said that preaching is *the* sacrament of the Church. It is *epiclesis*. By the power of the Spirit, the word is transformed into *hope*. Preaching is the leaven for the reign of God (Matt 13:33; Luke 13:21), the mustard seed that grows large (Matt 13:31; Luke 13:19), hope for the reign of God in the face of despair.

Throughout the Acts of the Apostles, preaching is *the* primary activity of the apostles and is directed to the hope for God's reign. Nothing else, as important as it may have been, was to interfere with preaching (Acts 6:2). The apostles are "witnesses to the resurrection" and "ministers of the word" (Acts 3:15; 6:4). For this reason, the Catholic Church associates the preaching ministry integrally with the episcopacy. Presbyters and deacons receive preaching faculties from the bishop. This institutional approach to preaching is important and even Christological. But the role of the Holy Spirit in preaching, and the eschatological hope for the reign of God, should not be forgotten by the Catholic institution, which in recent years has been too restrictive, in my opinion, of those "permitted" to preach in the liturgy. Women and laity "need not apply"—especially tragic in a post-Vatican II Church. Paul says, "There is no longer Jew or Greek, there is no longer slave or free, there is no longer male and female; for all of you are one in Christ Jesus" (Gal 3:28). Ordination is "required" for preaching the liturgical homily in the Catholic Church. But does this not restrict the work of the Spirit? Does this not quench the flame of the Sacramental Word? Is Christian hope preached where ordination is required and the "gifts of the Spirit" (1 Cor 12:4–11) are lost sight of?

I recently heard a story about a Catholic woman with a doctorate in Scripture who listened painfully as an ordained deacon—with little preparation—destroyed the Sunday readings exegetically and theologically. Karl Barth's words are still a timely reminder to those who believe that the Spirit *only* works through the institution: whether bishop or lay, presbyter or woman, deacon or pastor, the preacher *is* himself or herself *vicarius Christi* and *successor apostolorum*.[23] The Orthodox Church has

23. Barth, *Homiletics*, 67.

always spoken of preaching *primarily* as a charism of baptism, not ordination.[24] The Protestant approach is similar and likewise open to the
promptings of the Spirit. Dominican charism of the word in the Catholic
Church has been a constant prophetic reminder seldom heeded by the institution throughout the centuries. Newer indigenous and base ecclesial
approaches of Catholic communities in Latin America are indications of
where the Spirit is moving regarding the preaching charism. They remind
us that the Holy Preaching is not primarily an "office" conferred by the
institution through ordination, but a "way of life" conferred by the Spirit
through baptism.

Perhaps preaching is not an "eighth sacrament." But it is *the* sacramental activity of the Church *par excellence*. It is a sacrament of *hope*, a
sacrament of the reign of God. Edward Schillebeeckx reminds us of this
when he speaks of the word as the *forma* of the sacraments. The word of
God, and preaching, is sacramental, and the sacraments are word of God.
Preaching is a hopeful "sign" of the reign of God—the Sacramental Word
of the God of the poor through the ecclesial community entrusted with
the proclamation of God's reign.

I hope that these *estelas* are of some small help to those who preach
"Jesus Christ and him crucified" (1 Cor 2:2) from the perspective of
the imagination of the poor. The One whom we follow—the One who
"preaches the Good News to the poor" (Luke 4:18)—is the One who
chooses the poor and the exiled, the Word of God uttered in the Spirit to
all who will listen, the Sacramental Word who loves all unconditionally
but chooses the poor for God's own purposes. James tells us preachers:
"Listen, my beloved brothers and sisters. Has not God chosen the poor
in the world to be rich in faith and to be heirs of the kingdom that he
has promised to those who love him" (Jas 2:5)? But perhaps the words
of the great Paul of Tarsus are the best injunction to all who follow the
Sacramental Word in the Spirit—that in the Incarnation the "preaching
Word" of God, by the power of the Spirit, becomes poor, indigenous, and
pueblo: "For you know the generous act of our Lord Jesus Christ, that
though he was rich, yet for your sakes he became poor, so that by his
poverty you might become rich" (2 Cor 8:9).

---

24. See, for instance, *Encyclical Letter*.

Preaching Practicum Three

The following two homilies offer examples of preaching from the imagination of the poor while attempting to use methodologies from the experience of the base ecclesial communities and indigenous contexts. The first was preached on the feast of *Nuestra Señora de Guadalupe* (the vigil, also the Second Sunday of Advent, Cycle B of the Roman Catholic Lectionary, 11 December 2005), to the Mexican community at Sacred Heart Parish in Tacoma, Washington. The readings were Isa 61:1–2, 10–11; Luke 1:46–54 (Responsorial); 1 Thess 5:15–24; and John 1:6–8, 19–28. The preaching is an attempt to take one of the most important days in the Mexican community and give it a strong ecclesial emphasis. It was preached in Spanish. What follows is a rough translation of the original homiletic "moves." Indigenous words are explained in parenthetic italics. The introduction and first move retell the story of *Guadalupe* from the *Mexica* perspective using the *Nican Mopohua*, the indigenous account of the story. It also relies on the ecclesiology of Arias Montes, who says that the temple, or "little house," that the *Guadalupana* asked for on Tepeyac *really* refers to the people of God.

Introduction: As Juan Diego Cuauhtlatoatzin (*eagle who speaks*) was crossing Tepeyac for catechism on 9 December 1531, I wonder what he saw? Did he remember Tepeyac as a child? A jewel of Tenochtitlán (*pre-Columbian Mexico City and capital of the Mexica empire*), it overlooked the entire city—which Cortez himself described as more beautiful than any city in Europe. So why did he and the *conquistadores* destroy it? It was set on a large lake—where the eagle with the snake in its beak had arrived eons ago and rested on the cactus (*the symbol on the Mexican*

flag), that was where Tenochtitlán was to be built. On top of Tepeyac was a beautiful temple to Tonantzin, the *teotl* maternal expression of the sacrificial love of Ometéotl on behalf of the people. "Flower and song," he must have thought, *flor y canto*. "Oh, how I long the days when there were no *conquistadores*, when our priests, our *papahuaque*, our wise ones, our *tlamatinime*, and our authorities, our *tlatoani*, gave us wisdom and guidance." But those days were gone. Just ten years earlier, the Spaniards had killed valiant Cuauhtémoc (*nephew of Moctezuma*) and his warriors. "Do they now carry the sun to its place in the noonday sky," thought Cuauhtlatoatzin? That was what all warriors did who gave their lives for the people. "And the women who have died in child-birth—they are so many nowadays," thought Juan Diego. "Do they take the sun to its setting and gently place it to rest in mother earth?" But now Tepeyac was desolate, for in destroying the temple to Tonantzin the Europeans had murdered mother earth—no more trees, no more flower and song, no more life.

Move One: But then Cuauhtlatoatzin heard something, faint, distant. What could it be? One of the ancient songs of his *pueblo* so little heard these days? He went higher up the hill to see—now just a few old stones. Were they singing to him? And why are there roses here in December? "Could I have died," he thought? "Could I be in the paradise of Tláloc, the place of flower and song spoken of by the wise ones?" Cuauhtlatoatzin heard a voice, like he remembered from when his mother brought him to worship here. "Juanito, Juan Dieguito," it called to him. "I am your mother. I am the one who holds your people tenderly. I am the one who will give you compassion and protection. I choose you to be my ambassador, with dignity and honor, to bring the message of the God of justice to the bishop in Mexico City. Tell him I would like a little house built here so I can always be with the people so that I can build them into a *pueblo*." "But *muchachita linda* (*dear little woman*)," he said, "I am just excrement (*taken literally from the Nican Mopohua—what the people felt like after the Conquest*). Send one of our *tlamatinime* or *tlatoani*." "I place all my trust and confidence in you, Juan Dieguito," she told him. "It is you I will send to the bishop. Do not be afraid. You are worthy, blessed with the dignity of the *pueblo* you carry in your heart." And Tepeyac and the people were transformed that day by the God of life through the words of Santa María Tonantzin.

Move Two: John the Baptist is the "voice of the one who cries in the desert, 'Prepare the way of the Lord'" (John 1:23). We listen to the voice crying in the desert, because it points to Jesus. The voice of *La Morenita* (*"the little brown one"—another popular name for Our Lady of Guadalupe*) is soft and tender with Juan Diego. But it is a voice that thunders against the powerful. "God will cast down the mighty from their thrones and lift up the lowly. God will fill the hungry with good things and send the rich away empty." It thundered against the Spaniards who had desecrated the temple and caused so much death. The voice of Santa María Tonantzin points to Jesus. And she invites *us* to point to Jesus. John the Baptist says, "Behold the Lamb of God. I am not worthy to untie his sandals. He must increase, I must decrease." Where do we discern the presence of Jesus today? In our Tepeyacs that are transformed by flower and song? How can the desert we crossed to get to this country be transformed? What about the prejudice we suffer as a *pueblo mexicano*? How can our families be changed with the flower and song of the God of life? Where do we find the presence of Jesus? We look to who we are—the community, the people of God, the body of Christ, the Church. The temple is not only made of stone. The temple is not only the Basilica in Mexico City. The temple is . . . *us*. We are the temple. We are the *casita* that the *Morenita* wishes—not just a temple of stones, but a world of justice and peace built of hearts. The flower and song paradise, the reign of God we proclaim, the injustices we denounce like deportations of our sisters and brothers—*we* are the voice crying in the desert for the living God of Jesus in the Spirit—the living temple, the living Church, the living *pueblo*.

Conclusion: We see flower and song, like Juan Diego Cuauhtlatoatzin, on the barren hill of Tepeyac. Flower and song point us to Jesus, like Our Lady of Guadalupe, and transforms what is dead, what is "excrement," into ambassadors—a temple for Santa María Tonantzin, a Church community of Jesus, now living stones of the *pueblo*. We, the Church community, are the voice crying in the desert in the name of Jesus. Santa María Tonantzin shows us the way, for she points to Jesus present in the ancient culture of our ancestors, present in the *pueblo*, present in us. To Jesus be the glory forever and ever. Amen.

∾

This second homily was preached on the Second Sunday of Lent, Cycle B, 8 March 2009, at Holy Spirit Church in Kent, Washington. The readings were excerpts from Gen 22:1–18 (the story of Abraham and Isaac); Rom 8:31–34; and Mark 9:2–10 (the Transfiguration). It was preached in Spanish to a predominantly Mexican community of perhaps some fifteen hundred people, using methodologies suggested by José Marins for the base ecclesial communities and by Gonzalo Ituarte for indigenous Mexican communities. I am grateful to my friend and colleague, María Teresa Montes Lara, OP, for the co-preaching, and to the people of Holy Spirit Parish for the "*chit-chat*."

~

Introduction: (*Marins and indigenous community-style "chit-chat" for the first few minutes between two and three people in proximity. The question is posed: How do we live our baptism? Folks are invited to respond publically with one word or phrase. I listen especially for several things: God "Father," Son, Spirit, and the Church community "full of the Trinity" [Evdokimov]. I briefly review the words spoken out by the people: "grace" for "Father," and "pardon of sins" for the Son; the Holy Spirit is specifically mentioned by one person—I stress the connection to the community; and the word "community" itself is related to the "cloud" of the Spirit that make us "Church community."*) Last Sunday, we began a reflection on baptism. Baptism is our focus for the Lenten season. The catechumens remind us, in their journey, of our own baptismal call. There's an important question that we need to answer—how do we live our baptism?

Move One: At the Transfiguration, the disciples are bathed in the light of the Trinity. Peter's response is profound—"Master, it is good for us to be here." We usually give Peter a "rough time" because he wants to stay on the mountain. But the challenge for Peter was not really his desire to "stay on the mountain." It was, rather, how to bring the mountain on the journey! The challenge is "bringing" Mount Tabor with us wherever we go, wherever our baptism commitment leads us. Maybe that's what Jesus means when he says we can "move mountains" (Matt 17:20). Maybe it's "moving" the mount of the Transfiguration by responding, even on the road to Jerusalem, to our baptismal call. When we're bathed in the light of the Trinity and baptized into that holy name, we become a "royal priesthood," as Peter would say: "You are a chosen race, a royal priesthood, a holy nation, God's own people" (1 Pet 2:9). We are "transfigured" by the light who is Jesus, the Beloved One, to whom we listen. We, with Peter, James, and John, are taken up into the mysterious cloud to hear the voice and to see the light. We are immersed in that light by the waters of our baptism. We are "transfigured" with Jesus in the light of the Trinity by our baptism.

Move Two: I read an essay a few days ago by Benedictine Sr. Joan Chittister (16 February 2009, *National Catholic Reporter*). She talks about the recent announcement from the Vatican of the "apostolic visitation" of women religious (not *men*, she points out) in the United States. She says that perhaps it's good, for men in the Church rarely pay attention to the great work that has been done by women in consecrated life. When she was young, she says, there was at least one preaching a year on consecrated life. Not so anymore. I'm embarrassed to say I've not been much better. It's sad, because Catholic sisters are about the closest we Catholics get to women "priests." Oh, sisters are not "ordained." But they are priests, with all of us who are baptized. I am not a priest so much because of my ordination, but because of my baptism. My ordination makes me a "presbyter"—that's the word in the New Testament, and it means, simply, "elder." The older I get, the more I realize that it's true! The priesthood we celebrate on this feast of the Transfiguration is the call of our baptism.

Move Three: Sr. María Teresa shares some words about the priestly baptismal call of the consecrated life. She speaks of her own baptismal call. She will never be "ordained" because she is a woman—but her baptism, she says, makes her a priest. It begins in the journey up the mountain of the Transfiguration with Jesus, and she, like all the baptized, is bathed there in the light of the Trinity. She speaks of her baptism into a Church, and into an indigenous culture as well. She was baptized, she says, in the town of Yanhuitlán in Oaxaca, Mexico, a descendent of the Mixteca Alta *culture; she was baptized at the ancient font of the Church of Santo Domingo de Guzman—"I am a Dominican," she says. The ancient font was carved by indigenous workers centuries ago out of an old large ceremonial stone supported by four Quetzalcóatls, the plumed serpent* teotl. *The font reminds her of two things—the call, through baptism, to follow Jesus; and her indigenous roots.*

Conclusion: We are priests, sisters and brothers, by our baptism. Blessed be God, through Jesus, in the Spirit, who calls us to the Church community. Amen.

Conclusion
Word, Spirit, and *Pueblo*

Christian theology, along with the practice of preaching, has always considered Jesus the incarnate Word of the Triune God as essential to the theological and pastoral endeavor. Though the Christocentric imagination is not a unique innovation of contemporary theologians in the North Atlantic or Latin America, it is nevertheless being rediscovered by many today. The person of Jesus is central to the imagination of the poor. Jesus is the Sacramental Word of the God of the poor—*the* Good News for the *pueblo*. Jesus, the incarnate Word, becomes poor, becomes *pueblo*, by the power of the Holy Spirit. The Sacramental Word is *made flesh* in the imagination of the *pueblo*:

> Jesus evangelizes the poor because he himself is very poor: He is born in a manger, he lives without having a place to lay his head, and he dies stripped and naked on a cross. He evangelizes them because he dwells very closely with the marginalized *pueblo*, and because he has a merciful heart and takes compassion on their needs. He himself is the Good News for them. For this reason he has been consecrated and sent in mission, because he knows that the poor are less attached to riches and more open to the Word.[1]

When the word is transverbized into the poor through preaching, the *pueblo* are transverbized into Jesus Christ Sacramental Word of the God of the poor. The Spirit is "invoked" upon the *pueblo* through preaching that proceeds *from* their imagination. Preaching is an *epiclesis* from imagination to imagination—Sacramental Word to preacher,

1. Saravia, *El Camino de Jesús*, 125.

Spirit to Church community, incarnate Word to *pueblo*. For the preacher who accompanies the poor, the words proclaimed in *epiclesis* find their center in the Sacramental Word. The poor are consequently open to the Sacramental Word in communion, because the *pueblo* is, at its source, communion. The words, while necessary, are of less importance than this integral communion, which is Word, Spirit, and *pueblo*. If the preacher, in solidarity with the imagination of the poor, is deeply aware of this nepantlic communion, the words of the preacher become the words of the "preaching Word." The poor, through the power of the Spirit at work in their imagination, discern the presence of the Sacramental Word. How this happens is nothing less than miraculous.

The "miraculous" can summarize everything I have attempted to say. The word "miracle" has been among the most abused in the history of theology. Perhaps we have been wrong from the start in using it at all; for John the Evangelist prefers the word "sign." We have grown theologically accustomed to seeing the miraculous as the "extraordinary," the "super-natural." A miracle is something that takes place "outside of" nature. In this sense, we have even abused the word "sign"—"When the crowds were increasing, he began to say, 'This generation is an evil generation; it asks for a sign, but no sign will be given to it except the sign of Jonah'" (Luke 11:29). A miracle is a *sign* of God's love that happens in the midst of the ordinary—usually something to which we don't even "pay attention."

Gregory Heille has said that the most important thing to learn in a homiletic classroom is "paying attention."[2] Most preachers don't really "pay attention," though. We look for the supernatural, the magical—even without thinking—so that our preaching will "touch" (read "manipulate") the imagination of the people. Unfortunately, such preaching will never touch, will never "move," the imagination of the poor—or any imagination. Only preaching that comes out of concrete, everyday, ordinary life will do. Such preaching is "miraculous" because it learns to pay attention to life *as it is* and not to look for illusion and magic.

Unfortunately, North Atlantic imagination by and large still sees the miraculous, instead of something ordinary and natural, as "magic." But in the imagination of the poor, the "miraculous" is constantly around us, in the earth, in the sea, in the sky, in the very roots of our humanity. This is what *nepantla* expresses. To see the miracle as magic, as something extraordinary, is to tear it apart into the Western dualism that has been so

2. Heille, ed., *Theology of Preaching*, 11.

destructive in the history of theology—and continues to be perpetrated by our preachers and our theologians.

The early Church was on to something when it used the words "sacrament" and "mystery" interchangeably. Perhaps we need to recover the sense that the sacrament, the sign of God's passionate love, is not "supernatural" at all. It is a very ordinary, natural "mystery." "Mystery" is that which is not fully understood. It cannot be controlled and is solely dependent upon the grace and mercy of God. But grace is God's *life* in *communion* with the *pueblo*—nothing more, nothing less. Grace is *not* magic—but it *is* miraculous. There is nothing magical about the invocation of the Holy Spirit in the *epiclesis* of preaching that brings about the presence of the Sacramental Word in the *pueblo*. Through the preaching event, a miracle does indeed occur. The Sacramental Word identifies with the *pueblo*.

When Jesus Christ Sacramental Word of the God of the poor is discerned in the words of the preacher, it is not so much through the words themselves but in *miraculous communion*. The *pueblo* "drinks from their own well," says Gustavo Gutiérrez. The well is the source, the *ojo de agua*—the Sacramental Word transverbized in communion with the *pueblo* by the overshadowing of the Spirit:

> The image of a well is used here because a spirituality is indeed like living water that springs up in the very depths of the experience of faith. John writes . . . "Out of (the believer's) heart shall flow rivers of living water" (7:38). The life signified in the image of water comes to us through encounter with the Lord . . . That is what many Christians are now experiencing in Latin America. To be a follower of Jesus requires walking with, and being committed to, the poor: within such commitment Christians encounter the Lord.[3]

Without this source that is Word and Spirit, and this communion that is *pueblo*, our words as preachers mean *nothing*. This is, perhaps, the deepest insight of Latin American theology, the imagination of the poor, and the indigenous and mystical *pueblo*. For our God, the God of "mercy within mercy within mercy" (Thomas Merton), the God of the poor, wishes nothing more than self-communication with the beloved *pueblo*. God *chooses* the poor. This is the core meaning of the Incarnation of the Sacramental Word by the power of the Spirit. And God *chooses* our

3. Nickoloff, *Gustavo Gutiérrez*, 304.

feeble words if we but open ourselves to the Sacramental Word and to the poor and their imagination. Dead bones *live* by the breath of the Spirit (Ezek 37:9–14). Then the greatest miracle in graced nature occurs: our words are transverbized and become Word. Our words, in Jesus Christ Sacramental Word of the God of the poor, become *pueblo*.

Bibliography

Abbott, Walter W., editor. *The Documents of Vatican II: In a New and Definitive Translation*. With commentaries and notes by Catholic, Protestant, and Orthodox Authorities. Translation directed by Joseph Gallagher. New York: Herder & Herder, 1966.

Adam, A. K. M., editor. *Handbook of Postmodern Biblical Interpretation*. St. Louis: Chalice, 2000.

Aquinas, St. Thomas. *Aquinas's Shorter Summa: Saint Thomas's Own Concise Version of His Summa Theologica*. Manchester, NH: Sophia Institute Press, 2002.

———. *Summa Theologiae*. Online: http://www.newadvent.org/summa/.

Arguedas, José María. *Deep Rivers*. Translated by Frances Horning Barraclough. Long Grove, IL: Waveland, 2002.

Arias Montes, Manuel. *Y la Palabra de Dios Se Hizo Indio: Una Teología y Práctica Inculturada y Liberadora—Una Propuesta desde Oaxaca, México*. México, D.F.: Dabar, 1998.

Barth, Karl. *Church Dogmatics* II/2. Translated by G. T. Thomson. Edinburgh: T. & T. Clark, 1957.

———. *The Epistle to the Romans*. Translated by E. C. Hoskyns. New York: Oxford University Press, 1968.

———. *Homiletics*. Louisville: Westminster John Knox, 1991.

———. *The Word of God and the Word of Man*. Translated by Douglas Horton. New York: Harper, 1957.

Basilas, Elías, ed. *Jesús Nuestro Amigo*. Mexico, D.F.: Obra Nacional de la Buena Prensa, 1999.

Berryman, Phillip. *Liberation Theology: The Essential Facts about the Revolutionary Movement in Latin America and Beyond*. New York: Pantheon, 1987.

Bethel, Leslie. *The Cambridge History of Latin America, Volume 1: Colonial Latin America*. Cambridge: Cambridge University Press, 1984.

Biblia Latinoamérica. Estella, Navarra: Verbo Divino, 2004.

———. Madrid: Ediciones Paulinas, 1995.

Boff, Leonardo. *Jesus Christ Liberator: A Critical Christology for Our Time*. Translated by Patrick Hughes. Maryknoll, NY: Orbis, 1978.

Bonhoeffer, Dietrich. *Dietrich Bonhoeffer Works, Vol. 3, Creation and Fall*. Edited by John W. de Gruchy. Translated by Douglas Stephen Bax. Minneapolis: Fortress, 2004.

———. *Dietrich Bonhoeffer Works*, Vol. 4, *Discipleship*. Edited by John D. Godsey and Geffrey B. Kelly. Minneapolis: Fortress, 2001.

————. *Dietrich Bonhoeffer Works,* Vol. 1, *Sanctorum Communio: A Theological Study of the Sociology of the Church.* Edited by Clifford J. Green. Translated by Reinhard Krauss and Nancy Lukens. Minneapolis: Fortress, 1998.

————. *Letters and Papers from Prison: Enlarged Edition.* Edited by Eberhard Bethge. New York: Simon & Schuster, 1997.

————. "On the Question of Boundaries and Church Union." In *Testament to Freedom: The Essential Writings of Dietrich Bonhoeffer,* edited by Geffrey B. Kelly and F. Burton Nelson, 158–67. San Francisco: Harper, 1990.

Busto, Rudy V. "The Predicament of *Neplanta* [*sic*]: Chicano(a) Religions in the Twenty-First Century." In *New Horizons in Hispanic/Latino(a) Theology,* edited by Benjamin Valentín. Philedelphia: Pilgrim, 2003.

Buttrick, David. *Homiletic: Moves and Structures.* Minneapolis: Fortress, 1989.

Byassee, Jason. "The Health and Wealth Gospel: Be Happy." *The Christian Century* 144.12 (12 July 2005) 20–23.

Camorlinga Alcaraz, José María. *Dos Religiones: Azteca-Cristiana.* México, D.F.: Plaza y Valdés Editores, 1993.

Capon, Robert Farrar. *The Foolishness of Preaching: Proclaiming the Gospel against the Wisdom of the World.* Grand Rapids: Eerdmans, 1998.

————. *The Parables of the Kingdom.* Grand Rapids: Eerdmans, 1989.

Chauvet, Louis-Marie. *The Sacraments: The Word of God at the Mercy of the Body.* Collegeville MN: Liturgical, 2001.

Cleary, Edward L. "A New Social Structure: Grassroots Christian Communities." In *Crisis and Change: The Church in Latin America Today.* Online: http://www.domcentral.org/library/cleary_books/crisis/crisis04.htm.

Codina, Víctor. *Los Caminos del Oriente Cristiano: Una Iniciación a la Teología Oriental.* Santander: Sal Terrae, 1997.

————. *Creo en el Espíritu Santo.* Santander: Sal Terrae, 1994.

————. *No Extingáis el Espíritu (1 Ts 5,19): Una Iniciación a la Pneumotología.* Santander: Sal Terrae, 2008.

————. *Para Comprender la Eclesiología desde América Latina.* Estella, Navarra: Verbo Divino, 1990.

————. "Sacraments." In *Systematic Theology: Perspectives from Liberation Theology,* edited by Jon Sobrino and Ignacio Ellacuría. Maryknoll, NY: Orbis, 1996.

Comblin, José. *Called for Freedom: The Changing Context of Liberation Theology.* Translated by Phillip Berryman. Maryknoll, NY: Orbis, 1998.

————. *Tiempo de Acción: Ensayo sobre el Espíritu y la Historia.* Lima: Centro de Estudios y Publicaciones, 1986.

Conferencia Episcopal de América Latina. *Asemblea General de Medellín 1968.* Online: http://www.servicioskoinonia.org/biblioteca/bibliodatos1.html?CELAM.

————. *Asemblea General de Puebla 1979.* Online: http://www.servicioskoinonia.org/biblioteca/bibliodatos1.html?CELAM.

Congar, Yves. *The Mystery of the Church.* Translated by A. V. Littledale, Baltimore: Helicon, 1960.

Corbon, Jean. *The Wellspring of Worship.* Translated by Matthew J. O'Connell. San Francisco: Ignatius, 2005.

Craddock, Fred B. *As One without Authority.* Rev. ed. St Louis: Chalice, 2001.

De Lange, Frits. *Waiting for the Word: Dietrich Bonhoeffer on Speaking about God.* Translated by Martin N. Walton. Grand Rapids: Eerdmans, 2000.

De Las Casas, Bartolomé. *The History of the Indies.* Translated and edited by A. Collard. New York: Harper & Row, 1971.

————. *Los Indios de México y Nueva España*, con Edición, Prólogo, Apéndices, y Notas por Edmundo O'Gorman. México, D.F.: Porrúa S.A., 1993.

De Santa Ana, Julio, et al. *Beyond Idealism: A Way Ahead for Ecumenical Social Ethics*. Edited by Robin Gurney, Heidi Hadsell, and Lewis Mudge. Grand Rapids: Eerdmans, 2006.

De Santa Ana, Julio. *Good News to the Poor: The Challenge of the Poor in the History of the Church*. Translated by Helen Whittle. Maryknoll, NY: Orbis, 1979.

Elizondo, Virgilio P. *La Morenita: Evangelizer of the Americas*. San Antonio: Mexican American Cultural Center, 1980.

Encyclical Letter of the Holy Synod of Bishops of the Orthodox Church in America. Online: http://www.oca.org/DOCencyclical.asp?SID=12&ID=2.

Evdokimov, Paul. *In the World, of the Church: A Paul Evdokimov Reader*. Edited and tranlated by Michael Plekon and Alexis Vinogradov. Crestwood, NY: St. Vladimir's Seminary Press, 2001.

Fant, Clyde E. *Bonhoeffer: Worldly Preaching—Bonhoeffer's Finkenwalde Lectures on Homiletics*. New York: Nelson, 1975.

Florence, Anna Carter. *Preaching as Testimony*. Nashville: Westminster John Knox, 2007.

Forte, Bruno. *La Iglesia, Icono de la Trinidad: Breve Eclesiología*. Salamanca: Sígueme, 1997.

Galilea, Segundo. *Ascenso a la Libertad*. Bogotá: Paulinas, 1991.

Garibay Gómez, Javier. *Nepantla, Situados en Medio: Estudio Histórico-Teológico de la Realidad Indiana*. México D.F.: Centro de Reflexión Teológica, 2000.

Gaventa, Beverly Roberts. *Our Mother St. Paul*. Louisville: Westminster John Knox, 2007.

Gebara, Ivone. *Longing for Running Water: Ecofeminism and Liberation*. Minneapolis: Fortress, 1999.

————. *Out of the Depths: Women's Experience of Evil and Salvation*. Minneapolis: Fortress, 2002.

————. *El Rostro Nuevo de Dios: Una Reconstrucción de los Significados Trinitarios*. México D.F.: Dabar, 1994.

Godsey, John D. *Preface to Bonhoeffer: The Man and Two of his Shorter Writings*. Philadelphia: Fortress, 1965.

González, Justo L. *Mañana: Christian Theology from a Hispanic Perspective*. Nashville: Abingdon, 1990.

González Ruiz, José María, *La Teología de la Cruz en San Pablo: Su Eclipse Histórico*. Madrid: Sal Terrae, 1990.

Guenther, Titus F. *Rahner and Metz: Transcendental Theology as Political Theology* New York: University Press of America, 1994.

Guerrero, José Luis. *Flor y Canto en el Nacimiento de México*. México, D.F.: Librería Parroquial de Clavería, 1999.

————. *El Nican Mopohua: Un Intento de Exégesis*. México, D.F.: Universidad Pontificia, 1996.

Gutiérrez, Gustavo. *Compartir la Palabra a lo Largo del Año Litúrgico*. Salamanca: Sígueme, 1996.

————. *En Busca de los Pobres de Jesucristo: El Pensamiento de Bartolomé de Las Casas*. Lima: Centro de Estudios y Publicaciones, 1992.

————. *Hablar de Dios desde los Sufrimientos de los Inocentes: Una Reflexión sobre el Libro de Job*. Lima: Centro de Estudios y Publicaciones, 1986.

————. *Teología de la Liberación: Perspectivas, con una Nueva Introducción, Mirar Lejos*. Lima: Centro de Estudios y Publicaciones, 1989.

————. *A Theology of Liberation: History, Politics, and Salvation*. Translated and edited by Sr. Caridad Inda and John Eagleson. Maryknoll, NY: Orbis, 1973.

Hanke, Lewis. *All Mankind Is One*. De Kalb: Northern Illinois University Press, 1974.

Hanke, Lewis, and Jane M. Rausch, eds. *People and Issues in Latin American History: The Colonial Experience*. Princeton: Wiener, 2000.

Harrington, Wilfred J. *Parables Told by Jesus: A Contemporary Approach to the Parables*. New York: Alba, 1974.

Heille, Gregory, ed. *Theology of Preaching: Essays on Vision and Ministry in the Pulpit*. London: Melisende, 2001.

Hilkert, Mary Catherine. *Naming Grace: Preaching and the Sacramental Imagination*. New York: Continuum, 1997.

Howe, Reuel L. *Partners in Preaching: Clergy and Laity in Dialog*. New York: Seabury, 1967.

Janowiak, Paul. *The Holy Preaching: The Sacramentality of the Word in the Liturgical Assembly*. Collegeville, MN: Liturgical, 2000.

Küng, Hans. *Great Christian Thinkers*. New York: Continuum, 1994.

————. *Theology for the Third Millennium: An Ecumenical View*. Translated by Peter Heinegg, New York: Doubleday, 1988.

Lohfink, Gerhard. *Jesus and Community: The Social Dimension of Christian Faith*. Translated by John P. Galvin. New York: Paulist, 1984.

López Hernández, Eleazar. "Los Indios ante del Tercer Milenio." In *Revista Electrónica Latinoamericana de Teología*. Online: www.servicioskoinonia.org.

————. "Teologías Indias de Hoy." In *Revista Electrónica Latinoamericana de Teología*. Online: www.servicioskoinonia.org.

Maccise, Camilo. *Perspectivas Latinoamericanas de San Juan de la Cruz*. México, D.F.: Centro de Reflexión Teológica, 1991.

Machado, Antonio. *Poesías Completas*. Décimoquinta edición. Madrid: Espasa-Calpe, 1974.

MacNutt, Francis August. *Bartholomew de Las Casas: His Life, Apostolate, and Writings*. Cleveland: Clark, 1909.

Marins, José, y Equipo. *De Todas las Razas y Naciones*. Santiago de los Caballeros, R.D.: Pía Sociedad Hijas de San Pablo, 2004.

Marins, José and Teolide María Trevisan, *¿Valio la Pena?* México, D.F.: Centro de Reflexión Teológica, 1998.

Medina, Miguel A., ed., *Doctrina Cristiana para Instrucción de los Indios por Pedro de Córdoba: México 1544 y 1548*. Salamanca: San Esteban, 1987.

Memmi, Albert. *The Colonizer and the Colonized*. Introduction by Jean-Paul Sartre. Translated by Howard Greenfeld. Boston: Beacon, 1967.

Menéndez Pidal, Ramón. *El Padre Las Casas: Su Doble Personalidad*. Madrid: Espasa-Calpe, S.A., 1963.

Mesters, Carlos. *Las Parábolas de Jesús*. México, D.F.: Centro de Reflexión Teológica, 2005.

————. *La Persona de Jesucristo: Guía para los Grupos Bíblicos*. Estella, Navarra: Verbo Divino, 2004.

Metz, Johann Baptist. *A Passion for God: The Mystical-Political Dimension of Christianity*. Translated by J. Matthew Ashley. New York: Paulist, 1998.

Míguez Bonino, José. *Doing Theology in a Revolutionary Situation*. Philadelphia: Fortress, 1975.

———. "Love and Social Transformation: Base Ecclesial Communities in Latin America." In *The Promise of Hope: A Tribute to Dom Hélder*, edited by Daniel S. Schipani, and Anton Wessels, 89-104. Elkhart, IN: Institute of Mennonite Studies, 2002.

Mitchell, Henry H. *Celebration and Experience in Preaching*. Rev. ed. Nashville: Abingdon, 2008.

Muñoz, Rolando. *La Iglesia en el Pueblo: Hacia una Eclesiología Latinoamericana*. Lima: Centro de Estudios y Publicaciones, 1983.

Nazianzus, St. Gregory of. *On God and Christ: The Five Theological Orations and Two Letters to Cledonius*. Translations and introductions by Frederick Williams and Lionel Wickham. Crestwood, N.Y.: St. Vladimir's Seminary Press, 2002.

Nickoloff, James, ed. *Gustavo Gutiérrez: Essential Writings*. Maryknoll, NY: Orbis, 1996.

Pegis, Anton C., ed. *An Introduction to St. Thomas Aquinas: The Essence of the Summa Theologica and the Summa contra Gentiles*. New York: Modern Library, 1948.

Peñalosa, Joaquín Antonio. *Manuel de la Imperfecta Homilía*, Quinta Edición. México, D.F.: Obra Nacional de la Buena Prensa, 2004.

Pérez Fernández, Isacio. *El Itinerario Espiritual de Fr. Bartolomé de las Casas*. Santiago de Querétaro: Instituto Dominico de Estudios Históricos, 1996.

Perry, Ted, ed. "Chief Seattle Speech to Franklin Pierce." Online: www.synaptic.bc.ca/ejournal/wslibrry.htm.

Pita Moreda, María Teresa. *Los Predicadores Novohispanos del Siglo XVI*. Salamanca: San Esteban, 1992.

Rahner, Karl. *The Church and the Sacraments*. Translated by W. J. O'Hara. London: Burns & Oates, 1962.

———. *Foundations of the Christian Faith: An Introduction to the Idea of Christianity*. Translated by William V. Dych. New York: Seabury, 1978.

———. *Hearer of the Word*. Translated by Joseph Donceel, S.J. New York: Continuum, 1994.

———. "The Word and the Eucharist." In *Theological Investigations, Vol. 4*. Baltimore: Helicon, 1979.

Richard, Pablo. *Fuerza Ética y Espiritualidad de la Teología de la Liberación en el Contexto Actual de la Globalización*. San José, C.R.: Editorial Departamento Ecuménico de Investigación, 2004.

Rodríguez, Jeanette. *Our Lady of Guadalupe: Faith and Empowerment Among Mexican-American Women*. Austin: University of Texas Press, 1994.

Saravia, Javier. *El Camino de Jesús*. México, D.F.: Obra Nacional de la Buena Prensa, 2005.

———. *La Solidaridad con los Migrantes en la Vida y en la Biblia*. México, D.F.: Obra Nacional de la Buena Prensa, 2004.

Scheffczyk, Leo. "Word of God." In *Sacramentum Mundi: An Encyclopedia of Theology, Vol. 6*. Edited by Karl Rahner. New York: Herder & Herder, 1970.

Schillebeeckx, Edward. *Christ the Sacrament of the Encounter with God*. Translated by Paul Barrett. English text revised by Mark Schoof and Laurence Bright. New York: Sheed & Ward, 1963.

———. *The Church: The Human Story of God*. Translated by John Bowden. New York: Crossroad, 1990.

———. *The Eucharist*. Translated by N. D. Smith. New York: Sheed & Ward, 1968.

———. *I Am a Happy Theologian: Conversations with Francesco Strazzari*. New York: Crossroad, 1994.

Schneiders, Sandra M. *The Revelatory Text: Interpreting the New Testament as Sacred Scripture*. 2nd ed. Collegeville, MN: Michael Glazier, 1999.

Segundo, Juan Luis. *The Liberation of Theology*. Translated by John Drury. Maryknoll, NY: Orbis, 1976.

———. *The Sacraments Today*. Translated by John Drury. Maryknoll, NY: Orbis, 1974.

Sobrino, Jon. *Christ the Liberator: A View from the Victims*. Translated by Paul Burns. Maryknoll, NY: Orbis, 2001.

———. *Christology at the Crossroads*. Translated by John Drury. Maryknoll, NY: Orbis, 1979.

———. *Jesus the Liberator: A Historical-Theological View*. Translated by Paul Burns and Francis McDonagh. Maryknoll, NY: Orbis, 1993.

Sobrino, Jon., and Ignacio Ellacuría, eds., *Mysterium Liberationis: Fundamental Concepts of Liberation Theology*. Maryknoll, NY: Orbis, 1993.

———. *Systematic Theology: Perspectives from Liberation Theology, Readings from Mysterium Liberationis*. Maryknoll, NY: Orbis, 1996.

Tamez, Elsa, editor. *Through Her Eyes: Women's Theology from Latin America*. Maryknoll, NY: Orbis, 1989.

Taylor, Barbara Brown. *When God Is Silent*. Lyman Beecher Lectures on Preaching, 1997. Cambridge, MA: Cowley, 1998.

Traboulay, D. M. *Columbus and Las Casas: The Conquest and Christianization of America, 1492–1566*. New York: University Press of America, 1994.

Wagner, Henry R. *The Life and Writings of Bartolomé de Las Casas*. With the collaboration of Helen Rand Parish. Albuquerque: University of México Press, 1967.

Ware, Kallistos. "Seek First the Kingdom: Orthodox Monasticism and Its Service to the World." *Theology Today* 61 (2004) 14.

Webb, Joseph M. *Preaching and the Challenge of Pluralism*. St. Louis: Chalice, 1998.

Whitmore, Todd David. "When the Lesser Evil is Not Good Enough: The Catholic Case for Not Voting." In *Electing Not to Vote: Christian Reflections on Reasons for Not Voting*, edited by Ted Lewis, 62–80. Eugene, OR: Cascade Books, 2008.

Willems, Boniface. *Karl Barth: An Ecumenical Approach to His Theology*. Translated by Matthew J. Van Velzen. Glen Rock, NJ: Paulist, 1965.

Wilson, Roy I. *A Native American Liberation Theology: Healing for Both the Oppressed and the Oppressor*. Bremerton, WA: Wilson, 1997.

Wisdom, Andrew Carl. *Preaching to a Multi-Generational Assembly*. Collegeville: Liturgical, 2004.

Scripture Index

Subject Index

Base ecclesial communities
  (*comunidades eclesiales de base*),
  v, 70, 90, 96, 112, 119–23, 143,
  165, 185
  as "Abrahamic minority," 127
  and the Bible, 70, 96, 121
  and indigenous people, 144
  and "love motif," 126
  and preaching, 37, 162, 171, 174
  and *ver, juzgar, actuar*, 96
Better World Movement, 120
Bible, Bibles, 40–41, 42, 44, 70, 83, 89
  and base ecclesial communities, 70,
    96, 118, 121
  the book of the Church, 166
  as literacy tool, 121
  primary text for catechesis and base
    communities, 96
Bible Works, 41, 159
"Black Legend" (*Leyenda Negra*), 27
Bodiliness and Schillebeeckx, 57, 71

C

Cacique, 17, 24
Campesino, 82, 140
Cappadocians, the, xi, 50
Catechumens, 127, 174
Catechumenate, 23
Catequesis Familiar (Family
    Catechesis), 96
Causality, 67, 95
Cheap grace, 125, 165
Chiapas, 4, 27, 58, 119
Chief Seattle, 147, 185
Christology, xi, 36, 47, 51, 51–56, 58,
    62–63, 69, 72, 78–79, 115, 126,
    127, 134, 136 139, 143, 149, 161,
    169
"Christological ecclesiology," 5, 50, 68
Christian Scriptures, 138
Christianity, x, 10, 18, 28, 50, 90, 141
  ancient Christianity, 24
  "Conquering Christianity, conquered
    Christianity," 10, 13, 28
  institutional, 14
  Mexican, 137

as state religion, 125, 128
"Christic structure," 54–55
Church, 4, 5, 10, 16, 17, 22, 33, 47, 48,
    50, 53, 56, 65, 67, 70, 71, 72, 74,
    107, 110, 114, 119, 121, 122, 160
  analogous relationship to the Trinity,
    47–48, 161–62
  and the Bible, 166–68
  body of Christ, 53, 59, 63, 74, 85,
    103, 128, 139, 141, 142, 161, 173
  Catholic, 67, 104, 105, 124, 169
  "Christ existing as Church
    community," 5, 48, 53, 55, 127
  Communion of Saints, 5
  as community, 2, 10, 40, 45, 47, 48,
    63, 64, 67, 68, 78, 104, 105, 107,
    111, 113, 123, 127, 134, 142–43,
    166, 174, 175, 178
  confessing, 113
  creation of the Holy Spirit, 48, 62,
    63, 67, 70, 95, 103, 105, 161–66,
    174, 178
  denouncing and announcing,
    99–103
  early, 28, 51–52, 66, 69, 89, 113,
    127, 179
  Eastern, 66, 70, 139
  as *estela*, 161
  as Hearer of the Sacramental Word,
    89–103, 104
  "Hidden" Church (*ecclesia
    abscondita*), 128–29
  institutional, 101, 104, 107, 122, 123,
    137, 141, 149
  living, 35, 48, 161, 173
  local, 33
  marks, 104
  Mexican, 35
  mission, 110, 118, 126, 155, 169
  and *nepantla*, 143–44
  as "new creation," 168
  Orthodox, 50, 104, 105, 167, 169,
    170
  people of God, 53, 103, 141, 142,
    161, 173
  on pilgrimage (*iglesia peregrina*), 99

Theologian Index